ELUDING FAME

A Memoir

by
Allen Morris

eBook ISBN: **979-8-218-98248-5**
Paperback ISBN: **979-8-218-98249-2**
Hardcover ISBN: **979-8-218-98250-8**

Published by Penguin Publishing

Allen Morris
2020 Montrose Drive
Tyler, Texas 75701
allen@belaymedia.com
allenmorrisproducer@gmail.com
903-243-5228

DEDICATION

For my mother and father, without whom there would be nothing
To write about, regardless of achieving fame or not

ACKNOWLEDGMENTS

I wish to thank the people who made this book possible, all of the famous people with whom it was my honor and privilege to work throughout the past fifty+ years; especially the few who are included in this book. I am exceedingly grateful to Al Raya, who was first my teacher, then a business colleague, and always my friend. Al has kept me humble and helped me discover the nature of fame. Also, I owe a huge debt of gratitude to my high school classmate and friend, the New York Times' Bestselling author Suzy Spencer, whose guidance and assistance in editing was a tremendous contribution. The structure and style of this book is largely due to her expertise, patience, and knowledge. Suzy shone a light in the direction I needed to follow, making the journey so much easier.

Contents

Chapter 1
Prologue - Why Eluding Fame?

In a career spanning more than half a century (more impressive than merely stating "over fifty years"), it has been my privilege to work with famous people who have distinguished themselves in various occupations. From actors to athletes; writers and chefs; politicians and criminals (sometimes the same person); musicians and artists; to scientists and business leaders—the common denominator among the individuals with whom I worked is that they have achieved notoriety in their particular fields. What they have, that most of us don't, is fame.

My journey toward fame began with puppets. As ten-year-olds in Dallas, my twin sister Myra and I appeared in a talent show performing with marionettes. Jean Carson, who ran *Storybook Playhouse*, a school that taught children to dance, saw us perform. Ms. Carson approached our parents, asking if we would be available to perform our act at children's birthday parties. Naturally, Myra and I loved the idea. My father was supportive and had business cards printed that read: "Allen's Puppets and Marionettes, Available for Children's Parties." Below that was our phone number, Franklin 4-6382. Thus began our first foray as show-biz professionals, earning $2 for every fifteen minutes we were at the parties. It never occurred to Myra to question why her name was not on the card.

Fame is a double-edged sword. On the one hand, there were the perks that accompany fame, such as a better table at restaurants, moving to the head of the line, higher pay scales, and adulation from fans. On the other hand, there was the darker side of fame: interruptions at restaurants, lack of privacy, nagging by strangers to make investments, and the adulation from fans. While it is nice to get a better table at a restaurant, interruptions from autograph seekers dampen the dining experience. The adulation from fans can become dangerous, as occurred when John Lennon was murdered by Mark David Chapman shortly after signing an autograph for his attacker. Or when John Hinkley shot President Reagan to impress actress Jodie Foster. These are extreme examples, but relevant. Privacy comes at a premium when one achieves fame.

I admit, that about the age of five years old, fame was my goal. At that tender age, I learned that there were two types of people: those who were famous and those who were not. This fact came to me early in 1960 after meeting Mickey Mantle in a Dallas restaurant. The circumstance of meeting the baseball legend was brought about by my father who pointed him out to me as he sat at a nearby table. I sat in awe watching Mantle eat, realizing that he was the first famous person I had seen in the flesh. This took place after the 1959 season, when Mantle only hit 31 home runs, and 75 RBIs, and stuck out 126 times, ending the season with a batting average of .281. Mantle himself had said it was a lackluster season, his worst season in baseball, and that he wouldn't be surprised "if the Yankee management traded me to another club this winter."

Of course, I didn't know anything about Mantle's stats that season. I didn't know anything about baseball, and the only reason I knew his name was my father had told me who he was one afternoon while watching a game on television. Dad told me that he was one of the greatest players in baseball and that he had led the league with 42 home runs in 1958.

"What's a home run?" I had wondered without ever asking.

Sitting in that restaurant, staring at Mickey Mantle, the only thing I knew about him was that he played baseball, and that my Dad thought he was a great player, and that he was famous. It was only his *fame* that intrigued me. Throughout his meal (and mine), I sat transfixed, watching as he ate. Occasionally, he would glance my way, and I would grin and continue staring at him. When he finished his meal, he got up to leave, and then turned and walked over to our table. He held his hand out and said, "Hello, I'm Mickey. What's your name?" I shook his hand, never taking my eyes off his face, and said,

"I'm Allen."

"Well, Allen, I'm happy to meet you," he said and then addressed my father,

"Looks like you have a good Yankee fan there." My father laughed, shook Mantle's hand, and said,

"We'll see. Good luck next season."

And with that, the first famous person I had ever seen in the flesh winked at me and walked away. Later that evening, as I was getting into bed, my mother asked me what I thought about meeting Mickey Mantle that day, knowing full well that I had no idea who he really was. My response was to tell her that I wanted to be famous like him someday. "Maybe you will," she said in her ever calm, quiet voice, "but there are more important things in life than being famous. You should aspire to be a good person. Fame is fleeting. Character lasts."

My mother spoke to us using words like "aspire" in their proper context. She never talked down to us. She never sugar-coated things. She was always direct, and to the point, and assumed if she used words we did not understand, we would ask. And we did. Then she would explain the word's meaning and expected we would begin using that word as part of our normal vocabulary.

Although I understood exactly what my mother meant—that my aspirations should be directed toward becoming a better person—still, I wanted to be famous. I was willing to try becoming a better famous person. No matter what effort I made toward that goal, fame remained elusive. That is the subject of this book.

Chapter 2
Growing up with Television

To provide some context, these first few chapters are written as the background about how my journey seeking fame came into being. Television was just hitting its early stride in 1954, the year I was born into the Baby Boomer generation. Still a relatively new addition to American homes, television was then, and remains today, a pervasive force in my life. My birth took place at St. Joseph's Hospital in Dallas at 9:00 on the morning of April 23rd. Eight minutes later, my twin sister Myra was born. She has always told anyone who would listen, "I was tired of his feet in my face," frequently adding, "I gave him his first push into the world." Not only did our parents bring a pair of new babies home to our older brother Dalton, but they soon brought home a new television set; from Sears, a Silvertone black and white, of course. For the first fourteen years of my life, that Silvertone set graced the corner of our den. On it, we watched *Howdy Doody* every afternoon, which is where my love of marionettes was fostered. We turned it on every morning to watch *Captain Kangaroo*. When we got a little older, the family, which by then included our baby sister Brenda, sat on a curved sofa to watch *Saturday Night at the Movies* on NBC. There were only three channels available for viewing until September 1960, when the National Educational Television (NET) affiliate KERA signed on the air (and when I began the first grade). Throughout our elementary school years, television sets on tall stands were rolled into the classrooms, and we students "learned Spanish" by watching the instructional programs broadcast by KERA TV-13.

A major reason for becoming so enthralled with television was that every major event of the last half of the twentieth century became a televised event. From an early age, I was aware that television allowed me to be a witness to history. On November 22, 1963, I was a nine-year-old fourth-grade student at Mark Twain Elementary, which was located in the Glen Oaks neighborhood of Oak Cliff in Dallas. My parents had moved to a new house in that neighborhood when there were only a handful of houses built. It was an upper-middle-class area with an unusually large number of Catholic families. We lived on Haywood Parkway, which was across the street from the back side of the school's playground. On that particular fall day, I had gone home for lunch before going to a dental appointment. While eating lunch and watching the soap opera *As the World Turns*, the program was interrupted by a CBS Breaking News slide and the voice of Walter Cronkite telling viewers that three shots had been fired at the presidential motorcade in downtown Dallas. Almost immediately, Cronkite added that the president had been hit. My mother and I then left for the dentist's office and I turned on the car radio in her '55 Buick Special. By the time we arrived at the dentist, another bulletin came over the radio announcing that Texas Governor John Connally had also been shot.

I could sense the dental staff's confusion as I was settled into the chair in the exam room. Everyone was listening intently to the radio as reports continued to filter in regarding the president's condition. As we listened, a nurse was preparing me to have a tooth extracted. It was then that we heard the solemn announcement from Walter Cronkite, "From Dallas, Texas, the flash, apparently official, President Kennedy died at 1:00 PM, Central Standard Time, 2:00 Eastern Standard Time; some thirty-eight minutes ago." The nurse came in and grabbed my left hand; she was crying. Doctor McCullough came in and asked me to open my mouth. He probed around with a sharp tool and told me that he was going to extract my tooth. "You can watch what I'm doing in the reflection of my glasses." Then, he told me to relax for a moment and he left the room. The nurse continued holding my hand and spoke softly, "It's a very sad day. Our president has been killed."

The radio was still providing news bulletins when the doctor returned. He told me to open my mouth, and as he did, I looked at the reflection of my mouth in his glasses. He wore wire-framed glasses and the lenses were octagonal, like a stop sign. As he spoke to me, I noticed his eyes were red. He probed some more in my mouth and walked out again. What I'm sure was only a few minutes seemed like an eternity to a nine-year-old. Then, the doctor returned. "You'll feel a little pressure," he said, "but this will only take a moment. Just relax." Then, he placed the instrument in my mouth. I remember thinking that it looked like a fancy set of pliers, shiny and silvery. I watched as he placed them over the tooth he was about to pull. As he did, the nurse grabbed my hand even more firmly. I glanced at her, thinking how pretty she was with her blond hair pulled back on the back of her head. Her name was Donna, and she was my first crush. Then, Doctor McCullough pulled on my tooth. As he did, the most excruciating pain I have ever felt surged through my entire body. The pain started in my mouth, and I felt it instantly in my toes, the tips of my fingers, and the top of my head. It was like electricity racing throughout my body. I screamed and clinched my hand with all my strength around the nurse's hand. Although I did not know it, Doctor McCullough was immediately aware that they had skipped a step amid the confusion going on as the news of President Kennedy's assassination had distracted everyone on his staff. He had just pulled my tooth without benefit of Novocain. He immediately gave me a shot to stop the pain and told the nurse to monitor me closely, as there was a possibility of me going into shock. "Don't let him go to sleep," he said as he walked out.

What happened next is something I did not know until many years later when my mother recounted the story to me. She had been in the waiting room and had heard my scream. Doctor McCullough came out and asked her, "Ora Lee, can you come with me, please?" He took her into his office. The McCulloughs lived in our neighborhood and met our family at Glen Oaks Methodist Church when my mother was in charge of the children's Sunday School classes. Although, by this time, my family had started attending the Chapel in the Woods, a non-denominational church, they had remained friends. He had a daughter my age in my class and a son a year younger than my older brother. "Did you hear that scream a few moments ago?"

"Was that Allen? I'm sorry, he gets a little dramatic sometimes," she said.

"No, that's isn't the problem," he said interrupting her, "What college does Allen want to go to?"

"College?" she asked, trying to understand what that could have to do with her son screaming in the dentist's office. "That's not something we've thought about yet. He's only nine."

"Well, we made a big mistake today, and I want you to know that I want to make it right. Allen is fine. He's resting right now. We've treated him for shock and I've given him a sedative to calm him down and a shot to stop the pain. It seems that I pulled his tooth without first making sure he was completely anesthetized."

It took a moment before my mother fully understood what he was telling her. I'm sure she looked confused as he tried to explain what happened. "He's alright?" she asked, finally.

"He will be, but you are going to need to keep him still and keep him from going to sleep for several hours and watch him carefully. The sedative will wear off before the painkiller does. When he starts feeling pain again, you will need to give him one of these (he handed her a bottle of pain medicine) every six hours for the next few days. I suggest giving him these until they run out, and if you

8

think he needs more, just call me. I'm very sorry this happened. I can't tell you how badly I feel about this. This has never happened before. I have no excuse for this, and I want you to know that, although there is no way I can take away the pain I caused, I want to pay for Allen's college, when the time comes."

We had to stay at the dentist's office until he felt the risk of my going into shock was over. He then gave my mother explicit instructions about how to keep me awake for the next several hours. When my Mother got me home, she had me sit in the oversized chair beside the television, wrapped in a quilt. She brought me a chocolate milkshake and put a fresh pad of gauze over the hole that once held my tooth. For the next several hours, I was glued to the television watching the coverage of the events surrounding the Kennedy Assassination. When the report came across that a police officer, J. D. Tippet, was killed in Oak Cliff and that the alleged shooter was apprehended at the Texas Theatre, I imagined the scene on the TV screen in my mind. That movie theatre was only a mile or two away from where Dr. McCullough had extracted my tooth.

I sat snuggled in that chair riveted to the television for hours, fascinated by the historic events unfolding before my eyes. As I continued watching the news coverage, suddenly the live pictures were no longer coming from Dallas, but from Washington. I looked out our big picture window overlooking our patio and it was still light out. On the television, it looked like it was already night in Washington. I think that was the moment I realized that time was different in different locations. As a child, everything in my life happened in real time and centered around where I was. The day was day and night was night. Because television was covering events happening simultaneously in different locations, and because throughout the day Cronkite had been giving the time that events occurred in Dallas, followed immediately by stating the time in the

Eastern Time Zone, it dawned on me it could be a different time somewhere else. As I pondered this new revelation, I kept watching while new events were taking place, now in another time zone where night had fallen. I watched as Air Force One taxied across the runway in Washington. Then, as the plane stopped and several police cars and an ambulance arrived, I watched as dozens of men moved around the ambulance. The scene was chaotic as the door of the plane opened while a lift was moved into position and the casket was unloaded from the 707 at Andrews Air Force Base. I listened as Harry Reasoner's voice described the scene, explaining that Mrs. Kennedy was still wearing the blood-stained clothes she had been wearing earlier in the day. The camera panned with the car carrying the casket as it sped away into the darkness. My mother brought me a fresh milkshake and another pill for the pain. Then, President Johnson spoke to the nation.

President Johnson was a fellow Texan. He spoke briefly, asking for support from the American people and God's help in the days to come. He spoke with a thick, Texas accent, exactly the type of accent my mother worked hard to prevent any of her children from developing. As I listened to him speak, I understood why my mother had been so diligent in keeping us from developing such an accent. Listening to the commentators, I learned that Johnson had been riding in the car behind Kennedy when those three shots rang out, changing history and making an indelible impression on me. Just as Andrew Johnson had become president upon the assassination of Abraham Lincoln, Lyndon Johnson had become president upon Kennedy's assassination.

In the days to follow, much of the color commentary during the coverage included odd facts. Both Lincoln and Kennedy were elected to Congress in '46 and to the presidency in '60, a century apart. Lincoln and Kennedy were both shot in the head on a Friday. Lincoln had been killed in Ford's Theatre. Kennedy was killed while riding in a Ford Lincoln. Both were succeeded by vice-presidents named Johnson, both born in '08, a century apart. The names Lincoln and Kennedy both contain seven letters. The alleged assassins of them both were Southerners, in their twenties, born nearly one hundred years apart, and each had three names containing fifteen letters. Booth ran from a theatre and was caught in a warehouse. Oswald ran from a warehouse and was caught in a theatre.

Later in the evening, reports were repeated over and over that the Dallas police had arrested a suspect believed to be the assassin. Coverage from throughout the day was repeated ad nauseam. At some point, my body gave way to fatigue and I fell asleep. I was still wrapped in a comforter in that big chair when I awoke on Saturday morning. The television was still on, and the nonstop news coverage was still on. That morning, I vividly remember seeing Lee Harvey Oswald as he was paraded before the cameras, protesting his innocence. I remembered having heard his name the day before, but this was the first time I saw what he looked like. From my nine-year-old's perspective, he didn't look as I imagined a murderer would look. I had no idea how a murderer should look, but to me, he looked like a normal guy. I remember thinking how odd it was that every time the newscasters mentioned him, they always used all three names. At the time, it seemed that there was no question that Oswald had been the assassin, although, on the newsreel, he denied it. I spent the day watching every frame of news coverage.

Allen Morris

Chapter 3
Television the Chronicler

In my latter-day perception, the British Invasion—the advent of The Beatles—was more consequential than the excitement surrounding a young Frank Sinatra. I believe that to be true because of the advantage television created by broadcasting every minor detail concerning the "Fab Four." Although Sinatra's singing career began in the late thirties, his real prominence came during the Second World War. Radio was the most important broadcast medium for a few more years when Sinatra became a star performer. He established himself enough to be a full-fledged member of that generation of performers, bridging the gap from radio to television. As an idol for the generation of fans referred to as "bobbysoxers," Sinatra foreshadowed the hysteria surrounding The Beatles.

The early days of television included performers known to radio audiences. Jack Benny, Milton Berle, and even Lucille Ball had previously made the jump from movies to radio. *My Favorite Husband*, a radio program in which Lucille Ball starred, led to the creation of *I Love Lucy,* probably the most successful television show in history. The next generation of singers, following in the wake of Sinatra's success, began with Bill Halley and the Comets, Buddy Holly and Elvis Presley, the early rock and rollers who led the way for all the others who followed—all who became major stars, assisted because of the power of television. A television show, *American Bandstand*, introduced the new sound of Rock & Roll music to the boomers, and in the process initially made Dick Clark, who would eventually become one of the major moguls of the television industry, a star. However, television enabled Beatlemania to eclipse all comers. Their appearance on the *Ed Sullivan Show* drew a bigger audience than Elvis Presley's first appearance on September 9, 1956. In fact, the February 9, 1964, appearance on

Sullivan's show garnered 73 million viewers, at the time setting the record for the largest television audience ever.

Television and I grew up together. That box has been in the background of everything going on around me for my entire life. When I was a baby, television was a toddler. As I grew up, television was also growing up; but like my older brother Dalton, television was just a few years ahead of me. I was learning to read when television was teaching politicians the new tricks for running a campaign. I was only a six-year-old at the time of the Kennedy-Nixon debates, but I watched them with the same interest as I watched *Leave It to Beaver* or *Father Knows Best*. When Walter Cronkite became the leading news Anchor (a term reputedly coined to describe Cronkite's role), I was an avid viewer. Part of why I identified so closely with Cronkite was his resemblance to my father, right down to the neatly trimmed mustache and melodious baritone voice. On his way to becoming the "most trusted man in America," Cronkite was busy teaching me about the space program. He was a constant presence throughout the sixties, reporting about the ever-changing world in which I was growing up. When Cronkite mentioned someone, I had not heard of, I would look the name up in our *World Book Encyclopedia.* I did it when Eleanor Roosevelt died in 1962. I remember reading about Martin Luther King Jr., in *The Dallas Morning News* after he made the "I Have a Dream" speech, covered by Cronkite in 1963. I looked up Wernher Von Braun in 1967 after the Apollo 1 fire was reported on by Cronkite. As my family gathered around the television in 1969, to watch the historic moment as Neil Armstrong stepped onto the surface of the moon, Walter Cronkite was there with us, providing the commentary.

Television is as much a part of the Baby Boomer Generation as I am. While television existed as early as the late thirties, it was not a viable medium until after World War II ended. That is the reason

I say it belongs in the Baby Boomer Generation. As those of us who are Baby Boomers were growing up, the fabric of American life was radically changing. Unlike any generation before us, television was there serving as the chronicler of our times. Television's omnipresence had the most profound impact on popular culture and current events, blurring the lines between them. Each fed the other, no doubt in part due to the speed with which the growing audience of viewers received information through television's pervasive eye. Madison Avenue was quick to notice the power of television and its unparalleled influence over the largest target audience in marketing history. Baby Boomers spent their entire lives in a courtship instigated by the advertising industry. Starting with baby food and breakfast cereals, up through various fads in clothing, music, and fast foods, Madison Avenue blasted the commercials designed to trigger buying impulses into American homes, using television as their canon to deliver the messages to the Boomers. No generation in history has been so sought-after, so catered to, or so studied as we Baby Boomers.

Despite my youth, while growing up there was no doubt in my mind that I was living on the front row of history-making events. I was keenly aware that television news was coming of age. I had seen the newsreels of the Hindenburg Disaster, and heard the emotional coverage of Herb Morris describing the horrific event as he spoke the words, "Oh, the humanity!" (I wonder if we are related? I must look that up!). This was different, and I knew it. The Hindenburg newsreel was after the fact. The coverage was of the Kennedy assassination happened in real time—and I was there. I was part of it, along with millions of others, similarly glued to their television screens. At least that was how I felt. I was not merely watching the story unfold; the experience was visceral. I was there, a participating witness as the events unfolded. It was the same as watching Mickey Mantle hit a home run during a televised baseball game. Television placed me inside the ballpark and I ran the bases with Mantle. The coverage of the events happening in my hometown on November 22nd made me feel involved. It was happening right then, as I watched. I was there. It was a feeling magnified ten-fold on Sunday after church.

By the Sunday immediately following Kennedy's assassination, my extracted tooth was old news. I was no longer feeling any pain and our family went to the Chapel in the Woods for Sunday services. During church, several of us boys were allowed to sit outside in what had been the carport of the house, converted into a church. As long as we behaved ourselves, and did not make too much noise, we were allowed to sit outside and listen to the services over a loudspeaker. After church was over, several families from church arrived at the Alpine Club at about the same time. The Alpine was like a country club, except there was no golf course. We had a membership there and went swimming during the summer in the large pool equipped with a high diving board. Several kids lingered in the TV lounge while our parents went into the main dining room.

The reporter announced that Lee Harvey Oswald was being transferred from the city jail to the county jail. I stood there watching the screen. I saw J. R. Leavelle, a police detective wearing a light-colored suit and cowboy hat, as he walked into a crowded hallway. Handcuffs coupled Leavelle and Lee Harvey Oswald together. A man suddenly appeared in the foreground. I heard the sound of the gun on the television speaker. The reporter shouted, "Oswald has been shot."

Because of television, I witnessed a historic event as it happened. As I watched history unfold across the television screen, it occurred to me: that two days earlier, no one had heard of Lee Harvey Oswald. Now, the man who had been unknown just days before, whose name was now known around the world, had been shot by yet another unknown man, whose name was soon to become known around the world. In an instant, through the power of television, obscurity gave way to fame.

Five years after the assassination of President Kennedy, pop artist Andy Warhol used a phrase in the printed program for an exhibition of his works in Stockholm, Sweden. Warhol predicted that "In the future, everyone will be world-famous for 15 minutes." His remark has been studied by sociologists and quoted by television commentators ever since. The phrase itself entered our lexicon and became idiomatic. In 1968 society, fame could occur; but it might not last. The phrase also points out: that which becomes famous is not necessarily worthy of fame. Television helped increase society's capacity to achieve fame. The medium itself is conducive to catapulting an individual into the limelight for the slightest accomplishment. Perhaps, "notoriety" is a better word. An example of this phenomenon is Mrs. Elva Miller, known as Mrs. Miller professionally. She was a frumpy housewife, who sang in a pseudo-operatic style, slightly off-key and not quite on the beat. Despite that, in 1966 she managed to appear on *The Ed Sullivan Show* twice and sold 250,000 copies of her first album, entitled *Mrs. Miller's Greatest Hits.* The LP hit #15 on *Billboard's* Top Albums Chart and Mrs. Miller's cover of Petula Clark's song "Downtown" reached #82 on the Hot 100 Singles Chart. Capitol Records released two more albums, which failed to sell well enough, and the label dropped Mrs. Miller in 1967. Fleeting fame.

The year 1968 was one in which television news coverage reached adolescence. The year began with Cronkite reporting about the Tet Offensive, which would become known as one of the largest military campaigns of the Vietnam War. The images that accompanied the reports were stark. The expressions on the faces of the soldiers reflected the seriousness of Cronkite's tone of voice. The faces of Vietnamese women and children showed not only fear but desperation as well. On February 27, 1968, Cronkite filed an editorial based on his recent trip to Vietnam. After seeing a replay of that report, President Lyndon Johnson (as reported by Bill Moyers who worked as an aide on Johnson's staff at that time) flipped off the television set and stated, "If I've lost Cronkite, I've lost Middle America." One month later, Johnson ended a televised address to the nation with the startling remark, "I shall not seek, and I will not accept, the nomination of my party for another term as your President." Four days after that announcement, on April 4, 1968, civil rights leader Martin Luther King, Jr., was fatally shot on the balcony of the Lorraine Motel in Memphis, Tennessee. A clip from one of the most dramatic speeches uttered during that time made the news broadcast. It was of Robert F. Kennedy, the slain president's brother, addressing a crowd in Indianapolis shortly after the news of King's assassination broke. After announcing that King was shot and killed earlier in the evening, Kennedy made an impassioned plea for America to change the path down which we as a nation were heading. He appealed to the audience, "In this difficult day, in this difficult time for the United States, it's perhaps well to ask what kind of a nation we are and in what direction we want to move ... what we need in the United States is not violence and lawlessness, but is love, and wisdom, and compassion toward one another, and a feeling of justice toward those who still suffer within our country, whether they be white or whether they be black."

On June 5, 1968, two months and a day later, Sirhan Sirhan fired three shots, mortally wounding Senator Robert F. Kennedy, who had just delivered a victory speech after winning the California Primary. Kennedy died at 1:44 the following morning. Two days later, the alleged assassin of Martin Luther King was arrested at London's Heathrow Airport. James Earl Ray was extradited to the United States and charged with King's murder. Ultimately, Ray would plead guilty and spend the rest of his life in prison. Even evil people could achieve fame.

With each tragedy or triumph that year, television brought viewers the images of 1968, ranging from soldiers in battle during the Vietnam War; to Jesse Jackson pointing toward the direction of Martin Luther King's assassin; to busboy Juan Romero bending over the wounded body of Robert Kennedy. As the summer progressed, the news coverage included rioters in Chicago during the Democratic National Convention; Richard Nixon's acceptance speech when he became the president-elect; to the astronauts of Apollo 8 broadcasting a Christmas Eve message while in orbit around the moon. The year 1968 was a pivotal year for the nation, and for me, one that closed the chapter of childhood and opened a new chapter of my adolescence.

My family moved from Dallas to Lufkin, Texas, during the summer of 1968. Lufkin was then a small town of 23,000 people located in the piney woods of East Texas. The timber industry drove the local economy, which supported a paper mill manufacturing newsprint. When the wind came from the right direction, the foul smell of the paper mill wafted over the town. The stench inundated the entire town. It was impossible to escape and the memory of that awful smell remains with me as one of the distinctive aspects that, for me, is an identifying factor of Lufkin. The other major industry in Lufkin was a foundry, which manufactured oil field pumping equipment. Lufkin Industries had a separate division that manufactured the trailers that eighteen-wheelers pulled, transporting goods throughout the country. I had seen trailers all my life that had a white rectangle with the word "Lufkin" in red letters attached to their corners. A couple of blocks from where we lived was a Brookshire Brothers grocery store. There were Brookshires in some of my classes, and I would soon learn the Brookshire family was among the elite families of Lufkin. There were two radio stations and one television station licensed to Lufkin when we arrived. The single television station, KTRE TV-9, broadcast programming from all three networks, but had no affiliation with any particular network.

Cable had recently arrived in Lufkin, but its service was not available in every area of town. For the first year we lived there, Channel 9 was the only television we could receive at our house. There was a quaintness about Lufkin that appealed to me. I looked upon the move to this alien environment with anticipation. From my perspective, I thought of Lufkin as Mayberry, the imaginary town in South Carolina where Sheriff Andy Taylor, Aunt Bea, Deputy Barney Fife, Floyd the barber, and Opie all lived. Opie and I were the same age. In my mind, we faced many of the same problems in life. After watching the events of 1968, all of which never really affected me personally, but all of which impacted my view of the world, Lufkin seemed to me a safe place to confront life's problems as an undersized fourteen-year-old who was the new kid at school.

The most unlikely thing I expected to materialize out of my family's move to Lufkin was entering the world of television. It happened in the fall of 1969. Mrs. Pat Baldwin, known as Miss Pat on her local children's TV show, saw my twin sister Myra and me performing in a summer theatre program at Angelina Junior College. The father of one of our classmates, who was on staff at the college, directed a "Mellerdrama" every summer as part of a community theatre project sponsored by the college. Dr. Jimmy Tinkle became a mentor to us throughout high school and into college, even providing us both with scholarships. It was after a performance one evening in August 1969, that Dr. Tinkle introduced us to Miss Pat. It was during this brief meeting that Miss Pat told us her show, *Through Magic Doorways,* was to resume in the fall. She explained the program was live, one day each week, throughout the school year. The format was like an afternoon party for preschoolers. Each week, a different audience of children attended the program and took part in the activities Miss Pat planned for each week's show. These activities included sing-a-longs, simple games, and story-time, which usually entailed Miss Pat reading to the children and holding the illustrations up for the camera to catch for the children watching at home.

Speaking to my sister, Miss Pat blurted out, "It would help me out to have a sort of assistant; who could help corral the children and help me keep things moving. Wouldn't it be wonderful if you were dressed as a clown and sang a song with the children?" The other idea she had was for us to create puppet shows for the story-time segment. Her idea was for us to perform the stories with puppets, with Miss Pat narrating the story while Myra and I operated the puppets and created all the character voices and sounds. If I remember correctly, Miss Pat offered us each $10 per show. It is possible we split $10 per show. More than fifty years later, I don't remember. Regardless, my sister and I arrived at the studios of KTRE TV-9 in the fall of 1969, and my television career began at that small market station nestled in the piney woods.

Allen Morris

Chapter 4
The Early Influence of Women

My childhood memories include impressions of women with whom I feel somehow connected, in spirit if not through bloodline. One is my mother, for the obvious reason that she is my mother. Another is Queen Elizabeth of England. The third is Lucille Ball.

I always felt my mother bore an uncanny resemblance to the Queen, and although Mother is five years older (and prettier), part of the kinship I feel toward Her Majesty is no doubt due to the fact her children and my siblings and I are of the same generation. My brother is one year younger than Princess Anne. I am six years older than Prince Edward, and ten years older than Prince Andrew. I remember when both of those boys were born. Again, because of television, I was made aware of the lives of those young princes.

Lucy's daughter Lucie (I always felt I could call her Lucy) is my brother's age, and Desi Jr., is one year older than my twin sister and I. Lucy was ten years older than my mother, although she played the same age as my mother on *I Love Lucy*. The close bond I feel toward Lucy is because I grew up with her in my house on almost a daily basis. In addition to every Monday night at eight, reruns of *I Love Lucy* played every morning. I remember when I heard Lucy and Desi Arnaz were divorcing. My family was on a trip at the time, and the Arnaz divorce became a topic of discussion while we were eating dinner in some motel dining room. The news devastated me and I remember crying. My mother consoled me with assurances that she and my father were not going to be getting a divorce. Still, I went to bed that night thinking about poor Lucie and Desi Jr., and how sad they must have been that night.

In the case of my mother, we obviously share a bloodline. My mother was born May 9, 1921, in Kirksville, Missouri. Her father was Harold Dean Marlin (1880-1951), a Methodist Minister. Her mother was Esther Ann Parks (1882-1931). In order of birth, mother's siblings were Leonard, Alice, Howard, Pauline, Melba, Marian, Mary Olive and, finally my mother, Ora Lee. She was the eighth child of a Methodist minister and lost her mother to tuberculosis when she was only ten years old. I remember asking what it was like for her to grow up without her mother. Mother's memories of her mother, my grandmother, are sketchy. Her mother was sick the entire time my mother knew her. Because of that, most of the visits with her mother were at her bedside. There was little or no touching between them. She spoke matter-of-factly that she did not have her mother for long, but she knew her mother loved her and did not want to leave her. The tragedy of her childhood was only seeing her mother sick in bed, weakened by her illness and fighting for every breath. As her mother lay dying, my mother's older sisters took on the role of mothering her. She did not have the kind of relationship with her mother that she would later develop with her own children.

After my Grandmother Esther's death, my Grandfather Harold married a woman named Pearl, and they had another daughter, my Aunt Tennie Louise. I think the life-long lasting effects of her mother's death explain why my mother has always been reticent about public displays of affection. Despite that, Mother was affectionate and tender toward her own children. I remember once, at the age of three or four years, listening to my mother sing a lullaby that she said she learned when she was a child:

Lu, lu, lu, lulu, hush-a-by;

Dream of the angels in the sky.

Lu, lu, lu, lulu, don't you cry;

Mama won't go away.

24

Sleep in my arms while you still can,

Childhood is but a day.

Even when you're a grown-up man;

Mama won't go away.

Mother told me that when my big brother was little, and she sang that to him, he would cry. He misunderstood the words and thought she was saying that Mama was going away. Because her own mother had gone away, she was determined to reassure her eldest son that she would never go away.

My mother is never impressed by people because of their occupation. Certainly, never because of fame or fortune. What impresses my mother about people was how they conduct themselves. She likes people who are truthful, who live by the Golden Rule: treating others as they themselves want to be treated. Due to her father's profession, she grew up moving frequently and living in parsonages that were usually attached to the churches where her father had been assigned as pastor. She once told me that her family did not cook breakfast on Sundays because the smell would permeate the church. She didn't make close friends, probably intentionally, as she knew her family would eventually move away. I think she was a lonely child and that her mother's death was on her mind throughout her childhood. Early in life, my mother learned a cruel lesson: that life is not always fair, so, she learned to take each day as it comes, never making long-range plans.

As I write this (May 9, 2024), my mother is turning one-hundred-three-years old. She has lived an extraordinarily long life. The summer of my fourteenth year, as we were sitting together on our front porch swing, I asked Mother what her life's goal had been when she was my age. "I wanted to be a mother. I wanted to see my children grow up. I wanted to rear them to be good people. That's

25

all I ever really wanted." On a recent visit, as I was speaking to her, she leaned over to my sister and asked, "Who is this man that is annoying me?"

"That's Allen," my sister responded.

"I have a son named Allen," Mother replied giving me a sidelong glance.

"Yes. That's Allen, your son. My twin brother."

My mother looked at my sister, then toward me, and then back to my sister. In her calm, quiet voice, she spoke, "No it isn't." Despite the fact that my mother does not recognize me as the white-haired old man I have become, I know that the young black-haired boy of fourteen still lives in her heart and mind. I know that she took pride in whatever accomplishments I achieved through the years. And I appreciate the fact that she was never reticent about attempting to make certain I retained some sense of humility. When I told her about winning my first Emmy Award, her response was, "That's nice. But remember that awards are not important. What is important is how you treat other people. That is what matters; not accolades."

Another woman who was a great influence on my life is Shirley Ann Megarity. She was my teacher from the second through sixth grades and remained a lifelong friend after I was no longer her student. Today, she is in a nursing facility in Clifton, Texas, and no longer recognizes any family or friends. She taught Speech Arts at Mark Twain Elementary. It was her first teaching job after graduating from Texas Women's College in Denton, Texas. Her classroom was the school auditorium, where she taught us Public Speaking and where we learned to perform in front of an audience as cast members of the annual operetta she directed. My first acting experiences were guided by Miss Megarity, who taught me the importance of timing for delivering a punchline. In the sixth grade, I was elected president of the Student Council, a position I took very seriously. In that role, I was frequently asked to make the introductions of guest speakers at assemblies held in that auditorium. Officer Baker, a Dallas policeman, was a frequent guest at the school. He would make presentations about safety, subjects like not talking to strangers, looking both ways before crossing a street, not to get near a car if someone was offering to give us candy or wanted us to show them how to get to a certain street in the neighborhood. It was all basic information, but important safety rules for elementary-aged children to follow.

The years as a student at Mark Twain Elementary took place during the 60s. We watched the inauguration of President Kennedy on television and the constant coverage of America's space program every time the Mercury or Gemini space shots were made. We were fortunate to have real astronauts come to make a presentation, and it was my privilege to introduce them. Miss Megarity allowed me to hang out backstage with these men, which gave me the opportunity of peppering them with questions about traveling in space. Unfortunately, I do not remember the names of the astronauts who visited our school. I do remember serving as their assistant when they demonstrated the various experiment's they brought with them. One that stands out in my memory was showing how mylar, the thin, metallic-looking material that lined the space suits, could withstand extreme heat and cold. The astronauts used liquid oxygen, a pale blue liquid when oxygen transforms from its normal gaseous state into a liquid at -297 degrees Fahrenheit. They poured the liquid oxygen into a mylar bag. They asked me to touch the outside of the bag, and it was not cold. When the bag was opened, the ambient temperature of the room immediately caused to liquid to revert to its gaseous state, and the bag was empty. At least that is how I remember the experiment.

Allen Morris

Chapter 5
My Career Begins

Shortly after performing on *Through Magic Doorways* with my twin sister in the fall of 1969, I was offered a job running the camera for newscasts at the station. It was a job that not only included running the camera, but also cleaning the studio and a performing a myriad of other mundane tasks. Sometimes, I will admit it was boring and rather dull work. And much like the man sweeping behind the elephants during the circus parade, who was asked "Why don't you quit that awful job," and then replied, "What? And give up show-biz!"—that was my attitude. At a very young age, I was given an opportunity to enter the world of television as a professional. The greatest part of that opportunity was being able to learn virtually every job that was available. I took it seriously and was determined to learn everything I could from the ground up. I was sixteen and confidant in my abilities and assumed, that in time, better opportunities would be presented to me. And I was correct in that assumption.

The first thing the station's engineers (Tom Perryman, Chief; Jack Bryan; David Allen; Jerry Lamb; and Lee Walton, who was also the Production Manager) taught me was how to register the cameras so the pictures they produced were sharp and in focus. At that time, the color television cameras were large beasts with four separate tubes inside: white, red, blue and green. Those tubes had to be aligned properly to ensure that the resulting picture was correct. It was tedious work to make certain each tube was in proper register and that all four tubes were correctly aligned with one another. Complicating matters was the fact that the cameras were from two different manufacturers. One was the GE 350, a camera that could be found in almost every color studio in Texas at that time. The other was an IVC 500, known for its propensity to lose its registration after about half an hour of operation. It was impossible to get the two cameras to actually match one another, but since that was what we had, we made do with mismatched images.

The general manager of the station was Bill Carter. He was the father of one of my classmates. Bill became my mentor and remained a lifelong friend until his death in January 2022. Why he took such an interest in me as a teenager, I'm not sure. I suspected it might have had something to do with his having two daughters but no son. Whatever his reason, I am grateful that he did. Without his encouragement and guidance, I might not have made my career in television. Bill achieved fame in his own right for 60+ years in radio and television broadcasting. In 2010, he was voted Texas Broadcasting Pioneer of the Year and elected to the Texas Broadcaster's Hall of Fame. He retired from active and reserve military duty after thirty-three years of service to his country. He entered the broadcasting field in radio, where he learned to do every job that was necessary, from obtaining a First-Class FCC license and working as a studio engineer, to his work as an announcer behind a microphone.

When television was in its infancy, he was among the first of his generation to make the transition from radio to television. Eventually, Bill was a member of the Board of Governors for the FOX Television Network. After serving as GM at two of the Buford family-owned television stations, he worked for the Houston Astros in Broadcast Operations. When I was working for Metromedia in 1979, and I was traveling with the team as their broadcast producer, I introduced Bill to Raymond Shindler, who was in the process of building his own television empire. Bill became president of Shindler's Sage Broadcasting, helping to either buy existing properties or to build stations from scratch. He was responsible for the management of several Sage properties, which included TV and radio stations in the Southwest including KIDY-TV San Angelo,

KXVA-TV Abilene, KIDZ Abilene, KABB San Antonio, and KPOM Ft. Smith/Fayetteville, Arkansas.

When Bill took me under his wing, he was very much a hands-on station manager. Early on Sunday mornings, he and I would remove the IVC 500 camera from the KTRE studio and take it to the First Baptist Church in Lufkin to broadcast their Sunday morning service. Since he had an engineering license, Bill would handle the microwave link to the station and I operated the camera from the balcony of the church. Bill emphasized the importance of learning every aspect of broadcast operations. He encouraged me to follow the same course he had taken as I began my broadcasting career. His fatherly-approach stayed with me and is a contributing factor to my own efforts to share what I've learned with the next generation of broadcasting professionals.

In addition to operating the camera on Sundays, the other tasks I learned to perform were creating the lower third supers for the newscasts. This was accomplished by scratching little white vinyl letters off a sheet of Chartpak onto a black card. Then, using a Polaroid camera that made transparencies of the image, a slide was mounted into 35mm frames for use in the slide projector attached to telecine (a combination of two 16mm film projectors and one 35mm slide projector focused into a television camera). A multiplexer was used to switch a mirror system that determined which of the three projectors was aimed into the television camera. Eventually, the lower-third slides would be replaced by one of the first electronic character generators, the Vidifont from CBS Laboratories. I also had to learn how to operate the Vidifont during those early days.

Another job was learning how to use the machine that processed 16mm news film. It was unusual for such a small market station to have its own film processor, but we did. It was a Jamieson Compact. The Jamieson Film Company was a Texas company, founded by

Hugh Jamieson in 1916, that produced industrial films, television programs and commercials, thus establishing itself as a major contributor for Dallas becoming a major player in commercial television production. The company's biggest claim to fame was that it was the lab that made the original copies of Abraham Zapruder's film that had captured the assassination of President Kennedy. Eventually, the company patented and successfully marketed a machine that made it possible for local television stations to process their own news film. Prior to that, most stations had to send their film out to a lab and wait for it to be processed and returned. As television news gathering became more competitive, and a major source of revenue, a demand emerged to get filmed new stories on the air quickly. Jamieson's compact machine that made possible, and revolutionized the industry. As the first company to provide such a solution for local stations, Jamieson became the market leader as it sold its machines across the nation. For me, the next logical step after processing the news film was learning how to edit the film using a Moviola viewer and a splicer to cut the film and then glue the selected pieces together. At our station, sound film used a magnetic track, although the projectors were capable of reproducing sound from both the mag-stripe or an optical track (which is what all the film used for commercials employed).

To have news film ready for use on the six-o'clock broadcast, there was a three-o'clock deadline for "getting the film into the soup." I loved that expression from the moment I first heard it. There were so many industry terms I learned in the early days of my career. One of my favorites was "annoyance factor," referring to the irritating aspect of advertising copy that makes the message more memorable. A prime example is the phrase, "don't squeeze the Charmin," intended to demonstrate the softness of that brand of toilet paper. Many phrases that have become a part of industry jargon are logical. For instance, "2-shot" refers to a camera shot that includes two people at the same time. Another is "over-the-shoulder," indicating the primary subject of a camera shot seen from over-the-shoulder of another person. "Crossing the line" refers to an imaginary axis where one subject is facing right and the other is facing left. "Crossing the line" means you have positioned the camera where both people appear to be facing the same direction, which is confusing for the viewer of the scene where two people are supposed to appear talking to one another. Two terms that are often confused with one another are "dolly" and "truck," which refer to two different camera moves. One moves in and out, either toward or away from the subject, with a dolly move. To "truck" is to move the camera either right or left, perpendicular to the subject. "Subject," by the way, refers to the person or object being shown on the camera. "Hot" has two meanings. A shot is "hot" if it is over exposed. A set is "hot" if it is ready to be used. For continuity, nothing on a "hot set" is to be moved, because anything moved in the shot will be noticeable when cutting to a different angle within the same scene. A "scene" can be shot from several angles, then edited together from several sequences to create a unified whole (that plays out as it does in real life). For instance, a "master shot" is the entire sequence shot from one angle, showing all the actors at once. This is then "intercut," taking a close up of a speaker from one angle; a reaction shot of the listener from another angle; a "cut" to a different speaker, and so forth. "Cut" can also have two meanings. One, when the director says "cut" means to stop the action and the camera. Another meaning of "cut" refers to the physical aspect of making an edit, or a cut (because in the old days, we actually made a physical cut in the film to combine shots together). Electronic editing still uses the term cut, although nothing is actually cut anymore. When the director asks the camera operator, "will it cut?" what he means is will the footage that has been shot be adequate for editing the scene together. "POV" means point-of-view. Usually, this refers to the camera viewing the scene as it would be seen from the subject's point-of-view.

Because I am a director, I am finicky about the confusion between "director" and "technical director" when used in a television environment. In a live television event, the director watches the monitors of all the cameras and calls the shots (in other words, chooses which camera to take to air). The director is responsible for the pace and overall look of the program. The TD, or "technical director," actually punches the buttons on the switcher that "takes the camera to air." In a union house (a place where the technical crew are union members) the director is NOT allowed to actually punch the buttons.

When I first sat in the director's chair to direct a live newscast, at the age of seventeen, I called the shots and punched the buttons. KTRE was a non-union house. By the time I moved into directing, I had learned how to operate every piece of equipment in the station. Before I had graduated from college, I had a First-Class FCC Broadcast Engineering License, a requirement back then to operate a television transmitter and to take the required hourly meter readings on the transmitter log. Having that license was job security for many years. I signed on the log after directing the ten o'clock news as the engineer-on-duty for the last two years I worked at KTRE. I monitored the transmitter and switched the local breaks in the *Tonight Show Starring Johnny Carson* until we signed off at midnight.

As a small market station, we were also the training ground for on-air personalities who got their start at KTRE and moved on from there to bigger markets. Dan Rather had applied for a job there but was not hired. Instead, he landed at Channel 11 in Houston, where his coverage of Hurricane Carla slamming into Galveston got him noticed by the brass at CBS. Rather went to the network and was on the front-line of major stories, including being in Dallas on November 22, 1963. He covered the Vietnam War, and his heated exchanges with President Richard Nixon during the Watergate scandal have become legends in the news industry.

LeBaron Taylor was the first African-American on the air on KTRE. He was gregarious and charming. He also took the under-age me to a black club in Diboll, Texas, where I got to see Rufus and Chaka Kahn perform. LeBaron bounced around several medium markets, including WLBT in Jackson, Mississippi, but finally left broadcasting and became an Episcopal priest.

Another anchor we had briefly was Malcolm Landess, who was extremely good and spent his off-the-air hours putting together demo reels that got him noticed by bigger markets. Eventually, he changed his name to Mike Landess and worked in several major markets, including Dallas, Washington D.C., and Denver, where he spent the majority of his career. He retired and went back to his hometown, Tyler, Texas, where he runs the campus radio station at UT Tyler.

My first job, after graduating from Stephen F. Austin State University in 1975, was to leave KTRE and take a position at the independent (not-affiliated with a network) KDOG TV-26 in Houston. I was hired by the production manager, Al Footnick, to be an editor for their commercial production department. One of the reasons I got the job was because I had an FCC license and could also act as engineer-on-duty while I was working as an editor. The transmitter meters were located in the same room as the editing machines. On the occasions when it was necessary for me to sign the log as engineer, I had to break away from production sessions and take the meter readings. My willingness to do double-duty paid off in that it showed my new employers that I was a team player, willing to do whatever was necessary to help the station achieve success.

I also think they noticed that I had strong technical skills, as well as an artistic eye as an editor. My multidisciplined background from KTRE was proving to be the asset I had hoped it would! Within a year, I had worked on hundreds of commercials, edited on RCA two-inch quad machines using a TEP editor. One of the first national spots I edited started winning awards. My boss, Footnick, invited me to attend the local advertising awards show, and our spot won the top prize. To my surprise, I learned it was not only my first award, but also Footnick's. Later, it would go on to win a national Clio (four generations from the Rightmer Family each say how they had learned about Ford pickups from their father. The spot ends with the great-grandfather mentioning he came to Texas in a covered wagon and had to "learn about Ford's on my own. I'm a smart old bird ain't I!").

A local celebrity, Harold Gunn, became something of a cult figure with his *Captain Harold's Theatre of the Sky*, a series of short comedy sketches performed by a company of local actors Harold gathered together. Harold was the lead, dressed in the garb of a World War II U.S. air corps captain. Harold drove around town in an old, black Cadillac limousine. He was also host of *High Noon*, a live, midday talk show on KDOG. It primarily featured interviews regarding local events and people, however, when a celebrity was in town to plug a new movie, book, or an appearance at a local venue, they were frequently booked on Harold's show. In 1977, one of his guests was Jodie Foster, who was nominated for a supporting actress Academy Award that year for her work in *Taxi Driver*. However, at that time the fourteen-year-old actress was in Houston to promote *Freaky Friday,* a comedy about a mother (Barbara Harris) and daughter (Foster) who switch bodies when each simultaneously states, "I wish I could switch places with her for just one day."

I don't remember exactly how my conversation came about, but I remember calling her Miss Foster, and she replied, "Call me Jodie." I told her how much I admired Martin Scorsese's work and complimented her performance in *Taxi Driver*, and that I was sorry she did not win the Oscar, "you deserved it." She was gracious as she said,

> "It is really quite an honor just being nominated. Perhaps I will find out what actually receiving an Oscar is like someday."

Eighteen years later she found out when she accepted the Oscar for Best Actress in *The Accused*. I digress. I finally mentioned to Jodie that I had just received a promo video for *The Last Waltz*, Scorsese's as yet not released documentary about The Band's final concert on November 25, 1976. Jodie was intrigued and asked if I could show it to her.

I took her into the control room and loaded the two-inch tape onto one of my editing machines and played it for her. She watched the monitor screen intently, never looking away as it played. In the midst of her rapt attention, she made comments matter-of-factly of what a genius she thought Scorsese was and how much she was interested in seeing the complete film. After we viewed it, she told me that she knew he had been working on it and asked if it had a release date. I looked through the paperwork that had come with the tape and told her it had no definite date, but that it was slated for release sometime in 1978. The promo tape was cleared for use after July 1977. I was impressed with Jodie's polite composure as she thanked me for showing her the clip. I found her to be intelligent, engaging, and a good conversationalist. She was self-confident but not the least bit pretentious. What impressed me most was, that despite her own fame, she was still able to be awestruck by her colleague Martin Scorsese and displayed an almost giddy adulation for his work—as would any other teenaged girl lucky enough to be in the rarified movie-making atmosphere. I enjoyed the time I spent with Jodie and have continued admiring her work ever since.

I have been asked many times why Channel 26 had the KDOG

call sign. The general manager when I went to work there was one of the original investors, Leroy Gloger. He and Raymond Shindler, were the two largest investors when they put the station on the air in 1971, using the call sign KVRL. It was operating at a loss and Gloger was asked to step up and take charge in an operational role. He had previously had great success with KIKK radio, a station that played country-western music, affectionately known as "kicker" music, hence the call sign KIKK. Gloger, recognizing that his station was the underdog of the local television market, and with a penchant for using memorable branding in call signs, he made the decision to change its call sign, and on September 1, 1975, the station officially became KDOG. Two strategic moves helped turn the financial condition around. First was a programming move that revolutionized the marketplace: broadcasting Spanish-language program during primetime. At that time, the largest population growth in Houston came from an influx Latinos. Gloger recognized the Hispanic market as an untapped revenue-generator for the broadcasting industry. The second, not as controversial but just as significant, was the decision to expand the broadcast day to a full twenty-four hours. Prior to that decision, every television station signed off of the air between midnight and 6:00 AM. Gloger correctly assumed that shift changes at 12:00 midnight meant there were a significant number of people getting off work, and it was likely the only entertainment available at that hour could be television programming from KDOG.

At some point in late 1975, the station made a deal with an outside production company and began airing *The All-Night Show*. Not long after I arrived at the station in 1976, I heard rumblings that our local sales manager was not happy with the arrangement of outsiders producing the show, and I mentioned to Footnick that I would like a shot at producing the show if it ever became available. Not long afterward, Footnick invited me to lunch with Jo Edgel, the sales manager, and Johnelle Collura, who worked in the programming department producing public service spots. They explained to us that the station was considering starting a live, early morning children's show and revamping *The All-Night Show*, and that they were offering us the job of producing those new shows.

We were both excited at this new prospect, especially because it included a salary that guaranteed each of us whopping $800 a month! As I think back on that, it seemed like a small fortune (remember, this would be in 1976 dollars), as it was the most money I had ever made in broadcasting. My income was much higher in high school because I worked on commission every Saturday at my father's store selling sewing machines and stereos. My commissions eclipsed my income from KTRE by ten-fold. There was a point in time when my father made me split my commissions with the two salesman that worked for him, because as he said, "they had families to support." I thought it was unfair, but I understood his position. Still, I was making more money from Dad's store than the parents of some of my friends, so I was doing okay financially. KDOG was my first experience where I depended totally on TV for my income. I was fully aware that broadcasting could provide a living, but the only people who made any real money were those in front of the camera, the sales staffers who were real go-getters, and the execs who managed the business. It did occur to me that producing was another avenue through which it would be possible to make money.

The first thing that Johnelle and I did was sit down together and put our vision of the two programs we were about to create on paper. We decided that she would be the primary producer for *#26 Morning Place*, the children's show, and I would take the all-night show, which we decided to call *Paws for the Night,* pun intended in the title. *Paws* was slated to run Thursday-Sunday nights, 1:00 AM-6:00 AM. *#26 Morning Place* was scheduled Monday-Friday mornings, 6:00 AM–8:00 AM. We decided both shows would take advantage of our extensive movie and cartoon catalogs. The format for both shows was essentially an introduction segment from the in-studio talent, followed by a segment of the movie (*Paws*) or a cartoon (*Morning Place*), followed by a commercial break, followed by a live cut-in from the in-studio talent, then back to another cartoon (*Morning Place*) or the next segment of the movie (*Paws*). Cut-ins for *#26 Morning Place* would be educational in nature, and the cut-ins on *Paws* would include celebrity interviews, phone calls from viewers on a variety of subjects, and trivia games, where the viewers could call in to answer the trivia questions and win prizes.

For *#26 Morning Place,* we decided to hire a total of eight hosts, three boys and five girls, ranging in age from 10 to 14. We paired two hosts together for each day's program. In order to have segments in which all eight hosts could be seen together, we planned a series of field trips filming on location in places easily accessible to our viewers, for instance, the Hermann Park Zoo, The Natural History Museum, The Modern Art Sculpture Garden, Peppermint Park, and various sites in Galveston (Ashton Villa, the Beach, Strand Street, etc.). Basically, we would visit kid-fun locations through the Houston viewing area—an opportunity for the *#26 Morning Place* kids to show these places of interest to their audience. To help market the show, we planned to sell T-shirts similar to the collared shirts our *#26 Morning Place* hosts wore.

Our hosts were Julie Postle, Michael Tapley, Sonja Lloyd, Julie Roberts, Tim Poe, Caroline Durham, Kirsten Brown, and James Rowland. I lost touch with most of the kids, although I do know what became of a few of them. Michael Tapley's first professional job in the theatre was at age ten, appearing in *Kismet*, which starred Howard Keel. Much of his early training came from the children's theatre program at Houston's Theatre Under the Stars. At twenty-one, he was cast in a national tour of *42nd Street*, followed by a touring production of *Mame* with Juliet Prowse, *The Unsinkable Molly Brown* with Debbie Reynolds, *Evita,* and The Who's *Tommy,* in which he was understudy for the title role and performed the role at the Kennedy Center for a week. Later, he went to Broadway with *Tommy* and then to Germany. Most recently, he played Melvin P. Thorpe in *The Best Little Whorehouse in Texas* in Houston, back at his alma mater Theatre Under The Stars. In addition to his onstage appearances, Michael worked as director and choreographer for Goodspeed Opera House, the American Musical Theater of San Jose, the North Carolina Theatre, Kansas City Starlight, the Lyric Theatre in Oklahoma City, and Galveston Outdoor Musicals.

Caroline Durham also made a career in New York, acting in theatre and making appearances on television in *Law and Order, One Life to Live,* and *As the World Turns.* Her real passion is the art of burlesque dancing, performing occasionally at The Slipper Room in New York, and is, at this writing, working on a one-woman show about striptease.

Several years ago, I was in a meeting with the J. Walter Thompson Agency regarding a project for our mutual client, the Shell Oil Company, when a young man in the meeting spoke up, "Do you remember me? I was on a kid show you produced in the '70s?" That was James Rowland, who had gone into advertising when he grew up. I am proud of these kids who began their careers on *#26 Morning Place* and went on to make a name for themselves. I like to think that Johnelle Collura and I played a small part in their professional development.

We began our *Paws for the Night* host search at various local radio stations. One personality we considered was Crash Collins, who, in addition to his gig on the radio, hosted the television show *Crash's Jam* airing on KDOG. I edited a couple of those programs during its brief run and was familiar with Crash's ability to interact with his guests. The most memorable was when Leon Russell appeared. He arrived with his then-wife, Mary McCreary. Crash asked where he got inspiration, and Leon spoke about the various ways he got ideas. Then, noodling around on a baby grand piano, he played a melody and started singing lyrics he made up as he played. "That's how I write a song." It is possible the tune he was fooling around with became "Love Is in Your Eyes," a song that would be included on the album *Make Love to the Music* that featured Mary McCreary, released in 1977.

We also wanted a host who was good at comedy for *Paws for the Night.* We felt the logical place to look for such a host was to concentrate on "talk radio." After interviewing several local radio personalities, we offered the position to Roger Gray, who had a knack for getting the best reactions from telephone callers on his daily radio show at KQUE, and he also had a flair for writing funny bits to use on his show.

He brought that flair to *Paws for the Night*, along with a company of actors he met as a theatre student of Cecil Pickett's at the University of Houston. Brett Cullen and Robin Moseley were included in that group, both of whom achieved a modicum of fame in their respective careers. Other local actors included Mimi Rodgers, Tim Arrington, Tommy Rogers, and yours truly. Frequently, members of our production crew would be thrown into the comedy bits. Our director, Ric Castleberry, and the cameramen Gary Fones and Clay Jones were all pressed into service as actors. Hey, we weren't doing Shakespeare; as long as they could deliver the lines, they were good enough for our show!

Since we came on at 1:00 in the morning, it was after any of the groups playing at The Summit had finished their concerts. Our studio was not far from that venue, making it convenient for any groups willing to make a live appearance on our show. As the producer, I was actually surprised at how often we could get talent from The Summit to appear. Usually, it would only be a brief visit for an interview. Sometimes, they would take phone calls from viewers. However, on a few occasions, we would get someone actually to perform.

In addition to booking name acts from The Summit, several local bands were always willing to get exposure by performing on our show. We made friends with a local acoustic guitarist, Mike Whitney, who was always willing to show up on those occasions when I could not book a "name" act. His regular gig was as the lounge entertainer at one of the hotels near our studio. Mike would frequently stay all night, playing a set and providing bumper lead-ins as we resumed the evening's movies.

One of the methods used to get celebrities on our all-night show was to glom onto the guests who were booked on Harold Gunn's *High Noon* show. At first, Harold objected because he wanted their appearances to be exclusive to his show. However, once I explained to him that we had completely different audiences, he was gracious about giving us access to his guests—to the point that he would alert me to his bookings and provide me with the contact information needed to make the bookings for the extra interview. Thank you, Harold!

When their time permitted, we would walk the celebrities from Harold's set in Studio B onto our set in Studio A. A few of the guests who agreed to appear for the post-*High Noon* interview with Roger Gray on *Paws* were Robert Mitchum, Phyllis Diller, Joan Rivers, Ray Harryhausen, Sarah Vaughan, Dick Cark, Jay Leno and Kinky Friedman. This was in the days before the NAB made a ruling that required stations to identify videotaped segments as being pre-recorded, so we taped the interviews as if these celebrities were on the show live, making certain that Roger wore the same clothes on the nights the interviews were scheduled to air. On the day we interviewed Robert Mitchum, who was promoting *The Big Sleep* (his second movie in three years playing Raymond Chandler's detective Philip Marlowe), a young lady on our crew shook his hand, passing him a joint, to which he replied, "I'll save this for later at the hotel."

Paws for the Night not only provided me with an income but also presented an opportunity to rub shoulders with the famous (or the nearly-famous) personalities who came through Houston regularly. This was the era of dinner theatres, which purists looked upon as providing neither great theatre nor great dinners. Despite that, Houston had several thriving dinner theatres in the 70s. These included the Dean Goss Theatre located near the Astrodome, Marietta Marich's Dinner Theatre located in a Sharpstown area hotel in Southwest Houston, The Windmill Dinner Theatre located in the Town and Country Shopping Center, The Great Caruso located in a West Houston strip center on Westheimer Road, and the Country Dinner Playhouse located in the Memorial area. In the mid-70s, there were approximately 175 dinner theatres in cities across the United States. These were Actors Equity signatory theatres, hiring union-member actors.

To bring star power, which attracted patrons, these theatres often employed celebrity actors in the starring roles and filled out the rest of the cast with local actors from within the respective communities. Film stars from Hollywood's Golden Age, such as Mickey Rooney, Cesar Romero, Van Johnson, June Allyson, and Myrna Loy, toured the country playing in these theatres. Television actors such as Julie Kavner (Rhoda's sister) and Ester Rolle (the mother on Good Times) also found work in dinner theatres. Earl Holliman and Burt Reynolds both owned dinner theatres, The Fiesta Dinner Playhouse in San Antonio, Texas, and the Burt Reynolds Dinner Theatre in Jupiter, Florida, respectively. According to an article published in 1974 by the theater trade paper *Show Business,* "More actors work in Equity dinner theatres than work on

Broadway!"

For a time, dinner theatres were big business. Roger Gray's access to interviewing touring celebrities from the dinner theatre circuit gave *Paws for the Night* a huge boost. Our show became known for both the comedy sketches performed by our resident group of performers and for the insightful interviews Roger did with his celebrity guests. One of the problems we encountered in getting advertisers to support our show was the fact that we had no ratings. Not that we didn't have viewers; Neilsen did not offer its ratings service to programs on the air after midnight.

We did come up with a clever way to prove we had an audience. Since the show's beginning, we did segments with trivia questions and gave away prizes from our sponsors. The most frequent prize was a free sandwich from Papa Johns, one of our regular sponsors. I approached another one of our sponsors about providing the prize for a Grand Prize Trivia Game. It was to be a more difficult trivia contest with a Grand Prize of substantial value. The advertiser agreed to provide a Vespa Moped as the Grand Prize for our trivia contest.

Every night, Roger would ask viewers to answer a trivia question, and then he would take calls from viewers. He explained the rules of the game, which included which caller would get to play the game. Every time he asked the question, he followed it by stating, "Tonight, we will take the fifteenth caller." Every night, he would change the number. When the lights on the phone began to blink, he would answer by telling the number that the caller was, "You are caller number one, next caller … You are caller number two," and so forth until he reached the caller number for that night's game. When he reached the caller number for that night, he would banter with the caller for a few moments, and finally, he would re-state the trivia question, and the caller would respond. Naturally, the trivia questions were difficult, and no one answered correctly for several months.

This game became very popular with our viewers, and the people at the Vespa dealership were getting a lot of store traffic. We were getting so many calls when we did the Grand Prize Trivia contest that the phone service in our area was overloaded. Several times, phone service in the area around the studio was so jammed up with calls people trying to make a call that they got busy signals instead of a dial tone. Basically, our contest shut off phone service. It didn't take long before the telephone company sent a letter to the station complaining about how our show was responsible for the service interruption. I made copies of that letter for the sales staff, and they used it with potential advertisers to demonstrate how *Paws for the Night* did, in fact, have a substantial viewer base during the early morning hours every night we were on the air.

Eventually, we did have a winner for the Vespa moped. By then, we also had a ton of new sponsors advertising on our show. We kept the Grand Prize Trivia Game going for the duration of the time *Paws for the Night* was on the air, with prizes ranging from expensive wristwatches and diamond rings to all-expenses-paid vacations, with every prize given at no cost to the show because advertisers donated them.

Chapter 6
Carol Channing and Eddie Bracken: A Big Star and The Best Number Two Man on Broadway

It did not take long after I started producing *Paws for the Night* for me to realize that the show created the opportunity to meet and work with many celebrities. The proximity to the many stars who would eventually be guests on the show allowed me to gain a close-up view of how famous people behaved in the presence of their fans. I also got a glimpse of how they treated people who were peers in the business, the unknown minions, like myself, who gave these celebrities access to their adoring fans.

When the Houston Grand Opera produced the tenth-anniversary revival of Carol Channing's *Hello, Dolly!* she was a guest in our studio. Before the actual play arrived in town, she had come to Houston to produce a commercial that was used to promote the show (I appeared as an actor during the film shoot). In the commercial was a version of the show's signature song, with the lyrics changed to "Hello, Houston!" The soundtrack was produced by Robin Hood Brians and his co-composer Randy Fouts. It was produced at Robin Hood Studios in Tyler, a recording studio known for producing several hit records throughout the 60s. At the time the commercial for *Hello, Dolly!* was produced, ZZ Top had just completed recording their first platinum-selling album at Robin Hood's. When Brians and Fouts began putting the tracks together, they listened to the original cast recording of the musical from 1964. Carefully, they crafted the arrangement to match the original recording as closely as possible. The tracks were completed before Channing added the vocals. Upon hearing the tracks, she arrived for the recording session and said, "I can't sing in that key!" "It's exactly the same as the cast recording," Fouts explained. "Oh, honey, that was ten years ago. I could barely hit the notes then and certainly can't hit them now."

I managed to get Channing's co-star, Eddie Bracken (playing Horace Vandergelder), to appear live on our show, during which we played two of his most famous movies, *Hail the Conquering Hero* and *Miracle of Morgan's Creek*. Bracken was a one-time partner with Fred Nehas in an advertising agency in Houston. I met Bracken through Nehas at an anniversary celebration at Glenn McCarthy's Shamrock Hotel a decade before it was razed. Fred Nehas had been instrumental in producing the Shamrock's lavish opening night celebration on St. Patrick's Day, 1949. The evening included 150 Hollywood celebrities, including Bracken, Ginger Rogers, Hedda Hopper, Robert Preston, Errol Flynn, and Dorothy Lamour, whose performance singing on network radio was accidentally cut off, resulting in Lamour reportedly running from the stage in tears. Planned as "Houston's biggest party," a crowd in excess of 50,000 people showed up unexpectedly outside the hotel, causing the Houston Chronicle's society reporter to label the event "bedlam in diamonds." When I met Eddie Bracken at the Shamrock, the hotel was long past its prime. Eddie was, however, experiencing a resurgence in his career, which would lead to guest starring roles on television and character roles in several films during the next decade, most notably as Roy Walley in *National Lampoon's Vacation,* as the founder of Walley World, the film's fictional theme park based on Disneyland.

Eddie was extremely gracious toward me, and we developed a friendship. When I asked if he would do an interview that I could run on our show, during an evening when we would be showing his movies, it was Eddie himself who suggested that he should appear live on the show. He showed up at precisely 12:45 a.m. on the appointed night and stayed for almost the entire program. When we would come back from a commercial break in the movie, Eddie would tell backstage anecdotes about different scenes from the film.

Not only did he share stories about his career during Roger's probing interview, but he also took phone calls from the viewers. When Roger asked about his appearances on Broadway, Eddie explained that he took great pleasure in the fact that he had been cast in roles made famous by other actors, stating, "I'm the best number two man on Broadway." As an example, in *The Seven Year Itch*, Eddie replaced Eddie Albert in the role of Richard Sherman. Albert had previously replaced Tom Ewell, who had originated the role in the original production. Eddie played the role on Broadway and then in its national touring company before taking the production to London, where he starred opposite Rosemary Harris as Elaine. When Art Carney left the cast of *The Odd Couple* after playing the role of Felix Unger from the opening on March 10, 1965, Eddie took over the role in October 1965 and played the role for the rest of its original Broadway run, closing on July 2, 1967. Mickey Rooney made his Broadway debut in *Sugar Babies* opposite Ann Miller on October 8, 1979. Eddie took the role over from Joey Bishop and was then in the 1982 Bus and Truck Tour, with Jaye P. Morgan in the role originated by Ann Miller. Because of his reputation as a consummate performer with impeccable comic timing, Eddie was given the role of Horace Vandergelder for the revival of *Hello, Dolly!* staged by the Houston Grand Opera. That revival premiered in Houston, and Eddie played opposite Carol Channing in its 1978 Broadway run and throughout its London West End run in 1979.

During Eddie's appearance on *Paws*, I mentioned that my parents were coming from Colorado to see *Hello, Dolly!* Eddie made arrangements for us to meet at the stage door before the performance. I introduced him to my parents, and he graciously commented to them how well he thought I was doing my job as producer of *Paws for the Night*. He invited us backstage at the end of the performance, saying he wanted to be sure my parents could meet Carol Channing.

Meeting a celebrity, like Carol Channing, was not something my parents were wont to do. My father had a personality that was open and inviting. He could talk to anyone on any subject and always made the people he encountered feel at ease and comfortable. My mother, on the other hand, was introverted and shy. She was extremely quick-witted and could converse about various topics, but she was much more reserved than my father. She was not impressed by a person's fame and had a tendency to be judgmental based on how a person approached her. Both of my parents were keenly aware that Eddie was making an extra effort to be cordial. I believed part of his reasoning was to help me to impress my parents.

As he chatted amiably with my parents, he continually complimented me to the point it was becoming embarrassing. I appreciated what he was doing and accepted it as graciously as possible. Later, my father would tell me that what he was most impressed with about Eddie was his down-to-earth demeanor. "I would have imagined that he would be full of himself, but he was not the least bit arrogant or conceited," my dad said to me. "If I had just met him on the street, I think we would hit it off." Dad and Eddie spent some of their time together talking about the war. Dad fought in World War II as part of the infantry in the Texas 36th Infantry Division. During the war, Eddie spent much of the time making military training films and war-themed movies directed toward an audience that needed a diversion from the headlines coming from the front. Eddie expressed his interest in how serving in the war had affected my father. "I didn't like it, but it was a duty I was called to do, and I did my job as best as I could. The toughest part was being there when other soldiers were mortally wounded. In combat, the man next to you becomes your best friend. The most difficult thing to deal with is having that friend killed, and there is nothing you can do about it but be grateful it wasn't you," my father told him.

To a degree, Eddie felt his own contributions to the war effort were minor compared to those, like my father, whose lives were on the line every day. Although Eddie was only five and a half years older than my father, he was just beyond draft age. The films he made during the war years were comedies that successfully entertained the thousands of Americans who spent the war years stateside, each doing their part for the war effort. On one level, Eddie was aware that making films was an important contribution, but he did not feel it was nearly as big a contribution as those who were actually fighting. Based on how he talked about it, he obviously felt he had missed out by being stateside. "You made a contribution. We saw the films in the field. Those films helped keep the soldiers aware of what we were fighting for, a way of life that needed to be protected," my father assured him.

When the performance of *Hello, Dolly!* was over, we met Eddie backstage. As promised, he had told Carol Channing we were coming to meet her. Moments after the introductions were made and my parents complimented her performance, Carol looked at me and asked,

> "Do I recognize you from the shoot we did for the commercial?" That impressed my parents.
>
> "Yes, I was in that spot and also met you when you were on the *High Noon Show* with Harold Gunn," I replied.
>
> "And you did an impression of me?"
>
> So, as we stood backstage at Jones Hall, I launched into my impression of Carol Channing, "Why, yes, Carol. I spoke to you briefly, giving my best impression of you speaking. I hope you don't think I am too brash for doing that."
>
> "I don't know how much you sound like me, but you have the cadence right."

The rest of our brief meeting was devoted to talking about her performance. My mother mentioned how astounded she was watching her eat onstage (referring to a scene in which Dolly spends several minutes scarfing down potatoes at the Harmonia Gardens).

> "It's cotton candy. It melts as soon as I pop one into my mouth," Carol explained.

Because she played that scene so many times throughout the entirety of her career, I have often wondered whether she ever became a diabetic.

My last contact with Eddie Bracken took place just a few years later. I sent him a Christmas card, and he called me on the telephone. He asked how my career was going, and I told him I was on my way to Los Angeles for a meeting with a potential agent. He offered to put me in touch with some people he knew, but I never followed through. Several times in the intervening years, I thought of getting back in contact with him, especially after he had done the film *Home Alone 2: Lost in New York,* but I never made the effort. I regret that. When I read that he had died in November 2002, I felt a strong tinge of regret.

He had been so kind to me when my career was just beginning; I regretted that I had not made a better effort to keep in touch. I admired him as both a performer and a person. It would have been nice for him to have known how his early help had paid off in developing my career. I think he would have been pleased to know that thirty years after we met, I was making a decent living in the business and had developed a reputation within my generation of peers as a dependable, capable producer and director.

Chapter 7
I Remember Joan Rivers

The first I knew of Joan Rivers' death was reading about it in a crawler at the bottom of the cable news channel screen. Learning this tragic news prompted me to write about, a brief but personal, relationship I shared with Joan Rivers. Thinking that I might write a memoir one day, it was the first thing I wrote, and I stored it away.

Born as Joan Alexandra Molinsky in Brooklyn, she used her Jewish background as the basis for much of her early work, a combination of blunt sarcasm and self-deprecating humor, poking fun at herself as often as she targeted politicians and other celebrities. She was a funny person, a trailblazer, and a role model for women aspiring to perform stand up comedy at a time when the only women who succeeded as stand-up comics were Phyllis Diller and Totie Fields. Joan was different from either of them because she had a certain brashness that made her stand out. Part of the joke for Phyllis and Totie was their physical appearance. With Joan, there was more to it than that. Although she made fun of her looks, she always dressed like a million dollars and was actually very attractive. She had a vulnerability that she kept just out of reach from the audience. It made her self-deprecating remarks funnier because you knew they contained just a tad of truth smoldering between the punch lines and her wry comments about the way women were viewed by society in the days before women's lib took hold. To put my story in context, I need to give the background that led to our first meeting.

In 1977, Jimmy Carter was inaugurated President, and the United States was finally getting over Watergate. Having just completed shooting the pilot for *They'd Hang You in Nashville* starring Charlie Cudd, Phil Allen, Vickie Bergman, Tony Frank, and yours truly (based on the play by our college classmate William King Gleason), I rushed to the offices of MTM Enterprises located near the old Gunsmoke set at Studio City.

It was there that I met with Grant Tinker, who was, at that time, Mary Tyler Moore's husband. He was an interesting, no-BS kind of executive in those days. He was alone in the office when I arrived for our appointment. I stood in the empty outer lobby admiring posters of the various MTM Productions currently in production: *The Mary Tyler Moore Show, The Bob Newhart Show, Rhoda, and The Betty White Show.* I was admiring an Emmy when Tinker walked into the room wearing a pale-yellow sweater, beige slacks, and what I took to be Gucci loafers (although they may well have been Hush Puppies). He asked me where the receptionist was, and I immediately felt I was in trouble.

After explaining that I did not work there but that I was his 10:30 appointment, he politely led me into his office and offered me bottled water. We sat down, and he made small talk, asking how my parents were doing and what I had been up to lately. As I listened to his questions, it occurred to me he was confused about who I was, perhaps mistaking me for the son of some acquaintance. I told him my parents had retired to Colorado (he had not heard) and explained I had graduated from college in '75 and that after going to work at a studio in Houston, I put together the pilot for a new comedy show. He said he was excited to see my pilot and started to fiddle with the controls of a large 3/4-inch Sony Playback machine. It was one of the early models, the kind that had a transport that popped up with the aid of a slide lever. He had trouble getting the tape to go into the machine, which made me worry he was going to tear up my tape. It finally went down with a clunk, and I heard the mechanism grab the tape from the cassette and thread it through the capstan. He started the player and turned on the television set that was on the table beside the player. I swear, he winked at me and smiled before turning his attention to the opening sequence of what I hoped was to be my ticket to Hollywood.

We both stood there watching the screen. The only sound was from the tinny speakers on the television set. Naturally, I had heard these lines a thousand times. First, when we played in the original staging of the play in the Downstage Theatre at Stephen F. Austin State University; and then again at the time we filmed the pilot. And, again, over and over and over, as I edited this masterpiece, night after night—until it was absolutely perfect. There was always a rhythm to the laughter. Line, line, laugh. Line, line, laugh. I had been intimately involved with "They'd Hang You in Nashville" for more than a year. At the time, I considered it one of the funniest plays I had performed. After every performance, members of the audience would complain that they were in pain from laughing so much. I stood there trying to gauge Grant Tinker's reaction. I was in the presence of one of the most successful television producers in Hollywood, the man who ran a company that had four hit shows on CBS, the man who would, in the not-too-distant future, be the president of the NBC network, the man who slept with Mary Tyler Moore. And, here was I, the kid from Houston, whose star was destined to rise solely on the word of this one executive.

We stood watching in total silence. The lines came one after another. Line, line, line. Line, line, line. Not one laugh. I began to sweat. At one point, after my old friend Tony Frank cracked one of his funniest lines, Tinker took his eyes away from the set and looked at me and asked, "Who is the fat guy doing the bad Sheldon Leonard?" After about five minutes, Tinker turned off the television and ejected my tape. As he gingerly placed the tape cassette back into its case, he looked at me and asked, "How did you get an appointment with me?"

Instinct guided me; this was one of those sink-or-swim

moments.

"I called your office and asked to speak with you and your receptionist put me through," I said matter-of-factly.

"You mean that girl that's not sitting in the lobby, the girl that doesn't work here anymore?"

"Yes, I suppose she's the one," I replied.

"And I spoke to you? When?" Tinker demanded.

"Yes, about three weeks ago. You made the appointment. You told me to be here at 10:30 in the morning," I said, praying that my voice would not crack.

"Well, what is it you want? Do you want a job? Do you want to sell me this crap? Why are you here?"

"I think this is a good idea for a comedy series. I'd like MTM to produce it."

"You want to act in it? Direct it? Write it? What?"

"Whatever you think I should do."

"I think you should throw it in the Los Angeles River on your way out of town."

At that moment, I was absolutely crestfallen. A rush of emotions filled my body. It was similar to the feeling of pain I had experienced in the dentist's office many years before. I was instantly concerned about not letting my facial expression expose my feelings. I knew maintaining self-control was necessary and not allowing my reaction to betray me. I had to act like the professional I was pretending to be. I blurted out, "Don't be coy. Tell me what you really think." Have you ever had a moment when the words came out of your mouth without you intending them to? This was such a moment. All at once, it was as if my world had suddenly shifted into slow motion. In my mind, I was seeing the instant replay over and over and over— "Don't be coy. Tell me what you really think." "Don't be coy. Tell me what you really think." "Don't be coy. Tell me what you really think."

Tinker then sat down and spent an hour telling me how the business works. I had the graduate course in television production in that hour. "Allan Burns is in the office down the hall. He is one of the best comedy writers in town. I can tell him your idea; he can write it and I can have it on the air on CBS in the fall. And, you can't do anything about it."

By this time, I think he sensed I was slightly crestfallen.

"Am I the only appointment you have?" Tinker asked.

"No. I'm leaving here to meet with Norman Lear. Then late this afternoon I have a meeting with Judy Copage at Columbia. Tomorrow, I have a meeting at Metromedia Square, and then later in the week with Andy Cohen (not his real name) at CBS," I said, rattling off names as if I were reading Mary Tyler Moore's Christmas Card list.

"Andy Cohen, head of comedy development at CBS?"

"Yes."

"I can't get an appointment with Cohen. How did you get a meeting with Cohen?"

"The same way I got a meeting with you. His receptionist put me through."

"They must be sisters."

He stood there looking at me. I could not decide whether his expression was of mockery, sympathy, or amazement that I had meetings with some other high-powered names. Presently, he reached his hand out and, as he shook my hand, said, "I changed my mind. Don't dump that in the river yet. Go to that meeting with Cohen. When you get out, come back over here and tell me what he said."

I will not bore you with the details of my other meetings. Suffice it to say, they were almost as depressing as my meeting with Tinker. Instead, I will fast forward to my meeting two days later at CBS. I arrived exactly on time (which means ten minutes early) and got into the elevator at Television City. As I was pressing the button, a voice shouted, "Hold that car!"

A woman with the skinniest ankles I have ever seen got on the elevator. She was sharply dressed, and I recognized her immediately as Joan Rivers. She was much smaller than I would have thought. As the elevator began moving, I tried my best not to stare and cast my eyes forward, focusing on the numbered buttons. "You recognize me, don't you."

> "Yes, I do, Miss Rivers." We both stood there in silence, looking straight ahead.
>
> "Do you want an autograph?"
>
> "Thank you. No. But thank you. I really admire your work," I replied
>
> "What do you do?" she inquired.
>
> "I'm a television producer in Houston, Texas."
>
> "I'm a comic," she said.

Just then, we reached our floor. I held the door for Miss Rivers and followed her off the elevator. We both walked toward the receptionist, who immediately said, "Welcome, Miss Rivers, they're waiting for you." The receptionist hit the button that unlocked the gate. Joan Rivers turned to me and asked, "What is your name?"

"Allen Morris."

"It was very nice meeting you, Allen Morris."

"It was nice meeting you, Miss Rivers."

"Call me Joan." She shook my hand and then walked through the gate. As she did, the receptionist looked at me.

"I'm Allen Morris; I have an appointment with Andy Cohen."

Suddenly, I heard that famous Joan Rivers voice,

"Ooh, ooh, ooh… He's with me!" she said quickly. She came back through the gate, grabbed my arm, and whisked me alongside her.

"You have a meeting with Andy Cohen?"

"Yes."

"They're having a surprise party for me in his office right now. We're signing a contract this afternoon for a project at CBS. What is your meeting about?"

"I have a pilot for a comedy series."

"The schmuck probably forgot about your meeting. Don't you worry!"

When we walked into Cohen's office, there was a crowd of people. They all clapped as we walked in, and Joan turned on the

59

Joan Rivers charm. I stood back, out of the way, as a sea of people crowded around offering congratulations, with everybody kissing each other on the cheek or in the air near the cheek. Waiters began handing out glasses of champagne to the party-goers, and I started looking at the faces, trying to see who I might recognize. I recognized James Brooks. I think I saw Will McKenzie, the actor turned sitcom director, most famous as the nose in an early 70s TV commercial and as Larry Bondurant on The Bob Newhart Show. Allan Burns was also there. I was beginning to realize that nearly every comedy writer in Hollywood was attending this party.

As the initial chitchat began to die down, Joan Rivers noticed me, grabbed me by the arm, and dragged me to our host, Andy Cohen. "Andy, you schmuck, this is the appointment you forgot about this afternoon. Allen Morris, the producer from Houston."

Cohen looked slightly embarrassed, not certain what connection I had to Joan Rivers. He fumbled an apology, and said something about perhaps we should re-schedule, to which I replied, "Yes, perhaps we can get together in the morning."

Joan suddenly burst into our conversation with, "Ooh, ooh, ooh… this is perfect. Allen has this incredibly funny pilot, and we can all watch it right now!" Lowering her voice, she leaned over to me, "This could be your big chance. Don't blow it!"

I know why they give condemned men a blindfold when they are facing the firing squad. Her voice was ringing in my ears, "This could be your big chance. Don't blow it!" Then I heard Grant Tinker's voice, "Throw it in the Los Angeles River on your way out of town."

Joan, I know you were trying to help. You had not actually *seen* my pilot. It was for you, as much as for me, that I bailed out of that opportunity to show my pilot to that room full of Hollywood's funniest writers. "Oh, no, I think it would be best if I just leave you this tape, and I will call you in the morning," I said as I handed Andy Cohen my ticket to Hollywood, which, at that moment, I was beginning to think of more as my ticket to obscurity.

The day I walked into Grant Tinker's office chutzpah was playing a major role. When I recently described my actions that day to a friend, he asked me if I was able to "feel the moment" when I first met with Tinker. The answer is yes. I was very much aware that I was in the midst of a most unusual opportunity—one that could have given me my big break in Hollywood. When Tinker started "attacking" my project and then said he could steal the idea and put it on the air, and there was nothing I could do about it, I let my guard down and showed my vulnerability. I think that was due to a combination of inexperience, immaturity, and nervousness. I think the meeting would have gone much better had I not shown my vulnerability. If I could have kept up the charade, the chutzpah, he might have never seen the chink in my armor. But that is part of the point about having the goods to deliver. I went in there acting. When the scene changed from what I had planned in my mind before going in, I was not up to the task of ad-libbing my way through it. Sensing my vulnerability, Tinker went on the offensive. However, the more he attacked, and I sat there listening intently, his attitude slowly shifted. When we sat down, he explained how the business worked, telling a novice what reality was in Hollywood. By the time he was ready to end the meeting, he saw the need to give me a second chance by telling me to go to the other meetings and then come back and report to him.

However, I blew that. After several days of one rejection after rejection, I completely lost my nerve and did not go back to Tinker. I didn't even call his office. Instead, I got on a plane and went back to Texas. I should have gone back to Tinker's office. I truly believe things would have ended differently had I done that, but I obviously was not ready. I think, had I gone back and confronted the situation head-on, Tinker might have offered to mentor me. He might have given me the chance to prove myself in the business with his guidance. At some point during our meeting, he mentioned how things could change in Hollywood, and that one must be careful about protecting the relationships they build. "You never know, but I could be working for you someday," he had said in all seriousness. That was all I thought about on the flight back home. And for many years afterward. My timing was off. I think luck had been on my side, but I blew it. I was so close, very close to opening the door to fame and fortune in Hollywood, but I blew it and have regretted how I handled that moment ever since.

It was a little over a year later when I next saw Joan Rivers, this time on my home turf in Houston. She was on a publicity tour for a 1978 movie she directed starring a young and then unknown Billy Crystal. The movie was *Rabbit Test*. Joan was booked on the *High Noon* talk show and afterward was taping an interview for my late-night show, *Paws for the Night*. I escorted her into the studio and introduced her to the host of the *High Noon* show, local celebrity Harold Gunn. After that appearance was completed, Joan taped the interview with the host of my show, Roger Gray. We had some pictures made by a staff photographer (during that time in my career, I always had a photographer on the set who had been instructed to get my picture with any celebrities we had in the studio. I don't know where that picture is now). When the time came, I escorted Joan to her waiting limousine. As we were walking alone down the corridor toward the lobby, she grabbed my arm and stopped me in the middle of the hallway, "What happened when you went back to Cohen?"

"I beg your pardon."

"You thought I didn't remember you, but I do!" Joan said, winking at me.

I was flustered. "I called him the next morning, and he brushed me off. I got the tape back with a rejection letter about three weeks later," I told her.

"I told you he was a schmuck. Don't let it get you down. You just keep doing what you're doing. Thank you for having me on your show," she said with a smile and gave me a kiss on the cheek, or at least in the air near my cheek.

In the following years, my path crossed Joan Rivers' path twice more. Once was when I was directing a corporate show in Las Vegas, where she was appearing. The other time was in New York, at a party my client had invited me to attend. As my client was introducing me to various celebrities in attendance, Joan walked up. She immediately said, "I believe the last time I saw you was in Las Vegas. You were producing a show at Caesar's Palace. How have you been?" There was no question in my mind that Joan was trying to ensure my client was suitably impressed. She went out of her way to present our relationship as something more than it was; her way of helping me. That is what I admired about Joan. She was always gracious and knew how the game was played. If she thought a word from her would do some good, she was only too happy to oblige. When we were alone, she spoke to me as a colleague. She showed a genuine interest as she asked what I was doing and how my career was progressing. She asked if I was working on another sitcom, and if I was, would there be a part for her in it? Naturally, I told her anytime I had a project she wanted to be involved in, she was welcome. After nearly ten minutes, she nudged me and said, "I hope your client got enough out of this to do you some good. I hope to see you again. If you show up someplace where I'm working, be sure to let me know you are in town."

Not long ago, I was watching a cable channel that runs the old *Tonight Show Starring Johnny Carson.* I watched the episode from the mid-seventies, and Joan was a guest. This was taped long before she fell out of favor with Johnny. This was vintage Joan Rivers, and I enjoyed watching her work immensely. Her mind was so quick, and no matter what Johnny asked her, she would make a comment that caused the audience to roar. She worked hard to establish herself as a standup comedian, a career in which only a handful of women had succeeded up to that time. To say that she helped blaze a trail for other women in comedy doesn't give justice to her contribution. Most of the comedians (male and female) working today will readily acknowledge her influence.

I am saddened that Joan is gone. I liked her. I am glad I got to know her more than as a mere casual acquaintance. I always thought she was funny and knew she was tough. She, too, yearned for fame. She achieved it, and more importantly, she handled her fame with grace and charm. She never forgot her roots and never talked down to her audience. She also never apologized for her work when critics called it insensitive, stating, "I have no regrets about any jokes I've ever done." What I know that people not fortunate to have had a personal relationship with her may not know is that she was the genuine article. She truly cared about other people, even people she barely knew, or for that matter, people she may not have known at all. She believed in laughter. She gave us laughter. I will think of her often in the future.

Chapter 8
The Legend of Robin Hood Studios and the Merry Bands Who Recorded There

The road from obscurity to fame and fortune can be arduous. The turns and twists the road takes vary, based on imponderables such as education, experience, talent, and luck. Luck invariably plays a bigger role than it should. Suffice it to say fame and fortune in the music business is down a long and winding road (cue strings). I have known Robin Hood Brians for more than forty-five years. He is my best friend. We have worked together, played together, and gone to church together. We share several mutual friends and acquaintances, some in the business, but some are not. Robin Hood (as most people call him) dreamed of achieving fame and fortune in the music business. The degree to which he achieved either is up for debate.

Of course, there are degrees of fame and fortune. Some people have one or the other: fame *or* fortune. For instance, Mother Theresa had fame but no fortune. Then, there are those who have both fame *and* fortune. Bill Gates is in that category. So is Barbra Streisand. They both also have talent, although not the same kind of talent. Talent is not necessary for either fame or fortune, although it certainly does not hurt. Talent can certainly bring fame. Van Cliburn was talented and famous because of his talent, and Stephen King turned his talent for writing scary stories into a fortune. He also became famous. Another category is comprised of people who have fame *because* they have fortune. Donald Trump belongs to this group. Then, too, consider those who are famous simply for being famous. Kim Kardashian comes to mind. There is the prospect of making a fortune *because* of being famous. Again, Kim Kardashian comes to mind. It is possible to have absolutely no talent and still gain fame and fortune. Once again, Kim Kardashian (my apologies to Ms. Kardashian for taking such a cheap shot).

To set the stage properly, it is necessary to provide some relevant background information. If you are from Texas and are familiar with the Texas music scene, you are no doubt aware that *Austin City Limits* is the longest-running music program on television. Since 1975, *ACL* has brought the Texas music scene to the attention of fans, up-and-coming musicians, and industry moguls throughout the nation. Thirty-seven years ago, Austin hosted the so-called cosmic cowboy scene, later referred to as the progressive country sound or redneck rock. The genres showcased on *Austin City Limits* reflected the musical tastes of the entire state: a diverse mixture ranging from country, blues, and folk to Tejano, gospel, rock, and jazz. In addition to featuring prominent performers, the program showcased many talents who, if not actually born in Texas, at least made their musical mark here. Performers like Willie Nelson, Waylon Jennings, Jessi Colter, and Tompall Glaser (and others) developed a subgenre of country music known as Outlaw Country, a radical departure from the conservative Nashville Sound. Jerry Jeff Walker came to Texas in the 70's and started his career over. Guitarist Stevie Ray Vaughan was a teenage prodigy from Dallas playing in clubs he was too young to enter legally.

While PBS and *Austin City Limits* disseminated much of the Gospel of Texas Music to the world beyond the state's borders, the tradition of Texas-made music reaches back long before KLRN put the program on the air. Scott Joplin was born near Texarkana in 1868. His ragtime music started a musical revolution before the end of the nineteenth century, a revolution in which the tastes of common people influenced what music gained popularity. The advent of radio brought a wider audience for a growing variety of styles. Venues to accommodate smaller audiences sprang up: honky-tonks and nightclubs. Trombone player Milt Larkin and tenor sax player Arnett Cobb ushered the jazz age into Houston. Bob Wills and His Texas Playboys created the Western Swing sound, gaining nationwide popularity from the late thirties throughout the war years. Country Music Hall of Famer Tex Ritter starred in western movies and signed on with Capitol Records as their first Western singing star—a decade before Hank Williams recorded "Hey Good Lookin'."

The fifties changed the cultural landscape across America. When rock and roll hit the radio, Texas found representation in the movement with the likes of Buddy Holly, J. P. Richardson (The Big Bopper), and Roy Orbison. Holly, Richardson, and a teenage sensation from California going by the name Ritchie Valens died tragically in a plane crash, memorialized as "The Day the Music Died" in the song "American Pie" by Don McLean. It is a cruel irony that so many other young musicians fell victim to plane crashes (Otis Redding, Jim Croce, the Lynyrd Skynyrd Band, and Ricky Nelson, to name but a few). To understand the role (and influence) Texas musicians played in the continuing evolution of popular music, one must credit the enabling technological advances made in the broadcasting and recording industries. From the mid-twenties, recording music entailed crowding musicians into a large studio and recording live performances directly onto wax discs, from which an engineer made a metal master disc for use in "pressing" copies of the "record" for distribution. The ability to edit the recording or add separate "tracks" did not exist until the late 1940s, with the introduction of magnetic sound recording tape.

As rapidly as new technology arrived, a shift occurred in radio broadcasting. No longer was it necessary for musicians to perform live in a studio. Ampex introduced a small recorder that used seven-inch reels of quarter-inch tape. Soon after, multi-track recorders made it possible to discretely record several instruments and vocals simultaneously and then mix the sound levels to achieve a natural "live" sound. Almost overnight, the recording industry transformed itself. The improvements in the recording industry made it possible for "disc jockeys" to spin records. Teenagers listened to the radio and bought the records of their favorite songs. The demand for more products increased, and Top-40 was born. Just as quickly as the boom in the record industry occurred, the marriage of picture and sound added a new dimension to broadcasting.

Television became a pervasive new medium. When *American Bandstand* premiered on the ABC network in August 1957, the entire nation caught the dance fever ignited in 1952 by the local Philadelphia television program. By the late 1950s, the transistor further revolutionized electronics. Soon, nearly every teenage boy in America had a battery-operated AM radio in his pocket. The increasing popularity of rock and roll eventually led many teenagers to a more serious interest in music. Kids began forming bands, practicing in their parents' garages. The piano lessons many reluctantly endured provided a foundation as they began to pick up guitars and mimicked the three-chorded rhythms they heard on their radios. Just before the British Invasion of the '60s, regional bands proliferated across the country. Some of these garage bands scrounged together enough money to record 45-rpm demos. The lucky ones even got a little airplay. In the 60s, there were local television shows *Sump'n Else*, hosted by Ron Chapman in Dallas, and *The Larry Kane Show* in Houston, featuring "live" performances of regional bands that were beginning to get national airplay. Sometimes, one or two minor hits resulted, and the bands went on to work the hotel and honky-tonk circuit. They could then consider themselves as professional musicians. For some, that was as far as their dreams took them. They worked the circuit for a few years but eventually grew tired of the grind, married, and then settled down with a real job and a family.

There were others, however, with aspirations more serious. This is where we pick up our story. The setting is the town of Tyler, in

East Texas. Strategically located about halfway between Dallas and Shreveport, Tyler was first an agricultural center known for its peaches. When the peach blight devastated the crop in the early part of the twentieth century, local farmers switched to growing roses in sandy loam that was perfect for roses. Tyler became famous due to its roses, laying claim to being the Rose Capitol of the World because something like 50% of the commercially grown rose bushes sold in the United States come from Tyler. In the thirties, as was common practice in small towns throughout Texas, Tylerites felt their town needed a festival to celebrate. Thus, the Texas Rose Festival was born, which endures to this day—complete with parade, Queen's Coronation and other activities designed to attract tourists and give the locals a social event distinguishing the haves from the have-nots. It was also during the thirties when wildcatters discovered oil in East Texas, predominately on lands just east of Tyler. Oil brought fortune to Tyler and made it the white-collar town it is. Tyler became the banking center. It was close enough to the oil fields that it made a logical location for executives managing the drilling operations—and far enough away that they didn't have to put up with the roughnecks and riffraff that populated the boom towns.

The lure of possible riches from the oil fields gave Audrey and Bob Brians reason enough to migrate from Corsicana to East Texas after the oil boom years. Bob worked in the oil fields, and Audrey took care of their two children, Robin Hood Brians Jr. and Audrey Jr. At the age of five, Robin started piano lessons, and he continued studying classical music until he was in the ninth grade when he became bored and quit. "I had a teacher named Mrs. Durst," Robin remembers, "When she was teaching me a new piece, I would ask her to play it for me so I would know how it should sound. Instead of learning by the sheet music, I would remember it and improvise by ear." Robin laughs as he recalls how his teacher commented after hearing him play at his next lesson, "That was incredible. You could barely read music at your last lesson, and now you are transposing it into a completely different key!"

It was three years later, when Robin was a high school senior, that he heard "A Whole Lot of Shaking" by Jerry Lee Lewis. He loved its energy and beat and sat down at the piano to figure out how Jerry Lee Lewis played it. "Once I figured out how he did it, I was hooked," Robin recalls, "I knew I wanted to play that kind of piano." Just after graduation from Tyler High School in 1957, Robin's parents took him to Nashville for half of a two-hour recording session at Owen Bradley's studio. He shared the session with Dale Wright, a Dayton, Ohio, disc jockey signed to Fraternity Records (who charted twice with singles on the Billboard Hot 100 in 1958). Wright took an hour and a half to record two songs, leaving Robin half an hour to cut his compositions "Dis-A-Itty-Bit," a rocking novelty song on the A-side, and "Can it Be," a ballad on the B-side. Fraternity Records released the single, and it received moderate airplay in several markets, as well as substantial play on the local Tyler radio station. That was the beginning.

Robin is now 85 years old (as of this writing in 2024). The intervening years add up to thousands of hours in recording sessions and a lifetime as part of the Texas music scene. "That half-hour session sixty-five years ago was all it took, don't you know…" Robin smiles as he remembers that first recording session. "I knew then I wanted to build my own studio."

The first couple of years in the recording business consisted of taking a portable Ampex recorder to church basements and auditoriums or stringing microphones throughout the family's living room. Robin used portable, monaural equipment in the beginning. A spare bedroom was set up with a mixing console. To say the Brians' household endured some inconveniences for the sake of Robin's art is a gross understatement. In time, Robin expanded into two track, stereo recording. "Robie Morgan was an engineer at KDOK radio and, at the time, just about the most knowledgeable person in town," says Robin. "I went to Robie and asked him to build a ten-channel board with equalizers on each channel. Well, he didn't think that was necessary because we could EQ the final output on the mix. But I insisted, and he said okay and built a board to my specifications. That was in 1960. For its time, that was a hot board!"

Robin was making a living recording other people. In his spare time, he stayed busy writing songs and taking classes at Tyler Junior College. "It finally came down to decision time: go to school or get serious about the record business and write music," Robin thoughtfully stroked his graying beard, remembering a conversation he had with his father. "I told my dad what I wanted to do, and he agreed with me."

It had not taken long for Audrey and Bob Brians to get tired of the late-night recording sessions. The straw that broke the camel's back was one night when the police knocked on the door during a session. A neighbor across the street complained about the noises from her pipes. "Apparently, I placed the drum kit over the grate of the floor furnace. The grate captured the sound and then transmitted it through the gas pipes to the house across the street. When I went to investigate, I could hear the drums banging away through the pipes," Robin recalls, "and that was when we started making plans to build a real studio at the back of our house. My sister was an architect by then, and she drew up the plans. We did all the work ourselves, except for the Haydite blocks. We paid a crew to do that. It took nine months to complete the studio, but we were ready for business in June 1963."

They called it Brians Studio originally; however, the name soon changed to Robin Hood Studios because that was how clients referred to it. Word spread quickly about the new studio, and business was brisk. The first hit recorded at Robin Hood Studios was on Epic Records in 1963. It was David Houston's "A Mountain of Love," produced by Tillman Franks. Robin recalls those early days as hectic, "We stayed busy recording everything from garage bands to square dance records to people wanting to record themselves singing with just a guitar or piano."

Before the year was out, tragedy struck. On November 22, 1963, the same day as the assassination of President Kennedy in Dallas, Bob Brians collapsed. "It was either a stroke or a heart attack," Robin recalls, "He died early the next morning." Remembering that evening sixty years ago, Robin becomes reflective. His voice drops to a lower register and he gazes absently into the distant past as he speaks, "The real tragedy was Dad leaving us just as it looked like we were on to something that could be big." Not a hint of emotion in his voice as Robin recalls the impact that night made, "Dad never doubted the studio would be a success. He never questioned the decision to build the studio. I am sorry he wasn't here to watch it become what it did." One result of that tragedy was Robin's increased drive and determination to make the studio a success.

The Jewel and Paula record labels were owned by Stan Lewis from Shreveport. Abnak Records was a Dallas-based label owned by a successful Fort Worth insurance salesman, John Howard Abnor, Sr. Robin hooked up with both of these men and pitched them on using his studio to record. On the strength of David Houston's success with "A Mountain of Love" and the recommendation of its producer, Tillman Franks, both entrepreneurs gave Robin Hood Studios a chance. "When you record a song that becomes a hit, everyone wants on the bandwagon," Robin relates matter-of-factly, "It was important for us to have repeat customers in those early days. It helped that they both had acts that had a chance at really doing something. Once they had records getting airplay, then they had budgets to spend on recording."

Stan Lewis managed several acts that included John Fred and the Playboy Band, Nat Stuckey, Cheryl Poole, Mickey Gilley, The Uniques, Tony Douglas, Fontella Bass, Justin Wilson, and Ike and Tina Turner. John Howard Abnor's Abnak label had a group called The Five Americans, Jon and Robin (his son's group), and The In Crowd. Together, Abnor's and Lewis' acts became the primary source of the studio's income during those formative years. "There was a big difference between the groups from Louisiana and the ones from Dallas," Robin says. "The Louisiana groups reflected more influence from black artists and had an edgier sound. The Dallas groups imitated British rock or leaned more toward the bubblegum sound. I can't remember a group from Louisiana ever recording anything that had the pop, bubblegum feel of the material we recorded for The Five Americans or Jon and Robin."

That is not a criticism, just an observation from one who was an integral part of the popular music scene throughout the 60s and 70s. The biggest hit The Five Americans released was "Western Union." They had several other hits that charted "Say That You Love Me," "I See the Light," "Sound of Love," and "Zip Code." Jon and Robin hit the charts with "Do It Again A Little Bit Slower," "If I Need Someone – It's You," "Hey Girl," "You Got Style," and "I Want Some More."

The group from Baton Rouge, Louisiana, fared better on the charts. John Fred and His Playboy Band had hits with "Agnes English," "Up and Down," and "Judy in Disguise (With Glasses)," all recorded at Robin Hood Studios. "They were a well-rehearsed band," Robin reminisces, "and we were fooling around in the studio when the idea for 'Judy in Disguise' came about. It was really a parody of the Beatles tune 'Lucy in the Sky with Diamonds,' inspired in part when the band made a trip to Ft. Lauderdale and saw girls on the beach wearing large sunglasses." Legend has it that one of the girls took off her glasses, revealing she was not attractive—hence the title "Judy in Disguise (with glasses)." The four-track recording song incorporates strings, piano, horns, guitar, and bass, with breathing sounds and a sitar overdubbed at the end of the session. It was released and hit number one on the Billboard Hot 100, knocking the Beatles tune "Hello, Goodbye" out of the top spot for two weeks in 1968. It was the first million-seller and the first gold record winner to come out of Robin Hood Studios.

"I believe several factors combined to make the studio a success," a philosophical Robin Hood Brians elaborates on why musicians flocked to his studio in the 60s and 70s. "A main reason is nobody else was cutting hits in Texas at the time. We were. Another reason is the studio itself. It has a unique sound, like Muscle Shoals (another famous recording studio located in Alabama known for its unique acoustics and in-house rhythm section). From the beginning, I maintained the studio with the best possible equipment and instruments." Robin remodeled the studio five times over the years, updating the electronics to keep up with technology while maintaining the elements that produce the unique sound you cannot hear from any other studio. For instance, vintage Neumann tube mics have been in use since the beginning. Although the facility is now digital, it is still a studio where musicians can play together without having to overdub. That is because of Robin's foresight in the beginning, designing the studio with the musicians, not technicians, in mind. Musicians can look at each other while playing. Instruments can also be isolated when necessary. The studio also has an echo chamber, which is actually a chamber (a big empty room that creates the echo effect by sound waves moving through the air). Need a piano for a session? The Bösendorfer Imperial Grand has an extra nine keys on the bass end. Robin says he is glad he bought that piano when he did because not only does it add value to any recording session, but the instrument is now worth more than most people's houses.

Another factor for success is Robin Hood Brians himself. He has an affinity for musicians, and they know it. He *is* a musician. He is a superb technician with an incredible ear. Over the years, he learned every trick from every sound engineer he ever encountered. "It's funny when I think back on the number of people who came in and made a recording, paid their bill, and then later became famous. I don't remember them being in the studio," Robin laments, "Sometimes, I was just too busy taking care of business and getting the master ready to really pay attention to who was walking through the door. Don Henley is one of those. He recorded with me in 1964 or 65, before The Eagles."

Among the musicians who recorded at Robin Hood Studios are James Brown, Ike and Tina Turner, Tony Douglas, Johnny Horton, Bill Mack, Nat Stuckey, The Five Americans, Stevie Ray and Jimmie Vaughan, Jimmy Dean, Willis Allen Ramsey, Mouse and the Traps, Dale Hawkins, Gladstone, Bugs Henderson, The Boxtops, Southwest FOB, Joe Stampley and The Uniques, ZZ Top … take a breath. It might be easier to make a list of who *did not* record at Robin Hood's than to list those who did. In addition to musicians, Robin worked with a long list of voice talents, sometimes traveling to Los Angeles, Nashville, or New York to record voices, including those of Roger Miller, Charlie Pride, Orson Welles, Jim Finlayson, Bob Magruder, Carol Channing, and Charlton Heston.

Earlier in this piece, I wrote about my appearance in a commercial promoting *Hello Dolly!* involving Carol Channing. This is Robin's explanation about creating the soundtrack for that spot. "One thing I learned in this business is that you never know what will happen during a session. The Houston Grand Opera produced the tenth anniversary revival of *Hello, Dolly!* Randy Fouts and I made an arrangement based on the cast album. We pre-recorded the music so Carol Channing could sing special lyrics about Houston in a television promotional campaign. We played the track for her at the beginning of the session, and she complained it was not in her key. I assured her it was exactly the same key as the cast recording," Robin recalls that morning with a special fondness, "In that famous voice of hers she said, 'Robin, I had trouble singing it in that key ten years ago; I certainly can't sing in that key now.'" The solution was to record Channing singing a 'Capella and then re-doing the instruments to match her key.

In the 70s, a group called Moving Sidewalks booked a session and recorded several tracks. They left and threw out the recordings. When the group came back, they had a new name: ZZ Top. They recorded again, and once again, they did not like the sound and threw out the recordings. "When the group booked a third time," Robin recalls, "Billy Gibbons told me it might be the last session because their manager, Bill Hamm, did not think the sound they were recording was anything like what the band played live." Hamm's solution was not to overdub. "They came in with a drum kit, a guitar, and a bass. I told Billy Gibbons we needed to overdub and he told me Hamm would not allow it. It was frustrating." Robin looks back on that session and smiles a broad, mischievous grin. "Bill Hamm had promised to bring in barbecue from the Country Tavern. I looked at him and said, 'Bill, it's time for you to go pick up lunch while we lay down some tracks.' I gave him directions to get to Highway 31 and he left. As soon as the door shut, I told the guys, 'We have about an hour before he gets back because the Country Tavern is in the next county.'" With that admonition, Brians and ZZ Top began to lay down tracks.

The key to replicating a "recorded live" sound when actually playing live is to play loud. Robin told Gibbons to play a rhythm track so smooth he could easily double it. They recorded the track. Then, Robin went into the studio, grabbed the guitar strings, and gave a little tug, de-tuning them slightly, "Now," Robin commanded, "Play that same rhythm." Gibbons played it, and Brians recorded another track. "Now, let me hear some lead." After they laid down the lead guitar, they listened to the playback. Without saying a word, the three musicians all looked at Robin Hood Brians and smiled. The ZZ Top sound was born. "I told Dusty (Hill), 'When you play live, add a fifth on the bass.' Basically, all he had to do was play chords loud, and a live performance would sound just as good as the recording."

Bill Hamm returned with ribs from the Country Tavern after about an hour and twenty minutes. "Damn you, Hood! You didn't mention that place was thirty miles away!" "Is it really?" Robin replied and then punched the "play" button on the tape machine.

Billy Gibbons picked up a rib and said, "We stumbled on a sound we really like. See what you think." Everybody knew it was the right sound as they listened to the playback. Bill Hamm's mouth fell open as he listened. Finally, he yelled, "That's what I've been waiting to hear!"

> "You want us to record them all that way?" Robin Hood asked.

> "Hell, yeah!" Hamm replied.

They played the tracks repeatedly. Bill Hamm listened intently each time. Then he looked toward Robin and asked suspiciously, "Did you overdub?"

> Robin answered with the same patient tone he would later use when talking to his children, "Bill, you have one set of drums, one guitar player, and one bass player. Of course, we overdubbed." They argued for about an hour. To make his point, Robin explained, "When you have a little speaker about this big around on a little transistor radio, you have to

77

add some character to the sound that the room adds when you're playing live."

"You promise they can pull it off live?"

"As long as they play well and play loud, no one will miss the overdub."

To prove the point, Robin had band members pull the drums out of the isolation booth and set them up in the middle of the studio. They brought the bass amp in and set it next to the guitar amp. Then he asked Bill Hamm to take a seat right in front of the group. "Now, play it just like you did before, and play it loud!" Robin commanded.

Those first four ZZ Top albums were the biggest-selling albums recorded at Robin Hood Studios. Originally released on *London Records*, Warner Brothers re-released them on their label. To date, the band has sold over fifty million albums and has won four gold, three platinum, two double-platinum, and one diamond-certified album awards.

If there is anything said of Robin Hood Brians and his studio, it is that he spent as much time updating equipment to keep up with advancing technology as he did to keep the vintage equipment in proper repair. "Computers really transformed the business," Robin reflects, "I just recently recorded for several days in Nashville. At the end of the session, the engineers took about fifteen minutes to load all the tracks for eight songs onto a thumb drive. I brought it back to my studio in Tyler, and took about ten minutes to reconstruct the sessions and get everything organized for me to do the final mix. In the old days, it would have taken twenty or thirty hours just to get the tapes catalogued and ready to start making transfers for the backups."

When the recording industry first went digital, there were many purists who objected to the sterile sound it produced. "I was one of them," says Robin, "but I worked around the problem by taking the best of both worlds and combining them. I used the old tube mics and the analog equalizers and recorded them in digital format. I kept the warmth you get out of analog recording and gained the speed and convenience from the digital realm."

Building a successful recording business in a small town like Tyler, Texas, is a remarkable feat in itself. "One thing that helped us was being located about midway between Dallas and Shreveport. That made it more convenient for those small regional groups to record here," Robin explained. "As many demos as we did for little garage bands, and the records we recorded that actually got airplay, there was still not enough cash coming in that we had to worry about what to do with all the extra money."

To supplement his studio income, Robin and a partner, Randy Fouts, started Brians & Fouts Music. They targeted advertising agencies in Dallas and Houston and began writing music for commercials. "Randy was a great session player who came from Hawkins, Texas, a little town just north of Tyler. He had classical training on the piano and was one of the finest technical musicians I ever worked with in the studio," Robin spoke fondly of his partner in the jingle business. "He could write charts for all the players in just a few minutes, and he could play the piano as well as anybody in the business."

For nearly thirty years, the music of Brians & Fouts blasted out of car radios on a daily basis. The commercials they produced were not just in Texas, but many were for national companies. Robin remembers one of their biggest contacts in advertising, "Tracey-Locke was a big agency located in Dallas that handled several big accounts. One of their largest accounts was Frito-Lay, a national snack food business that was part of PepsiCo. They had several hundred million-dollar brands: Fritos Corn Chips, Doritos, Cheetos,

Tostitos, and of course, Lays Potato Chips. We did several campaigns for many of their brands."

As more of their jingles went national, the reputation of Brians & Fouts grew, leading to more business with other agencies. In 1980, they wrote the music for a campaign titled "The Bus Brothers" for Greyhound Bus. It was a national spot that won a Clio Award, the Oscar of Advertising. Jud Chapin, the lead on the Greyhound Bus account for the Glenn, Bozell & Jacobs Advertising Agency became a lifelong friend to Robin. "I did more campaigns with Robin Hood Brians than with any other music producer," Jud boasts. "After I left Bozell & Jacobs and started my own agency, we did some award-winning work for amusement parks like Six Flags and White Water, a memorable campaign with Roger Miller and an inspired spot for Chili's Baby Back Ribs (a jingle you hear in an Austin Powers movie)."

Many of Robin Hood Brians' contemporaries retired long ago. "I've been doing this for over sixty years," Robin says with the energy of a man half his age, "Since my children are grown and out of college and on their own, my focus has shifted. The pressure to book every session that comes along no longer exists. Now, I am spending more time creating projects of my own." Specifically, he and Jud Chapin teamed up to write several songs. "We just finished a session in Nashville where we laid down something like sixty-five tracks for about twenty songs," Robin explains. The plan is to mix those tracks at his own studio and turn those recordings into demos for use in marketing the songs. The target of the marketing campaign is established artists looking for a new hit and film producers who want a unique soundtrack for their next movie project. "It's time to cash in," a broad smile creeps across Robin's face.

Another project is working with his little girl.

"She may be a young woman in her late thirties," Robin

says in a fatherly tone, "But she is still my little girl."

As children, Michelle and her older brother, Christopher Robin, spent many hours at the studio behind their grandmother's house. Exposure to every type of music imaginable, and the variety of personalities recording there made for a unique musical education. Both of the Brians children took piano lessons. Christopher took up the horn and Michelle concentrated on the violin.

> "Naturally, I was a great believer in nepotism," Robin confesses, "Anytime I needed a child's voice, reading or singing, the job went to one of my children. We saved the money they earned for their college fund."

Allen Morris

Chapter 9
Bob Woodruff: An Accident of Fate

While many of the famous people I worked with have been connected to the entertainment industry in some way, there have been others who achieved their fame in fields that one could consider related to entertainment but are distinctly set apart. This would be true of Bob Woodruff, whose field was journalism but whose fame derived from the fact that he was a broadcast journalist. His work was seen on the ABC television network, where the line between journalism and entertainment is blurred. In Woodruff's case, that blurring increased when he became the news story, he covered.

That life can change in an instant proved true on January 29, 2006, when ABC reporter Bob Woodruff and Canadian videographer Doug Vogt sustained major injuries as an improvised explosive device (IED) exploded near the Iraqi MT-LB in which they were riding. They were standing with their heads outside the hatch when the bomb went off. Despite wearing body armor and protective helmets, shrapnel struck both men in the head, causing severe injuries. Vogt's recovery was swift; however, Woodruff's injuries required a medically induced coma lasting thirty-six days to facilitate his recovery. The personal account of this life-altering experience was the subject of Woodruff's presentation as part of the Cowan Center's Distinguished Lecture series.

I had the privilege of interviewing Woodruff when he was invited to make that presentation. Meeting him and discussing how the experience changed his life was inspiring. Inspiring because it was such a devastating occurrence that happened as he was simply doing his job. Woodruff is not a reporter. He is a journalist. And there is a difference between those labels. Most journalists who choose to go into combat zones are usually kept away from the direct danger that their subjects face daily. In this case, Woodruff and Vogt were in the wrong place at the right time. Instead of reporting from a distance, they were in the midst of the action, on their way to cover the story, without any knowledge that a bomb was embedded in the roadway. Such was the nature of the type of enemy the soldiers were facing. IEDs were wreaking havoc across Iraq, maiming and killing not only soldiers but also civilians including old men, women and children ... and, journalists. That Bob Woodruff had survived was a testament to the quality of medical care he received. That he was making the presentation at the Cowan Center at all was an accident of fate. Katie Couric was the scheduled speaker for the evening, but a family emergency forced a last-minute cancellation. Woodruff graciously accepted the invitation to replace his colleague. "It is important to take advantage of every opportunity to explain the plight thousands of service members endure while returning from Iraq and Afghanistan," Woodruff said, referring to military personnel with similar injuries to his own.

Becoming a journalist was another accident of fate. After earning a law degree in 1987, fate guided Woodruff to China, where by 1989, he found himself teaching law in Beijing. His fluent command of Mandarin was especially useful when the protests at Tiananmen Square broke out. CBS News hired Woodruff as an on-air interpreter. Life changed in an instant again as journalism suddenly sparked his interest.

"I was hired by CBS News to be a fixer for them, to translate on the streets," Woodruff recalls, "In the midst of that massacre at Tiananmen Square, it was my first exposure to working in television news, and it was the most moving and interesting story. So, I decided to get out of law and become a journalist." It took a little time before he was working at a network again. He spent time learning the ropes of television reporting at several local stations: KCPM, an NBC affiliate in Redding, California; WTVR, the CBS affiliate in Richmond, Virginia; and finally, KNXV, the ABC affiliate in Phoenix, Arizona. In 1996, Woodruff joined ABC News in their Chicago Bureau.

For the next few years, Woodruff covered various stories throughout the country and around the world. In December 2005, network management named Woodruff as co-anchor of "ABC World News Tonight." One month later, he was in Iraq.

Woodruff does not remember much about the incident itself. He remembers passing palm trees on either side of the tank and that he and Doug Vogt decided to film an intro to his story as they were driving along the road. About the actual incident, he remembers little, "but I heard later that our Iraqi driver told us we should get down because it was getting more dangerous. Just a couple of seconds later, there was an explosion." He remembers the concussion knocking him from his perch. He remembers grabbing Vogt's legs and pulling him into the tank. He remembers asking, "Are we alive?"

The next memory he has is of waking up thirty-six days later. He saw his wife, Lee, and asked her where she had been. She had been by his side. When he speaks of his injuries and the experience of going through recovery from a serious traumatic brain injury, Woodruff maintains a sense of humor. When he was asked what he would do differently if in that same situation, he quipped, "Next time, I will duck." A sense of humor is an asset for a journalist.

There are two things critical to Woodruff's recovery. The support provided by his family is paramount, "Of all the things I've learned, keeping everything in perspective—being able to laugh, is crucial for recovery." The second is sharing what he learned with others, "There are many service personnel with injuries similar to mine, and some of them go through the recovery alone." That is one of the reasons he immediately started working on a documentary about his experience in the early days of his recovery. "It was necessary for me to be able to make people aware of the thousands of troops whose lives have been changed by a serious brain injury," he explains, "I had to get back to work as quickly as possible."

Thirteen months after the incident, ABC News aired the one-hour primetime special "To Iraq and Back: Bob Woodruff Reports." The Peabody Award-winning program details not only Woodruff's painstaking recovery but also, more importantly, highlights the needs facing thousands of service personnel who are returning to their families with similar scars. In addition to airing the documentary, Bob and Lee Woodruff wrote a best-selling memoir, aptly titled *In an Instant*, chronicling how their family persevered through the intense trauma and uncertainty brought about by Bob's wounding in Iraq. They also formed the Bob Woodruff Foundation to assist in raising money for injured service members, veterans and their families.

As we talked, I mentioned that I had been in Israel shooting footage during the early days of the first Iraqi conflict in the early 90s. This was during the period of time when Saddam Hussein was lobbing scud missiles toward Israel. "So, you understand what it feels like to be under fire?" Woodruff asked.

> "To a degree, but not to the extent you do. I never really felt any great danger because the scuds didn't have the range to get much beyond the border," I replied. "Most of what I filmed was after-the-fact, going to the locations where scuds had exploded on Israeli soil. Most of the time, when our crew got there, the Israelis had cleaned up most of the damage, and there was very little damage to see. Prime Minister Rabin told us that cleaning up after a scud attack was important for the morale of the citizens. They

didn't want anyone to feel that the Iraqis were making any real impact on the country."

"What did you think about Rabin?" Woodruff asked, journalist-to-journalist.

"I liked him. His most important statement to us was that he would consider a land for peace initiative as long as he felt the offer was genuine."

"Throughout my career, there have been individual moments when I was working on a story that gave me an affinity for the people I was covering. Did you have any particular experiences that made a personal impact when you were covering that first war?"

"We were attempting to get interviews from both sides of the conflict," I answered. "We spent a lot of time in the West Bank with Palestinians and in Jerusalem. We hired a young Palestinian to work as our guide and interpreter. He was called Hammad and was fluent in Arabic and Hebrew, as well as English and French. Hammad understood our desire to cover both sides of the issue and to let the public understand more about both attitudes. He was also anxious for us to get as much of the Palestine perspective as possible. One incident that stands out in my memory is when we pulled up to park outside the gates of the Old City. I was driving and saw a spot right by the gate, which I thought was perfect because it meant we wouldn't have as far to lug all that heavy equipment. As I pulled in to park next to another car with a Star of David on its door, Hammad told me not to park there, pointed to a spot much farther away, and told me to park there instead. We unloaded our gear, went into the Old City, and filmed a b-roll and several interviews with people Hammad had arranged for us. We heard an explosion at some point during the day, and I asked Hammad what it was. 'Probably a car bomb. It happens frequently these days.' When we wrapped for the day and returned to the parking lot, the car with the Star of David on its door was demolished and sat there smoldering. It had been the target of the car bomb we had heard earlier in the day. I looked at Hammad and asked, 'Is that why you wanted us to park over there?' To which he shrugged his shoulders and replied, 'Inshallah,' which is a common Arabic expression meaning 'the will of God.'"

When asked whether the story he had been covering was worth the trauma he endured, Woodruff was quick to reply that he believed his role as a journalist, covering the transfer of power from the US military to the Iraqi military, was important. He was steadfast in his belief that journalists play a vital role as witnesses to the events they report. "Perhaps we made some mistakes, rushed out too quickly," he admits, adding rhetorically, however,

"Would I do it again?" For a moment, he becomes pensive and sighs loudly.

"My wife has asked that question many times. I said many times that I would. Not because it's an addiction for me, but I think somebody had to do it." Thinking for a moment, he continues by explaining that he was not a rookie; he had covered combat areas before. He was wearing the best body armor and helmet available. He states simply, "We made a mistake."

He returned to Iraq after his recovery. He met with people he knew from the 4th Infantry. He met with the tank driver, who he credits with saving his life. In fact, he helped that man get out of Iraq and immigrate to America. Returning to Iraq was something

Woodruff needed to do in order to complete his recovery. It provided closure by coming full circle. "I won't cover wars anymore," he explained, "My wife told me I can't. ABC doesn't want me to cover wars anymore. Maybe we'll compromise and go to refugee zones outside of Assyria."

He laughed as he said it, but the look in his eyes indicated he was seriously thinking about another story. That's something I've noticed that all journalists have in common. They are always thinking about the next story. Once a story is turned in, they tend to be anxiety-ridden until they start the next one. There is something in the DNA of a journalist that does not allow them to relax and rest simply. They are driven to be working on another story. A bigger story, perhaps. Every new story they begin seems more important than the one they had just completed. To be a good journalist requires curiosity and an insatiable appetite for getting the facts. Sadly, too many reporters today are not journalists. Woodruff is a journalist.

Allen Morris

Chapter 10
Tom Perryman: An Influential Voice in Radio

I have known two people named Tom Perryman during my career. The first was the Chief Engineer at KTRE in Lufkin, who was instrumental in my early training in broadcasting. The other Tom Perryman was an acknowledged pioneer in the early days of radio. Getting to spend time with *that* Tom Perryman was akin to a master's course in the history of broadcasting. I felt privileged to be in a position to ask him what the early days of radio were like from his perspective. He was more than willing to share his experiences, and I think he was somewhat appreciative to have someone who was genuinely interested in what he had to say.

As a kid growing up during the Depression, in a place aptly called Rural Shade, Tom Perryman remembered how he, his brother Bill, and their friends wore overalls all summer, "No shirt, no shoes, and no underwear… just overalls." In those days, kids worked in the fields as soon as they were big enough to drag a cotton sack. At the end of the day, Tom said he and the boys would "get to running down to the tank, unbuckle, and dive out of them overalls and into the tank."

When his family moved onto that cotton farm in 1933, Tom was six years old. His father was a geologist working in the oil fields. People knew the place they lived on as the Morris Perryman Farm. Before that, the family lived on the farm where his mother grew up, about eight miles south of Kerens, Texas, not too far from Rural Shade. Tragedy struck the family a couple of years later when Tom's father died in an auto accident on Highway 31, just east of Corsicana. "A timber fell out of a derrick and hit him in the head," Tom recalls what the adults told him, "After that, he would black out sometimes … They think he blacked out and hit that concrete bridge."

One thing Tom learned from his days spent picking cotton was that there had to be a better way to make a living. One thing he did like was listening to the radio. "I listened to the radio a lot, but not so much hillbilly back then or Opry, but more or less the pop music of that big band era," Tom recalls.

That is when the seeds were sown which led Tom Perryman to become one of the country music trailblazers. When I met Tom, he was eighty-seven years young and was heard from nine until eleven weekday mornings on 104.1 KKUS. Called "The Ranch," the radio station played many of the "Classic Country" standards Tom helped make famous. In a way, working at "The Ranch" brought Tom full circle. His first radio job was at Jacksonville's KEBE in 1947.

It is necessary to back up a little to tell Tom's story properly. When Tom was sixteen, doctors at Scottish Rite Hospital in Dallas performed spinal fusion surgery in an attempt to fix a back problem that had plagued him throughout his childhood. While he was laid up for four months recuperating, he listened to the radio, paying particular attention to the disc jockeys. "I got to listenin' to those disc jockeys and took a liking to them. I thought then that I might like trying that."

It was 1945 when Tom graduated high school. By then, his mother had remarried, and the family had moved to Trinidad, where Tom was able to play football because of the successful surgery. When school was out, the war was still raging in the Pacific, and Tom and a buddy joined the Navy. They went to San Diego, but Tom was sent back home because of the back surgery. Soon after that, the war was over. Tom enrolled in Tyler Commercial College and started studying to get a First-Class FCC Radio Engineering License.

While taking the radio-engineering course, Tom lived in a boarding house on Ferguson Street in Tyler with three roommates. One of them had a picture of a girl he had graduated with from Buffalo High. Her name was Billie Joyce Watson, and Tom was immediately smitten. Just before Christmas, Tom arranged to travel with his roommate to Buffalo to meet Billie. Tom remembers they had a date, went to a movie or something, and then she left on the train to go back to college, where she was dating one of the Navy boys, home from the war. It was not long until Tom's roommate received a letter from Billie asking, "Why did you bring that long, tall drink of water down here? He's funny, and he's got pretty eyes." Tom read that letter and told his buddy, "Hell, I'll just go down there and marry that gal!"

They married on September 14, 1946, beginning their life's journey together—a journey that continued for more than sixty-eight years. Unlike so many couples, the Perrymans had been able to share their careers together. Throughout all the moves they made following Tom from one radio station to another, Billie also frequently went to work at those stations. "I called Billie my special angel. I would never have been anything without her," Tom said. Billie returns the sentiment, calling Tom "The love of my life and a Star, as they say in the music business." Within months after getting married, Tom was hired at KEBE in Jacksonville.

"I was working about sixty hours a week and making about sixty dollars a week," Tom remembered with a laugh. It was while working for two years for KEBE General Manager Bill Laurie that Tom got one of the best pieces of advice of his early career: "If you can't whistle it, don't play it." In addition to becoming a disc jockey, it was during this time that Tom began promoting live music shows. His first show was at Jacksonville's Tomato Bowl in 1949, featuring entertainers who performed frequently on the Louisiana Hayride in Shreveport. "Hank Williams, Johnny and Jack, Kitty Wells, and

Slim Whitman were on the show. We had a big crowd, and I took a liking to it right then and there," Tom recalls.

Soon, Tom was offered bigger and better things, and the Perryman's packed up and moved to Gladewater in 1949 to work for daytime KSIJ radio. "That is where I really got started in country music and the promotion of country artists of the Louisiana Hayride, The Big D Jamboree, The Cowtown Hoedown, and some from the Grand Ole Opry," Tom says. At KSIJ, Tom was selling airtime, doing an on-air shift, calling play-by-play for sporting events, and by the time he turned twenty-three, he became station manager. During the evenings, when the station was off the air, he would help local artists record their songs and cut demos. He worked with before-they-were-known performers like Jack Rhodes, Big Red Hayes, Jim Reeves, Johnny Horton, Bob Luman, and Johnny Gimble. During this time, Tom and Billie welcomed children to their household: Vicki, 1951; Marilyn, 1953; and Thomas King, 1954.

Many of the performers booked on the Saturday night broadcasts of the Louisiana Hayride would come to Gladewater and perform live or sit in the studio with Tom as he played their records. Tom would book these performers throughout the week at schools, rodeo arenas, ballparks, honky-tonks, or whatever. The list of performers reads like a history of country music and includes Johnny Cash, Carl Perkins, Sonny James, the Wilburn Brothers, Ferlin Husky, George Jones, Roy Acuff, Ray Price, Willie Nelson, Roger Miller, Don Gipson, Ernest Tubb, Faron Young, Jean Sheppard, David Houston, Red Sovine, Loretta Lynn, Floyd Tillman, Charlie Walker, Lefty Frizzell, Tex Ritter, Floyd Cramer, Hank Thompson, Jerry Lee Lewis—and so many others.

One popular rising star Tom booked for his first appearance in Texas was Elvis Presley. That was in 1954 when Elvis and two other players did not have enough money to get home. Tom promoted them for three days on his radio show, and they appeared at The Mint, just across the river from Gladewater. "We made ninety dollars, charging a dollar a ticket. I usually took fifteen percent, but I gave it all to Elvis that night. He never forgot that," Tom said. It was a year later when Tom booked Elvis at the Mayfair Building in Tyler. After that performance, Elvis would come and spend a week at a time with Tom and Billie, experiencing their hospitality between shows.

In 1956, Tom was lured to Nashville to be the all-night disc jockey for WSM and to start the Opry Star Spotlight Show. "There was Billie with those three babies, and I took a job making less money than I was making in Gladewater. I tell everybody I went to Nashville and the Opry to become a star, not realizing it would be spelled STARVE," Tom said, only half-jokingly. He stayed in Nashville until 1959 when he heard his old station in Gladewater was for sale at a fair price. He did not end up buying that station, but he and his friend Jim Reeves did buy KGRI in Henderson.

They made it an all-town-and-country format, one of the first in the East Texas area. In fact, it was one of the few all-country stations in the country at the time. Tom and Billie both worked at the station; Tom remembered, "I would open it up, sold advertising, did sports, and booked shows. Billie ran the office and did the books and logs while raising three kids." Five years after they bought the station, Jim Reeves died in a plane crash. "He was just beginning to be a real superstar," Tom says, "We had talked about Billie and I returning to Nashville to run his office. But on July 31st, Jim Reeves flew his plane into a thunderstorm outside of Nashville and crashed."

After a few years, Jim's widow Mary called, and Tom, Billie, and the kids moved to Murfreesboro, Tennessee, outside of Nashville, and went into partnership with WMTS radio, which became one of the top country stations in the nation. The station won a CMA in 1969 and again in 1970. Tom and Billie remained active in the music business throughout the decade, but by 1978, the business was changing, and Tom was beginning to get tired of it. They sold WMTS in 1978 and "retired."

During this retirement, Tom spent much of his time as vice president of Jim Reeves Enterprises and helped Mary Reeves build the Jim Reeves Museum. Tom produced a syndicated radio documentary on Jim and his music that won a gold medal in 1984, at the International Radio Festival in New York. In 1988, Tom received recognition for his contribution to Country Music, with his induction into the Country Music Disc Jockey Hall of Fame in Nashville. The Texas Country Music Hall of Fame inducted Tom in 1999. Of all the accolades Tom received, the one that means the most to him is the Pioneer Award from the Texas Association of Broadcasters, "Because that award comes from my peers in the business," Tom explained.

In 2001, Dudley Waller of Waller Broadcasting in Jacksonville called and asked Tom if he ever thought about coming home to East Texas. "Just about every day," Tom replied.

That is what brought Tom and Billie out of retirement and back to East Texas. Tom is quick to point out that most of today's country music is not to his liking. "There are a few I think are good. They record like we used to record, doing material similar to what we did in the fifties… their style of recording and their instrumentation, fiddle, and steel… without so much of the psychedelic sounding, distorted guitars and overpowering rhythm and drum beat and the artificial synthesizers. These artists should be getting more exposure."

If anybody has earned the right to criticize the direction country music has taken, it would be Tom Perryman. After all, in his day, the disc jockey, disc jockey promoters, and the jukebox operators played a big part in the success of a recording. There can be no denying that country music increased in popularity from 1947 until the late 1970s, becoming mainstream in so-called sophisticated markets like Chicago, Las Vegas, L. A., and New York. A big reason for that increase in popularity is the quality of the recordings produced and the emergence of "The Nashville Sound." It became a success due to the contributions of promoters and disc jockeys, like Tom Perryman, who knew if a song would be a hit from the first moment they put it on the turntable.

When Billie and Tom came home to East Texas in 2001, a big part of their motivation was the opportunity to be back on the air, doing a radio show the way it was done in the fifties, "Which is really when Country Music came of age," Tom spoke about that time like it was just yesterday. "There was a period when hillbilly music was really popular. Bill Haley was performing hillbilly and then came out with 'Rock Around the Clock' and that led to Elvis Presley and a new type of music they called 'rock n' roll.' A lot of that history took place right here in East Texas. That is the era we refer to as the Golden Age of Country Music. I am proud to say I was part of that transition in music and radio. It's rare that a day goes by when someone who was listenin' as a kid back then doesn't mention they remember hearing me on the air. Those kids are grandparents themselves now, and they grew up during that time when Country Music was growing up. That's why I like doing the show I have now. A lot of old-timers enjoyed it, and now we have a new generation who are becoming familiar with the giants of that time in music. Patsy Cline, Roy Orbison, and, of course, my good friend Jim Reeves, and so many others. The kids are beginning to listen to those recordings, and they are becoming fans of that music, just like the kids fifty years ago."

What did Tom think about a man his age working so hard? When asked, he did not think twice about it, "You stay sharp by working, by keeping active and keeping your brain busy. It's all right to get older, just don't get old. You are only as old as you feel, and you are not old 'till you don't feel."

Editor's note: Thomas Eugene Perryman passed away on January 11, 2018, at age 90.

Chapter 11
Conductor Richard Lee: The Power of Music

Another thing to ponder about fame is the nature of fame itself. It can come from different sources and is affected by circumstances that include location and timing (right place, right time). It is also affected by one's particular skill or talent. Culture is another factor. All of these factors coalesced for Richard Lee.

At the age of seventeen, Canadian native Maestro Richard Lee passed the piano and violin exams at the Royal Conservatory of Music in Toronto. Briefly studying physics, he followed his true passion and pursued a degree in Music Performance at the University of Toronto. He taught middle school students for five years before returning to earn a Master's degree as the Victor Feldbrill Fellow in Orchestral Conducting. His illustrious career included serving as the resident or assistant conductor with symphony orchestras in Winnipeg, Quebec, and Thunder Bay, as well as Music Director for the Korean Canadian Symphony Orchestra. For Lee, his first taste of fame came in his own backyard, so to speak, first becoming noticed as the talented kid whose Korean mother introduced him to music and made certain he went to his lessons and practiced every day. In May 2012, Lee was introduced as the new Musical Director and Conductor for the East Texas Symphony Orchestra.

The first impression I had upon meeting Lee was how open and approachable he was, just a regular guy who followed sports, enjoyed an occasional cigar, and drank hard liquor or wine when it was offered. Had I not known he was a musician, I could have easily pegged him as an insurance salesman or the manager of a restaurant or bar. His engaging sense of humor was obvious, as was his ability to make conversation easily. I'm not sure what I expected. I think, perhaps, I was prepared to meet an elitist snob. I don't know why.

Since taking the reins of the ETSO organization, Lee says one of the things he tried to do was to meet as many people in the community as possible. "I don't know of a better way to get to know the audience than to meet them, talk to them, and get tuned into the local culture," Lee says. In his official capacity, Lee frequently attends civic events and receptions, not the least of which are fundraising events organized by the Women's Symphony League, which directly benefit the East Texas Symphony Orchestra. "I wear many hats as the Musical Director, and among them is that of being one of the chief fundraisers for the Orchestra," Lee confides. "I attend as many of the fundraising events as possible. Many times, there is a student quartet playing background music at those events," Lee explains, "I always make it a point to introduce myself to the musicians, to thank them for playing, and perhaps spend a few minutes chatting with them."

Lee remembers a group of young high school musicians he met soon after taking charge at ETSO. "They were a really young group who played fairly well, especially considering how young they were. I thought one of the pieces they played was perhaps a little slow." Lee, being who he is, mentally changed into his teaching hat and approached the quartet, asking them if they had considered what the dynamics of the piece would be if they played it at a different tempo. "At the age high school players are, they tend not to think for themselves. They rely on their teacher to tell them what do. I wanted to plant the seed for them to analyze the music on their own, to consider what the composer intended," says Lee. "After a moment of discussing it with the kids, explaining how a piece of music has a character that can change by the way it is played, they agreed to humor me by playing it again at a faster clip. After that, I think they understood what I meant about the character of the music."

Lee says working with kids is one of the greatest satisfactions he gets out of life. He says it is fun and that he relishes those "teaching moments." One thing he learned when he was a young student was that there came a moment when a student's relationship with the teacher changed when the teacher began to take the student more seriously and, in so doing, began to share ideas about music instead of merely dictating how a piece should be played. "With very young students, you don't do that, and there is no reason to. The very young are learning the basics. However, there is a moment when the light bulb goes off, and suddenly, it becomes obvious that the student is translating the musical articulation without help from the teacher. That is the moment when the composer begins to speak directly to the student through the music."

Attracting students to attend concerts was a primary goal for Lee when he arrived in Tyler. Richard Lee knows exactly what he envisioned then and what his hopes are now: "I want the students to take music seriously. One of the ways to accomplish that is for them to go to all the concerts they can. To experience the performances of the various soloists and, when possible, to meet them and have a dialogue exchange with individuals who have made the transition from being a member of the school orchestra… to the ranks of a professional musician. It is all part of the training and should begin early in the student's music education."

Lee recently had a realization: here he is, the conductor of the East Texas Symphony Orchestra, and the only place he had been in East Texas was Tyler. "I took it upon myself to take a little tour of East Texas," Lee explains his four-day hiatus traveling through the region. He went to Longview and attended a concert at the Belcher Center, getting a sense of what a Longview audience is like. From Longview, he went to Jefferson, "Which I found to be surprisingly different. It did not look like East Texas, but I would compare it as more like Mobile or New Orleans, much more Southern in attitude than Tyler," says Lee. In Marshall, Lee was able to spend some time on the East Texas Baptist University campus, where he could interact with students and faculty members. In Nacogdoches, he was impressed by the beauty of the Stephen F. Austin campus and the quaintness of the downtown area. "I learned that SFA has the largest music program of all the schools in our East Texas region. I also learned that while there are similarities in these towns, there are also cultural differences that give each town its unique character. Just the way each piece of music has a unique character of its own!"

Lee came back from this tour, his mind brimming with ideas for ways to establish some type of collaboration with the different areas of East Texas that lie beyond Tyler's borders. "I don't know what, if anything, will come of it, but I definitely have the feeling that there is a genuine interest in our symphony expanding its presence throughout East Texas. Perhaps a tour throughout the region, or some kind of performance involving students from the other colleges and universities, similar to the Side-by-Side concert," Lee remarks. For those who are unaware, Side-by-Side refers to the opportunity for student musicians to sit beside and play with professional musicians in a concert designed specifically for the purpose of exposing those students to the world of professional music. It is a concept Lee has introduced to East Texas as a major part of his educational outreach for ETSO.

One thing is certain, his tour of the region showed Lee that a myriad of reasons exists for supporting the East Texas Symphony Orchestra. Whether it is pride of place (East Texas), or the grander aspirations of some residents to be seen with the professional musicians and the guest soloists who perform, the bottom line has to be the music itself. According to Lee, his most important role is to expose as many people as possible to the glory of music.

"There is a baseline awareness among many of our audience

members. Most can recognize the difference between Bach and Tchaikovsky, but there are some gaps in knowledge. Two generations ago, I believe people were better informed than today. It shows me the need for us to work harder as educators, not just for the appreciation of music but for a deeper understanding of how music can transport us to a different time and place. Music is the universal language. The earlier we can reach the younger members of our community with its message, the more likely they will be to adopt and cultivate a love for the art of music. Whether playing an instrument or sitting in the audience listening, the power of music is transformative and cuts across cultural lines better than anything else. We need music in our lives."

When I first interviewed Lee, I asked an unfair question: What his favorite music was? Without missing a beat, he responded, "The politically correct answer is to say whatever piece I am conducting at the moment. I must love it to conduct it." Pressing further, he sidestepped the issue by stating, "Bach is one of my favorites. His music has a timelessness that speaks to the soul." To give his answer a better context, he shared a personal incident. "At my sister's wedding and my father's funeral, we played the same piece by Bach. On one of the most joyous occasions and one of the saddest of my life, the same piece of music. It was appropriate for both." That illustration provides an excellent insight into how Lee prepares a music program for his audiences in East Texas.

Music did not always speak to him the way it does now. As a youngster, he says he hated practicing. "I would rather have been outside playing baseball," he confessed. However, his attitude changed when he was about thirteen. His teacher had him play an étude by Rachmaninoff in a studio recital. "As I played, I suddenly had an awesome feeling." The light bulb went off for him, just as he hoped it would for the young players he encountered now in his role as Musical Director and Conductor for ETSO. "I suddenly realized

I was creating this atmosphere with my fingers and making a sound that people could respond to." As he explained that pivotal moment in his life, he pantomimed playing the piano. "It was an expression of great art and great beauty. I had never felt it before. Not before that moment."

Lee's priority is for the orchestra to play music the way the composer intended, as much as possible. It is not about the personality of the conductor but rather the personality of the music. "In the musical part of the job, my personality matters very little. Dealing with donors and the musicians, personality does matter. If I am conducting Beethoven, the audience should experience Beethoven, not Richard Lee. I am no one. When I am conducting, I should let the personality of the music become my personality. It's not me. It's the music."

It is refreshing that a person in Lee's position should be able to keep his personality set apart from the work itself. Lee was well-known in his native Canada. He was a famous conductor who had achieved a following, along with the orchestra he conducted. Certainly not as well-known as Leonard Bernstein or Arthur Fiedler, Richard Lee's fame is growing—now in East Texas and will expand further. I imagine that his efforts to expand the reputation and the audience for ETSO will cause Lee's personal fame to increase, definitely on the local level. On the national level, his name is likely to be known among other musicians. The professional music world is a small community. It is not uncommon for musicians from one region of the country to be aware of their counterparts in other regions. And conductors seem to be more well-known than the members of the orchestra. While Lee appreciates the fact that he has some degree of fame, he does not actively seek it. For Lee, fame is merely a byproduct of his chosen profession.

Watching Lee at the rostrum, baton in hand, reminds me of a

logical comment he made shortly after accepting the position, "The community, the musicians, and the conductor need a little time to get to know one another." Sitting in the audience during a performance that had a tentative start, my admiration for the maestro rose tremendously when he stopped the performance and began again. It reminded me of another important comment he made during our first interview, "I am willing to get my hands dirty and work hard to make the orchestra better." It took courage to stop the performance and begin again. Far more telling was the way he handled that critical moment. He turned to the audience and said matter-of-factly, "We need to start that again." He then surveyed the musicians with his eyes, set a tempo, and began the performance. "It was not a good moment, but it was necessary. Playing a symphony is, by its nature, quite difficult. Error correction needs to be fast. A really good orchestra can recover almost immediately; when they do, it is a mere hiccup. I expressed my disappointment that we messed up and included myself in that."

I admired Lee's poise under pressure and his leadership skill in getting the orchestra back on track. When the evening's performance ended, the audience members rose from their seats and gave thunderous applause to everyone on the stage. Regarding standing ovations, Lee told me, "Growing up, my teachers were adamant that a standing ovation was a rare occurrence, reserved for those moments when a performance was so extraordinarily moving that it was impossible to remain seated. I have never witnessed one in London, and I have only witnessed one in New York once. In Texas, however, a standing ovation is de rigueur. I often wonder if it is because the audience is so starved for good entertainment or if they simply do not know any better."

In my opinion, it is not that Texas audiences do not know any better, nor are they starved for quality entertainment. I believe they stand while applauding because they appreciate the efforts made on their behalf by all those musicians on the stage.

I ponder what lessons about fame can be learned from Richard Lee. The most obvious is humility. Here is a man who is very secure in his ability and talent and outwardly humble. He is not one prone to flash. Instead, he is steadfastly dedicated to doing what he does well. More importantly for the ETSO organization, he is dedicated to ensuring that the public gets more exposure to the music his orchestra creates. And, of course, he is dedicated to raising awareness of the beauty and grandeur of music among the community's youth. He is introducing the works of the most famous composers, past and present, to a younger generation, who will, in turn, continue to spread the power of music to yet another generation.

Chapter 12
Orson Welles: Boy Genius

In a career filled with highlights, one of the greatest for me was that Orson Welles narrated one of my films. Of all the people who impacted my career in some way, Welles is among the most famous of the famous. It came about when I was preparing to go on location in Arizona to shoot a project for Frito-Lay. My association with Welles came about as we were in the development stages for what was going to be an extremely high-profile project. My client, Albert Raya (the company's Manager of Internal Communications), off-handedly remarked, "I wish we could get a big name to narrate this piece."

"Who would you like?" I responded.

"It would be great to get somebody like Orson Welles," Al said wistfully.

"We can do that."

It was 1984 when we began working on an idea for a film about a new management process being implemented by the snack food giant. The company had opened a new plant in Casa Grande, Arizona. The plant featured state-of-the-art facilities designed specifically for manufacturing and producing the company's six core brands of products made from corn and potatoes: Fritos, Cheetos, Doritos, Tostitos, Ruffles, and Lay's Potato Chips. Nearby the plant were the remains of a structure, built more than a thousand years ago, known as Casa Grande. It was all that remained of a community once inhabited by the Hohokam people, members of a Native American Pima tribe that once flourished in the region. The structure was about three stories high and was protected by a canopy structure erected overhead in 1932 to protect it from the elements.

The Hohokam had established a remarkably advanced civilization centered on cultivating corn as a food source. Researchers discovered an elaborate system of irrigation canals during excavations at the site during the late nineteenth century. It is believed that the villages of the Hohokam existed from roughly 100 BC until 1450 AD, with its most prolific period lasting for a century before the once-flourishing culture completely disappeared. Why their civilization ended remains a mystery. However, descendants from that ancient culture can be found among Pima and Tohono O'odham tribes today.

We decided that our film would draw parallels between the ancient and modern communities as it now exists. I hired a writer with whom I had worked on other projects, a Dallas writer named Marshall Riggins. Riggins conducted extensive research about the region and the people who once lived there. From that research, he developed a script that effectively captured the essence of the ancient community and its similarity to that of the modern-day food processing facility.

Now that I had a script, I began tracking down Orson Welles. This was before the Internet existed, which meant much of the work was accomplished by making phone calls. A lot of phone calls. My first call was to the Screen Actors Guild in Los Angeles. I thought locating the talent agent representing Welles would be the most efficient way. To my great surprise, SAG had no record of Orson Welles having an agent. My next attempt was to call the Player's Guide. Again, no luck. I thought perhaps Actor's Equity in New York would have the information. I was informed that Welles was listed among their members, but his membership was marked as inactive, and they had no further information available. I was beginning to get frustrated. By happenstance, one Sunday morning while reading the *Dallas Morning News,* I ran across an article referencing the magician Mark Wilson, who had learned the art of magic as a teenager living in Dallas. In the article, there was a brief sentence referencing Wilson's recent meeting with Orson Welles in Las Vegas.

Taking a huge leap of faith, I telephoned the information operator in Las Vegas and asked for a listing for Orson Welles. To my great delight and astonished surprise, the operator said, "Please hold, and I'll connect you." The next voice I heard was a single word,

"Hello."

I was silent a moment, certain that the voice who spoke that single word was unmistakably none other than Orson Welles himself. Somewhat flustered, I managed to speak:

"Hello, this is Allen Morris. I'm trying to reach Mr. Orson Welles."

"This is Orson Welles."

When he spoke the words, he paused slightly between "This is" and saying his name, "Orson Welles." Of course, he did. He spoke his name almost as reverently as I did. In the microsecond elapsing, after he spoke his name, I thought, "Orson Welles has a listed number, and he answers his own phone." He spoke again: "Hello?"

"Yes, Mr. Welles, I have been trying to locate your agent…"

"I don't have an agent," he interrupted,

"Yes," I replied, "I found that out. The reason for this call is regarding a film I'm producing for the Frito-Lay company. I was hoping you might be interested in narrating my industrial film."

"Do you have a budget in mind?"

"Yes, my budget is $50,000."

"That will do. Do you have a script?"

I suddenly thought this was all going too quickly. He thinks I just offered him $50,000. "Oh, no. My entire budget is $50,000. That's all I have to produce the entire film."

"I see," said Welles.

There was another somewhat awkward pause as I was feverishly trying to calculate in my head how much I could offer for his services. "How much do you have budgeted for a narrator?" he asked. Thinking quickly, but not particularly accurately, I blurted out, "$15,000."

There was another pause. Remembering the adage that he who speaks first in negotiating loses, I remained silent. Finally, Welles broke the silence. "Before I commit, can you send me the script? I'd like to read it and then get back with you," he said.

"Certainly," I said, thinking it made perfect sense that he would want to read the script before committing: "Where shall I send it?"

"Send it right away, and I'll take a look at it as soon as it arrives." He gave me an address in Las Vegas and said: "May I have your name again … and your telephone number?"

I repeated my name, spelling it for him: "A-L-L-E-N, the Welsh spelling," and gave him my phone number. "Thank you for taking time with me. I'll send it first thing in the morning," I said.

"Allen, with the Welsh spelling, may I call you Allen?"

"Of course."

"Allen, it was nice speaking with you. I look forward to reading your script and getting back in touch with you," he said.

"Thank you, Mr. Welles, goodbye," I said.

"Call me Orson, the French spelling."

As I hung up, I thought to myself, "One of my longtime idols, a man I have admired since I was old enough to understand movies, the man who made *Citizen Kane* just told me to call him Orson." I put a copy of the script into an envelope, addressed it, and rushed to the post office. The deal was not done yet. I had to get him that script, and if all went well, I'd be able to call Al and tell him he got the narrator he wanted.

We arranged to begin shooting in the Arizona desert late that year. As was my routine when going on location, I provided my wife with numbers at the various hotels where the crew and I would stay throughout the two weeks we planned to be away. This was taking place before cell phones existed. I was on location when the news came that Welles was willing to record the narration. The phone rang at my home, and my wife answered:

"Morris's residence"

"May I please speak with Allen Morris?"

"I'm sorry, he isn't here. He's shooting on location in Arizona. This is his wife. May I ask who's calling?"

"This is … Orson Welles."

Believing the call was a prank from some friend, she replied, "Yeah, right. This is Rita Hayworth." There was a pause.

"You don't sound like Rita."

"Maybe not, but the red hair is the same."

"This really is … Orson Welles."

"How do you spell that?"

"O-R-S-O-N-W-E-L-L-E-S," he spelled his name out slowly.

"Well, *Orson*, Allen won't be back for a couple of weeks. May I give him a message when he calls in?"

"Yes, please. Tell him that I called and said I would be willing to record the narration for his film. He can reach me at my Las Vegas number."

"I'll tell him when he calls. Does he have your Las Vegas number?"

"I gave it to him when last we spoke. But just in case, I'll give it to you." He dictated the number.

"Got it! Allen should be calling in late this evening, and I'll give him your message."

"Very good. Thank you, Rita."

"You're welcome, *Orson.*"

Later that evening, I called home, and my wife recounted the conversation she had,

"Some guy claiming to be Orson Welles called and left you a

message. He said he was willing to narrate your film and asked that you call him on his Las Vegas number."

"That really was Orson Welles." At first, there was silence, then a high-pitched squeal.

"You're kidding! I thought it was some prank."

"No prank. I spoke with him last week and gave him our number. I sent him the script and asked him to call me after he read it."

"I told him I was Rita Hayworth."

The next day, I telephoned as soon as I thought it was a reasonable hour. I didn't want to call too early for fear that he might not be an early riser. "Hello," said Orson Welles.

"Good morning, Mr. Welles. This is Allen Morris."

"Good morning, Allen, with the Welsh spelling. This is Orson."

"My wife told me you called to say you would narrate my film."

"Yes, I did. She was quite charming, although I don't think she believed me when I told her who I was. I thought the script was quite good. It was not at all what I expected in an industrial setting. I found the comparison between an ancient farming culture and that of a modern plant facility quite a novel approach. Very well done."

"I'm glad you liked it, more so that you are willing to be part of the production. What do I need to do next? Shall I send a contract and make arrangements for studio time?"

"Is the script you sent final?"

"Yes, it has been approved by the client and their lawyers. It is ready to record as is."

"That's fine. I have time booked tomorrow for another recording session, and I can tag this on to that session. How does that sound?"

I did not presume to direct the mighty Orson Welles, but I was interested in meeting him in person and attending the recording session. There was no way I could leave my shoot to go to a recording session on such short notice. So, I asked him about sending a contract.

"I don't think that will be necessary," said Orson. "How about this? I'll go into the studio tomorrow and record your script. Then, I'll send you the tape from the session, and you will send me a check for $15,000 made out to Idiom, Inc."

"That sounds fine," I said somewhat reluctantly since it was obvious that I would not get to be at the session.

"There is one thing I'd like to caution about, and that is the proper pronunciation of Hohokam. The accent is on the first syllable. HO-ho-kahm."

"Yes, HO-ho-kahm," he said pronouncing it correctly. "Is there anything else?"

"No, sir. That is all. I'll look forward to getting your tape."

When I arrived back in Texas, the tape was already there. I had all the footage and was ready to edit. I booked editing time over a weekend in Jackson, Mississippi, at WLBT, a television station managed by my close friend, Frank Melton. I had used that facility on a couple of other projects and was pleased with the atmosphere and the crew. The biggest advantage of using that facility was that I got it at a rate about half the cost I would pay in the DFW Metroplex. Normally, I do a rough cut on my Avid system and then complete the online edit elsewhere. Time was getting critical for this project, so I decided against doing a rough cut and went straight into the final post. The first time I heard Orson on the tape was when we put it on the machine to transfer it to the one-inch machines we used to make the final master. The first sound I heard was a hacking cough and an engineer's voice over the talkback asking if Orson needed some water.

Once the engineer started recording, the tape was never stopped. Literally, everything that went on during that recording session was on the tape I had received. The coughing and hacking worried me. Listening to that made me think Orson might have a heart attack at any moment. I could hear his cough, and then the engineer would come over the talkback and ask if Orson was alright. "I'll be fine," Orson said and erupted into another round of coughing. I heard him take a drink and clear his throat. And then, "Are we rolling?"

"You have speed, Orson."

Then, he read the opening lines of the script.

I was shocked as I listened to Orson read those lines. They were supposed to grab the viewer's attention. They were supposed to set the tone to match the majesty of the visuals opening the film. What I heard was a lackluster reading devoid of emotion and utterly boring. I cannot express the disappointment I felt when I heard it. My mind was racing as I listened to the first paragraph. How could I show this to my client, who expected perfection from one of the world's most famous voices? Then, the coughing started again. Orson cleared his throat and asked for another glass of water. The tape kept rolling for about a minute, and there was nothing but the sound of Orson Welles clearing his throat and gulping down water. Then, nothing but silence for another minute. Finally, Orson cleared his throat once more and spoke into the mic, "I don't like that. It was all wrong. Let's do it again."

"We're still rolling," said the engineer.

"There is a place in the Arizona desert called Casa Grande..." Orson began.

And he kept going. His reading was understated. As he read the words, the pictures I imagined would open the film filled my mind. His voice painted a majestic scene of members of an ancient culture going about their daily routine, making masa by hand. "Nearby is another structure built in our own time..." With his voice, the transition from the ancient civilization to the present day seemed magical. This was what I had imagined a narration from Orson Welles would be. His inflection was perfect. His cadence varied as he allowed the words to set a rhythm that would guide how the visuals would be edited into the final film. How could I have doubted this genius?

Throughout the session, he would pause occasionally and then re-read a line. Every time, the reading was an improvement. I was thrilled listening to how he would make changes, just slightly changing his tone of voice or the inflection, which always gave individual words a specific emphasis needed to bring the script to life. The only thing wrong with his reading was a mispronunciation of Hohokam. He said ho-HO-kahm. But who am I to complain? Orson Welles narrated my film.

The editing session went smoothly. There were graphic sequences for which the staff at WLBT was able to create animations that added a layer of value to the overall production. The on-location sound sequences were recorded in camera and required only minor equalization to bring them up to the standard of quality exhibited by the rest of the production. The color timing process went much faster than I originally planned, saving valuable time in our production schedule. The only thing left to do once I left Jackson was to take the film to Robin Hood Studios in Tyler, Texas, for post-scoring and final sound mixing.

I had adopted a habit of post-scoring my films early in my career. Some people like to cut to the soundtrack. I like to cut the film and then create a score that matches the visuals. Either way works; I just feel a post-score is better for achieving my goals as a director. Having worked with Robin Hood Brians and Randy Fouts on nearly one hundred projects, we had developed an excellent process for scoring to the picture. They understand my vision and how to enhance it through the music. Working with a soundtrack that combines narration with on-screen talking heads and natural sound from the shooting environment takes a keen ear. Having a music track that doesn't overpower the story is also imperative. Brians and Fouts were masters at that. They also understood the value of adding a foley track. When you see layers of potato chips bumping their way down a conveyor belt, the natural sound enhances the viewer's experience. You can almost smell the product when you can see the product and hear the sounds as the seasoning is being sprayed on.

Once completed, I took a copy of the film to review with my client. "I love it. This is going to be a big hit at Frito-Lay!" Al then picked up the telephone and made an appointment to present the film to his bosses later that afternoon.

While waiting for the reaction from the bigwigs at Frito-Lay, I drove to the original location of Campisi's on Mockingbird, which was near the Frito-Lay headquarters. The restaurant was across the street from the famous Art Deco Dr Pepper headquarters building. Campisi's is a Dallas institution and my favorite Italian restaurant. It was the perfect spot to have a light lunch and a cocktail while awaiting word from my client.

The location was founded as a piano bar called The Egyptian Lounge. Carlos Campisi established the restaurant for his sons, Joseph and Sam, to run. When he bought the location in 1950, he didn't have enough money for a new sign, so he merely replaced "lounge" with "restaurant," which explains why it was called Campisi's Egyptian Restaurant. There was a malicious rumor circulating in Dallas after the Kennedy assassination that Joseph Campisi was somehow involved in planning the assassination in the back room. Reputed members of the Mafia frequented his restaurant. Carlos Marcello frequently had dinner meetings there when he was in town. Jack Ruby was also a regular customer. And because Joseph was friendly with Carlos Civello, the reputed head of the Dallas crime organization, the rumor gained credibility.

Of course, it was nonsense. Just like other people who considered Campisi's to be one of the best places to eat in Dallas, so did certain members of the community—who happened to be criminals. It was not until the 1979 House Select Committee on Assassinations published the findings from their investigation that the rumors were quelled. I ordered veal and a scotch and waited for Al to show up.

The reaction from the brass at Frito-Lay was positive, as expected. Al told me they wanted copies for every plant location and twenty extras to be available whenever they needed them. He also asked to have 16mm prints made so the film could be projected for large groups. They wanted the title changed from *Our Desert Heritage* to *Managing the Future*. I immediately booked time to get the opening title changed and ordered the copies. I had additional copies made to submit the final film to various film festivals.

It did extremely well on the festival circuit. It won a medal at the International Film and TV Festival of New York, was recognized as the Best Corporate Film/Video Production by the Dallas Press Club's Katie Awards, and won two awards from the Texas Public Relations Society. I think it would have won other awards, but I was out of money by the time I completed the film and only entered those three competitions. As it turned out, this film turned out to be a prestigious production, enhancing the careers of everyone involved. The reason the film was so well received is due to the team of production professionals who worked on the project. Marshall Riggin's script was superb. The on-location crew was comprised of all Dallas film professionals: Director of Photography was Gerald Cain; his wife Doris did location stills and worked as a PA; Bob Dracup did lighting; location sound was from Bruce Sherin; we had two assistants, one for lighting and one for sound, whose names I have forgotten, regrettably. And there is no doubt that the narration from Orson Welles was a major reason for the film's success.

After its release, I called Orson, telling him I thought it had turned out well and wanted to send him a copy. He graciously told me he was anxious to see it and would be happy to give his critique if I wanted it. Naturally, that was exactly what I wanted. A couple of weeks later, he called me back and said he had seen my film and thought it was a promising example. Then he asked when I would be in Los Angeles or Las Vegas. I told him I had plans to be in Los Angeles in October, and we made plans to meet for lunch and spend the afternoon together eating, drinking, critiquing my film, and getting to know one another better. I was thrilled and looking forward to meeting with the only Hollywood celebrity I have ever considered to be my idol.

Orson Welles achieved fame at an extremely young age. It was his fame that haunted him throughout his career. He was once quoted as having said of critics, "They don't review my films; they review me." Sadly, he is the prime example of someone whose fame may have been his downfall. After making what is considered by many to be the greatest American film ever made, *Citizen Kane,* he forever spent his lifetime in the shadow of his masterpiece. Often both maligned and praised by critics, at the same time, that film remains as controversial today as it was during its production. The thinly disguised portrait of William Randolph Hearst brought forth the wrath of the newspaper mogul, who used his power in every way possible to make certain *Citizen Kane* would never be exhibited publicly. Welles' name was banned from mention in any of the Hearst publications across the country. Hearst went so far as to offer RKO the cost of the film and a small profit if they would destroy every existing print of the film. The offer was refused, and the film was released in 1941 for mixed reviews.

The Academy of Motion Pictures Arts and Sciences nominated the film in nine categories, including nods for Orson Welles as producer for Best Picture, Best Director, Best Actor, and Best Screenplay (with Hermann Mankiewicz). Its single win was in the writing category, which led to criticism against Welles by several claiming he had nothing to do with the script. As late as 1971, Pauline Kael wrote a *New Yorker* article in which she accused Welles of trying to deny credit where credit was due to cinematographer Gregg Toland, writer Hermann Mankiewicz, and the writing contributions of John Houseman, who disputed this claim despite having parted ways with Welles due to some other disagreement. People present during the production have frequently defended Welles, saying he generously praised the work of others on the film.

Film and television writer Stephen Farber wrote, "Looking back over American movie history—a history of wrecked careers—you begin to see that the critics have a lot to answer for. The classic victim is Orson Welles." Too much too soon? Perhaps. But when you look at the entire body of his work, there is no denying that the films Welles directed, now considered classics, have earned their place. One cannot deny that Gregg Toland's work on *Citizen Kane* was groundbreaking. However, one must also consider where his inspiration came from.

I think the inspiration came directly from Orson Welles' vision for the story he wanted to tell. Before production began, he spoke to associates about the look he wanted for the film. He was upfront about his desire to break barriers, to make an unconventional film that bore no resemblance to what had been seen before. Without Welles, I think an argument can be made that Toland's work would not have reached the new levels that it did. Even Welles himself often stated that the film turned out the way it did because of the craftsmen who did the best work of their careers to that point in that film.

I read many books written about Orson Welles and his career. I have never been deterred in my admiration for him and his work. Much of the negative criticism is merely how some journalists work their craft. Tearing down the reputation of someone who has attained great prominence becomes a challenge for many who are bereft of a great level of talent themselves. While I understand that Welles may have been difficult to deal with and was probably abrupt with many of his associates while working, it is an understandable part of the personality of a genius, which Welles was. It is a character trait I have witnessed hundreds of times throughout my career when I have been in contact with famous people. I have seen that type of behavior in people who are not geniuses, merely people who have a certain talent and are fortunate to have an audience that appreciates that talent. I don't like them any less because they have talent and human frailties.

I understand the kind of trouble that followed Orson Welles every day of his life. Achieving the level of success he had at such a young age was unprecedented. Shirley Temple had tremendous talent at a young age and was recognized for that talent. But, unlike Welles, hers was not a talent that could sustain a lifetime as a performer. Welles spent the greater part of his career, post-*The Magnificent Ambersons,* looking for financing to complete other projects. As a result, he started many films that were never completed. Those films languish somewhere in storage vaults, never to be seen. Some view his career as an unfulfilled promise.

For me, my relationship with Orson Welles became an unfulfilled promise. Shortly before we were to meet in Los Angeles for a leisurely afternoon of lunching, drinking, critiquing, and getting to know one another better, Orson Welles died of a heart attack on October 10, 1985. The news of his passing brought sadness and filled me with grief. Although we had only spoken a few times, I felt a kinship with him. He had been witty and kind to me, which I appreciated. He narrated one of my films, and when he saw it, he told me he thought it showed promise. And he told me to call him Orson, with the French spelling.

Chapter 13
Mickey Rooney: Talented, Professional, and Kind

Back in the 70s, when an entertainment celebrity was in town, either working or promoting a new book or movie, it was common for the heads of some local charitable organizations to ask them to appear in a public service announcement. That is how I met Mickey Rooney.

If my memory is accurate, Rooney was in Houston performing at the Windmill Dinner Theatre. He had graciously agreed to appear in a spot promoting an upcoming fundraising benefit for one of Houston's local charities. Which one, I do not remember. Having someone famous act as a spokesperson was thought to be a big advantage for the charities, especially when they were trying to raise money for their worthy causes. At that time, I had been engaged several times to direct various PSAs, primarily because they were frequently shot on Saturday afternoons when nothing else was going on at our studio. The station's Program Manager was Jim Monahan, who was also in charge of placing public service announcements into the rotation on the program log. Monahan knew of my interest in directing and would give me these assignments to help build my resume. Monahan gave me a big boost as I came into contact with so many in the early stages of my career. He would later stand as Godfather at St. Martin's Episcopal Church when my first son, Asher, was born.

In directing these PSAs, part of my job was to rustle a crew together to work the gig without pay. We would shoot these small productions with a skeleton crew, just the absolute minimum number of people needed to pull it off. Since we were a non-union house, getting a crew was fairly simple. I used the control room staff already on duty, and the cameraman was the only person who needed to be brought in for the production. It was our contribution to the charity. Usually, the crew consisted of the cameraman, the tape operator who was already on duty, who would also monitor the sound levels, and the transmitter engineer, who would help by setting the camera levels.

Although we had a TelePrompTer, we frequently did not use it for these productions. Instead, we wrote the copy onto the posterboard for cue cards. On this particular day, I asked a friend who was working at a different local dinner theatre to come in for makeup. I arrived at the studio an hour and a half early to get the boom mic in place and turn on the studio lights. We were shooting on the set for my *Paws for the Night* show, so the lighting did not need to be focused. As would occasionally happen, when the staff knew that a celebrity would be in the studio over the weekend, five or six extra people would be in the studio. Naturally, when this happened, I would press them into use, holding the cue cards, bringing in water for the talent, or whatever other tasks might be needed.

About fifteen minutes before we were scheduled to shoot, the client arrived with Rooney. There were five other people, presumably big donors, making the client-side entourage larger than I had expected. Jim Monahan greeted them at the front entrance who escorted them into the studio. Once I saw the size of the group, I asked my impromptu extra staff to bring in more chairs so they could sit and watch the production that was about to unfold. As I was instructing them where to place the extra chairs, Monahan came up to me from behind and began the introductions. "Mr. Rooney, this is your director, Allen Morris." He had a huge grin on his face as he reached out with both hands and shook mine vigorously.

> "I'm honored to meet you. I am a big fan," I said in total sincerity.

"The honor is mine," he said while still vigorously shaking my hand. "I always like working with new people, especially a youngster like you, just beginning your career."

I wondered if he was sincere in that statement or disappointed there was not a more seasoned director helming this little production. At that moment, as I looked into his twinkling blue eyes, I couldn't help but think he would be ideal to play Santa Claus. He was short, about 5'2", and plump—a right jolly, old elf! As we continued making introductions, I introduced the cameraman and the girl who was going to hold the cue cards. "Oh, we won't need cue cards. I know the script, and I'm ready," Rooney said.

While the guests were being seated and the girl was dusting Rooney with makeup powder, I had a moment to make small talk with Rooney. "My father met you in Europe during the war. He loaned you a pen to sign autographs and never got it back." He laughed.

"I had a blast doing USO shows. I think it was very important being able to bring a bit of home to the troops who were out on the front line," he said with a serious tone of voice.

"I think my father would agree with you."

"Do you know what outfit he was with?"

"The Texas 36th Infantry Division. He was in North Africa and then the invasion at Anzio."

"John Huston shot a documentary around Anzio, I believe."

"The Battle of San Pietro. My father was there."

"That was some tough fighting, as I understand."

"That's what my dad said. He didn't like being shot at, but he took great pride that he did what needed to be done. I think the toughest part was when he helped liberate the camps. He was one of the few G.I.s with a camera, and he took pictures. His commander said they needed evidence because no one was going to believe what they found at the camps."

"The camps may have been the biggest surprise of the war … I mean a surprise for everybody back home. You should be proud of your dad," Rooney commented.

"I am."

About that time, the cameraman shouted out that the control room was ready to begin. I showed Rooney where to stand, and we did a mic check to set the levels. I took my place beside the camera and pulled my stopwatch out of my pocket. "Let's try one for a time. Roll it, please."

After a brief six seconds, the cameraman shouted, "Speed."

I looked toward Rooney and then quietly gave the command, "Action."

Rooney looked directly into the camera and began reciting the copy. At the same time, I started the stopwatch. When he finished the copy, I stopped the watch and said, "Cut." I looked at the watch, and it read thirty-eight seconds. "That's eight seconds over. We need you to speed up the read just a little."

"Alright," Rooney said and adjusted his stance, looking toward the floor for a moment. Then he looked up and said, "I'm ready."

"Roll it," I said.

"Speed," shouted the cameraman.

After a slight pause, I said, "And... action."

As Rooney began the second reading of the script, I was transfixed watching him work. It was a simple piece of fluff about raising money and promoting the date of the event. But he was putting great emotion into his reading as if this was the most important message the people watching on television would hear that day. As I watched him, I thought about what a pro he was and what a multitalented performer he was. I had seen nearly every film he had made. He could sing, dance, and play comedy and extremely difficult dramatic scenes. I was thinking about that as he began reading the line near the end of the script, which was the money appeal. I was thinking about how his performance in *Boys Town* had been hailed as "hammy and histrionic." He finished the line and stood there, holding his facial expression. I was mesmerized. I just stood there looking at him, holding that expression, not moving. "Okay, CUT IT," he said loudly. Then he motioned toward me and said, "May we speak for a moment?" I walked over to him, and he turned us both away from the crew.

"Okay, here's the deal. Your job is to say 'action,' then my job is to do the spot. Then, your job is to say 'cut.' I'm not budging until I hear cut, see?"

"I am sorry. I got caught up in how you were saying the lines, and then when you stopped and didn't move, I was fascinated watching you hold that final moment."

"Look, kid, don't be intimidated by me. I'm just an actor reading the lines. You're the boss on the set. Direct me. Tell me how you want the thing read. Tell me to give you more, give you less. Let your crew see that you are in

127

charge. It's your set."

Then, he pulled a crumpled piece of paper out of his pocket and handed it to me and he turned toward the crew. "Act like you are looking at the script and telling me how to read it," Rooney said quietly so only I could hear. "It's like this is what we've been talking about."

I did what he said, looking at the crumpled script in his hand, I saw the last line, and I looked up at him, "I'd like to suggest that you pull back just a little on this line. Less Whitey Marsh in *Boys Town*, more *Andy Hardy*."

"Good direction," he said and smiled. Then he raised his voice so the crew could hear, "I got it. Let me try another take. I know what you want."

I walked back to my position by the camera and called, "Roll it." When I heard "Speed," I said "Action" and started the stopwatch. This time, I paid attention as he did another take. This time, it was much less dramatic than the previous take. When he finished, I glanced at the watch, waited two seconds, and then called, "Cut."

"How was that?" Rooney asked.

"Timing is right on. Did you like it?"

"Only if you did."

"I'd like another take. This time, let's bring the emotional level up a bit at the end."

"How much do you want?"

"If that last take was a five, make it eight. Do you know what I mean?"

"I think so," he said and stepped back onto his mark.

Once again, I called "Roll it," and when I heard "Speed," I quietly said "Action." Rooney went through the copy again, this time adding more emotion to that last line but without going over the top. The time was right. As far as I was concerned, it was all we needed. "Cut," I said and walked to the set.

"I think we have it. Did you like your read?"

"I thought it was good. But let's do it again. Act like you're telling me how to read that last line again," Rooney said. I could tell he was acting now for the benefit of the crew. I went along.

"Okay, one more time. Roll it."

Six seconds later, the cameraman shouted, "Speed." I looked into Mickey Rooney's blue eyes, smiled, and quietly said, "Action." As it turned out, he made a few changes to his reading, which made it better than before. Then, he nailed that final line with just enough emotion to make it believable and compelling. When he completed the script and held his look into the camera, I waited a beat and then called, "Cut."

Rooney took a few steps toward me as he said, "I think that was perfect. Just right. What do you think?"

"Let's do one more." He wasn't expecting that, and it registered on his face.

"Alright, what was wrong with that take, my friend?"

"Nothing. I want one more to play with. This time, let's have a little of that Mickey Rooney ham at the end." Then I looked at the cameraman, "Go in extreme close up for the whole take. Fill the screen with his face."

"You're going for the drama," Rooney said as a huge smile came across his face. "You're going to cut in when it gets emotional. Good idea," he said to me with a wink.

"Back to one and roll it," I said.

"Speed."

"Action."

I watched him intently, seeing how a consummate professional who has been doing this for nearly fifty years plies his trade. I was thinking to myself, "I'm a twenty-three-year-old rookie working with an actor who has been doing this nearly since birth, and he's treating me like a pro." I was extremely grateful for the consideration he was giving me. He finished the read, looked into the camera with the same engaging smile, and held the moment until I called, "Cut. That's a wrap." I walked over to the set and asked,

"Would you like to see the recordings?"

"Yes, that would be great."

"Ask the control room to replay everything from the beginning, please," I told the cameraman.

The cameraman came back with a message from the control room. They were in the middle of a break and would play the tape as soon as the break was over. I turned to Rooney and explained that our control room crew was also working the on-air breaks, and we would have the playback momentarily. In the meantime, the crowd of donors that accompanied the client to the studio were all busily gushing over Rooney, and he was politely taking in all their praise. Within a couple of minutes, the cameraman told those of us in the studio that the playback was ready, and I told him to roll it. We all gathered around the studio monitor and watched the replay of each take. As it played, various members of the client entourage made comments: "Great reading," "Love your expression there," "I am amazed you didn't need cue cards," and so forth. Rooney was paying careful attention to his look. As I watched him watch, I could see when he liked or didn't like something in each take. When it was over, and the final version in extreme close-up played, he looked at me, saying, "Take three with the ending from the final works for me," he said, and then added, "Will you ask the control room to join us out here?"

I motioned to the cameraman and said, "Mr. Rooney would like for the control crew to join us in the studio." He repeated my request into his headset.

"Mr. Rooney, they'll be here in just a moment."

"Call me Mickey, Allen," he said. "Pros like us don't need to be so formal with each other."

When the entire crew was assembled, Mickey shook hands with each member of the crew and thanked them for their good work. Then he added, "Watch out for this guy," pulling me to his side and putting his arm around my shoulder. "This guy is going places. He's a good director, and you all should pay attention to him. He'll be someone about whom one day you can say, 'I knew him when.'"

"Thank you, that's very kind of you. On behalf of our entire crew, we appreciate having the opportunity of working with you this afternoon," I said to Mickey as he reached out, and we shook hands again, and he smiled that huge smile, gave me a hug, and said quietly,

"I meant what I said. I wish you the best of good fortune in your career. I'll look for you someday in the future!"

As the entourage was leaving, Mickey turned around and walked back toward me. Reaching into his pocket, he pulled out a pen. "Give this to your father. Tell him I'm sorry it took so long to get his pen back. There was a war on. I'm sure he'll understand." And with that, he turned and walked out the studio door.

Looking back on that afternoon, I remember how impressed I was with how Mickey Rooney handled himself and others around him. Here was a man whose career had been in decline, now doing dinner theatre and appearing in a public service announcement that I directed. What impressed me most was that he approached every project with the attitude of a true professional. He was not relying on his fame and past glory; instead, he was working to give every project the same effort, using his remarkable talent to bring whatever he could to help make the project a success.

Keenly aware that he had been famous for his entire life, since playing as a nine-year-old in the *Mickey McGuire* series of shorts beginning in 1929, and then as Puck in 1935's *A Midsummer Night's Dream,* followed by *Captains Courageous,* the *Andy Hardy* series, *Boys Town,* and all the musicals he did with Judy Garland, his filmography is a history of Hollywood itself. In the not-too-distant future, his career would have a resurgence with a hit show on Broadway, *Sugar Babies*, and the presentation of an honorary Oscar at the 1983 Academy Awards. In Mickey Rooney, I saw a man of immense talent doing his job professionally and making an effort to help a young director who was just beginning his career. He treated me as a professional, on his level, and wanted to be sure the crew saw me that way as well. I appreciated his kindness. With his guidance, I became a better director that day.

Allen Morris

Chapter 14
Mark Kennedy Shriver on his father
Robert Sargent Shriver, Jr.

Some people are born into great wealth. They may add to that wealth, or they might squander it. My point is this: they started their lives rich because their forebears had fortunes. The same is true for people who are born into a famous family. The chances of becoming famous are significantly improved if one happens to be born into a famous family. Being born into a wealthy, famous family is akin to hitting the trifecta at the racetrack. Frequently, although not always, wealth and fame seem to go hand-in-hand. Have one, and your chances of having the other are greatly improved.

Growing up in the sixties and living in Dallas at the time of the Kennedy assassination, I was aware of the many members of the Kennedy Family and their extended family. I think it is fair to say that beginning in the last half of the Twentieth Century, the Kennedy Family ranks as one the most famous families in the United States. Perhaps THE most famous. They were to the 60s what the Rockefeller, Roosevelt, and Vanderbilt families were to the last half of the nineteenth century. While Kennedy's wealth was not nearly as substantial as that of the families who came to prominence during the Industrial Age, one can easily argue that the newcomer Kennedy's fame became far greater. The marital union of Joseph P. Kennedy and Rose Fitzgerald Kennedy produced nine children. Three of their sons became United States senators. One became president in 1960. It was the election of John Fitzgerald Kennedy as the 35th President of the United States that created the most fame for the family, a fame that continued to grow throughout the remainder of the Twentieth Century. The Kennedy Family's influence on American politics and culture, as well as Jacqueline Bouvier Kennedy's direct impact on fashion, helped drive their fame further.

One of the members of the extended Kennedy family is Robert Sargent Shriver, Jr. Although an outspoken voice against American involvement in World War II, he joined the United States Navy before the attack on Pearl Harbor. He served for five years in the South Pacific, most notably participating in the Battle of Guadalcanal, during which he was wounded and received the Purple Heart. After his discharge from the service, he worked as an assistant editor at *Newsweek*, where he met Eunice Mary Kennedy, the fifth child of Rose and Joseph Kennedy, Sr. They were married in 1953. After his brother-in-law was elected president in 1960, Sargent Shriver (as he was more commonly addressed) became the driving force in the creation of the Peace Corps. Following the death of President Kennedy, Shriver became an important member of President Lyndon B. Johnson's administration. He served as Ambassador to France from 1968-1970. In 1972, when Thomas Eagleton dropped out as the Democrat nominee for Vice President, Shriver became his replacement, losing in the landslide election that put Richard Nixon in the White House. Shriver briefly pursued nomination for president on the Democrat ticket in 1976, dropping out of the race after a poor showing in the first few primaries.

Mark Kennedy Shriver is the son of Sargent Shriver. When I heard that Mark Kennedy Shriver was to be speaking at a luncheon for the Alzheimer's Alliance, I wanted to take advantage of the opportunity to interview him. What better opportunity than speaking with a member of the family to learn first-hand knowledge about the family, and in particular about Sargent Shriver! Mark Shriver has himself had a distinguished history of public service, having served two terms as a member of the Maryland House of Delegates from 1995-2003. Since 2014, he has served as President of the Save the Children Action Network, working on campaigns to end child mortality, and served as Senior Vice President of U.S. Programs & Advocacy of Save the Children. In 2021, he became president of the Don Bosco Cristo Rey High School. His father would no doubt take great pride in the fact that Mark has continued the work he started with Save the Children!

As Shriver began his presentation, the "Kennedy/Shriver Charm" was in full force. "When I arrived this morning, someone walked up to me and said, 'Has anyone ever told you that you look like a Kennedy?' I replied that sometimes it does happen, and he shot back with, 'And I bet that makes you mad.'"

The crowd burst out with laughter. Shriver flashed the famous smile he and so many of his siblings and cousins inherited from his mother's side of the family. After a moment to allow the crowd to realize he was joking, he brushed the hair off his forehead—in the same manner as his Uncle Bobby did—and launched into his presentation, "Let me say a couple of words about a book I wrote about my Dad and Alzheimer's."

That was the morning of September 16, 2013, in the main dining room at Tyler's Willow Brook Country Club. Just the week before, the Alzheimer's Alliance of Smith County released butterflies at the Tyler Rose Garden in a gesture symbolizing setting loved ones free, once held captive by the devastating disease. The gesture is a way of letting go of the anger, pain, and frustration felt by many people tasked with caring for a family member who has Alzheimer's. For those with a belief in the afterlife, it is also a symbolic gesture welcoming the spirit of their loved ones into the presence of God. I interviewed that annual luncheon's guest speakers for roughly a decade. Every time, I found their stories to be inspirational and poignant.

The title of Mark's book is *A Good Man,* subtitled *Rediscovering My Father, Sargent Shriver.* That Mark was a member of a famous family held little meaning to him as an eight-year-old whose father was on the Democrat ticket in the 1972 presidential election. Four years later, at the age of twelve, the 1976

Democrat primary race gave Mark Shriver a role in the campaign process, but still, the impact of fame was overshadowed by the force of his father's personality. "Dad exuded joy every day of his life guided by three principles: faith, hope, and love," is the way Mark describes his father. "He had one of the most brilliant minds of the twentieth century."

The Alzheimer's Alliance of Smith County invited Mark Shriver to speak at this year's Butterfly Hope Luncheon because of the book he wrote in his search to discover the source of his father's joy, sense of purpose, and devotion to helping others. "For me, there was a period of anger after Dad's diagnosis in 2001," Mark confides, "We first noticed something was wrong when Dad would get Orioles player's positions mixed up when he talked about the games. Alzheimer's slowly took him away over ten years." The other reason the Alliance invited Mark to speak was that the Shriver Family's story of coping with Alzheimer's could help others who are dealing with a similar situation. As his book points out, helping others is the underlying theme of Sargent Shriver's life.

The great tragedy for the Shriver family, as with so many families, was slowly losing a father, husband, and grandfather who had been the solid rock within the family. The guiding light of the family was beginning to dim, and just as importantly, they were watching a man slip away that had been such an integral part of so many other people's lives.

Born on November 9, 1915, Sargent Shriver played a major role in many of the major events shaping the 20th Century, beginning with his service in the United States Navy. Sargent Shriver's personal relationship with Dr. Martin Luther King began in the early 1950s. It was Shriver who convinced his brother-in-law, then-Senator John Kennedy of Massachusetts, to make a phone call offering help to Coretta Scott King after her husband's arrest during the 1960 presidential campaign. King's later endorsement of the Kennedy ticket helped the Democrat Party narrowly win the election that November. Shriver created the Peace Corps as part of the "New Frontier" administration. His leadership profoundly affected not only the young people who served in the Peace Corps but millions of people around the world who benefitted directly from their work. Shriver's service to the country continued with LBJ's "Great Society," in which he was considered the "architect" of the Johnson Administration's "War on Poverty." This included developing the Head Start Program, VISTA, Job Corps, Foster Grandparents, Upward Bound, Neighborhood Health Services, the National Clearinghouse for Legal Services, and other programs designed to provide assistance to the least fortunate segment of American society.

"My father had two great priorities in his life: his relationship with God and his relationship with my mother," Mark explains the source of his father's joy, "Everything else came after." The elder Shriver was a devout Catholic who attended Mass every day. It was his strong faith in God that Mark credits with his father's ability to face Alzheimer's with the courage and fortitude he always exhibited.

Mark believes the joy his father exhibited most of the time came from his strong relationship with God. His faith was unwavering. Constant. Strong. There is no doubt to Mark that his father lived the admonition of St. Francis to "preach the gospel always, even if you must use words." Sargent Shriver was a man of action who got things done. His daily actions reflected his belief in the teachings of Christ. To Mark and his siblings, it was important that the disease (that took hold of their father) not prevent him from living his remaining years as fully as possible. "We kept him active. He participated in a Men's Club run by the Presbyterians near our house. We took him on field trips to the museums. When the time came for him to be in a facility where he could be cared for, we took him home every day for dinner with the family." Another thing Mark points out is that his family was fortunate to have the means to provide their father with the best care possible. Not all families do, which is exactly why an organization like the Alzheimer's Alliance of Smith County is necessary to the community

"People need to understand that they can only do what they can do. Do not be afraid to ask for help. No one can take care of someone with Alzheimer's alone," Mark turns serious for a moment, "We all need organizations like the Alzheimer's Alliance of Smith County to help us cope with this terrible disease. We all need a network of strangers and friends."

Mark made a subtle distinction because of what he learned about his father while writing the book, "I don't like the term 'caregiver.' I think it is more important for us to be 'love givers.' My father dedicated his life to helping others because he had a true and abiding love for his fellow man. After he died, I constantly ran into people who would offer their condolences, and frequently, the final thing they had to say about my father was that he was a good man." Mark is emphatic that his father was not concerned about his legacy. His concern in life was getting things done and changing the world. He wanted a better world for all people, and he worked to make that happen so everyone might have the opportunity to realize their dreams. Mark flashes that smile again, and his bright blue eyes sparkle as he says with conviction, "If I learned anything from my parents, it is that doing for others is a great job."

When Sargent Shriver died, a number of people spoke at the funeral Mass, including each of his five children, Vice President Joe Biden, and former President Bill Clinton. They all spoke about the attributes that made him a good man. They celebrated the outward accomplishments of his lifetime of public service. Before his turn to speak, Mark remembered a phrase his father had spoken to him often, "I'm doing the best I can with what God has given me."

That sentence sums up how Shriver lived his daily life. According to Mark, he let God guide his footsteps every day, and he did what he thought God instructed him to do each day. His passion and joy for life were gifts from God, gifts he repaid through his service to others and the example he set for his children. He did the best he could with the gifts he received from God. The message Mark Kennedy Shriver shared with those of us who are now facing the burden he and his family faced as they cared for their father is a simple one, "Be love givers and do the best we can with the gifts God has given us to ease the way for our loved ones on the path of their final journey."

Coming from a family famous for its competitiveness, Mark shared a story with the audience at the Butterfly Hope Luncheon about calling his sister Maria to brag about the invitation to speak at the event for the Alzheimer's Alliance of Smith County:

> "I just wanted you to know that I am going to be the luncheon speaker in Tyler, Texas, at a luncheon for the Alzheimer's Alliance of Smith County in September."

> "Mark, I turned down an invitation from Mary Lauren Faulkner two weeks ago inviting me to speak at that luncheon," Maria quickly informed her younger brother.

> "Are you serious?"

> "Yes. Definitely. You have three kids, I have four. You've written one best-seller; I've written four or five. I work for NBC, and you work for Save the Children. I'm a big shot; you're not."

> "So, I hung up on Maria."

You have to love sibling rivalry! Mark's sister Maria may make jokes about his accomplishments, but the reality is that he is taken very seriously for his contributions to society. He holds five Honorary Doctorates from La Roche College, 2016; Seattle University, 2015; Wheelock College, 2013; College of the Holy Cross, 2010; and Loyola College in Maryland, 1994.

Other honors include: Legislative Sponsor Award, Maryland Children's Action Network, 1999, 2000, 2001; Environmental Leadership Award, Maryland League of Conservation Voters, 1999, 2000, 2001; Leadership Award, Maryland Alliance of Boys and Girls Clubs, 2001; Award of Excellence, Mothers Against Drunk Driving, 2002; Outstanding Legislative Leadership Award, The Arc of Maryland, 2002; and Father of the Year Award, Mother's Day/Father's Day Council, 2008.

Mark Shriver's self-deprecating sense of humor is ingratiating. It comes from his father, he says, proudly. That his father is his hero is evident. Writing the book, which won a Christopher Award in 2013, by the way, was a labor of love. It was Mark's way of ensuring that his father's legacy would endure. It was a way for his children to know their grandfather better. It was a way for Mark to know his father better. Having the opportunity to meet with him and talk with him about his family and his passion for helping others, especially those who cannot help themselves, was not merely an honor for me; I found it to be inspirational. I hope our paths cross again someday.

That is true of most of the famous people I have encountered throughout the years. Whether making a film, directing a concert, or writing an article, the opportunity to meet them gave me insights into their personalities. I knew them better as individuals who were not so different from the regular people I encountered daily. I have always been somewhat amazed at how quickly famous people will let down their guard and behave like normal people when they spend enough time to feel comfortable and not threatened. For so many who live their lives in the glare of spotlights and photographer's flashbulbs, there is a tendency to maintain an aesthetic distance, so to speak. They are careful about what they say and how they say it. I suppose it is a defensive mechanism that kicks in automatically to prevent being misquoted or falling into "gotcha" traps that so many yellow journalists use to exploit them. But that changes when you can gain a little trust and establish a level of rapport. There have been several times when my paths did cross again with a few of the famous people I got to know, even if only slightly. That many of them honestly remembered me was a frequent and pleasant surprise.

Chapter 15
Charles Nesbitt Wilson: Before Good Time Charlie!

There was no sense of surprise when meeting Charles Nesbitt Wilson after our first meeting. It was in his nature to develop a rapport with everyone with whom he came into contact. Putting constituents at ease and making them feel they were one of his best friends was one of the most important tools Wilson used when stumping for votes. I called it glad-handing. Wilson called it job security.

I first met Charlie Wilson during his first campaign for a seat in the U. S. Congress from Texas's 2nd Congressional District. Everyone called him Charlie. Even then, he had a self-proclaimed reputation as a lady's man. It was well-known throughout his constituency that he had graduated from the Naval Academy, where he had the distinction of receiving the second most demerits ever. His roommate was the first with the most demerits. Wilson graduated 8th from the bottom of his class with a B.S. in Engineering and then served in the U.S. Navy from 1956-1960, where he eventually made the rank of lieutenant aboard the USS John W. Weeks.

It was in the early summer of 1972, and I was working at KTRE-TV 9 in Lufkin, when Vic Kopycinski dropped by the station to introduce himself and announced his intention to open a new advertising agency at some unspecified date in the future. Vic was a man of many varied interests, one of which was fishing, and another was political campaigns. The first placement he intended to make through his new advertising agency was for Charlie Wilson's campaign, and he asked the sales manager for the political ad rates. He booked time to produce a commercial and scheduled a date for the production to be done at the KTRE studio. Sensing that I was a potential vote, the first thing Charlie said to me when he arrived at the station was, "How old are you?" When I told him I was eighteen, he replied enthusiastically, "That's wonderful! You'll be able to vote in the election this coming November!" He asked me how someone as young as I happened to be working at the station, and I explained I had started there as talent on a kid's show and worked my way up from sweeping floors to running the camera and finally directing the news. "How long have you been directing the news?" he asked. "About a year," I replied. "Then, you must know a lot about my plans after the election. Bob Browning (who was our lead reporter) has interviewed me several times."

It was the first political commercial I ever worked on. I helped shoot the footage and then was responsible for editing the final spot that was aired on our station, the only local television station in the area. The 1972 election was the first time I voted. The election was held after I had graduated from Lufkin High School and six months after I turned eighteen. I voted in the Democrat Primary and supported Charlie Wilson, but in the general election, my vote for the presidency went to Nixon, contributing to his landslide victory.

From the 1972 election until 1988, I was involved with producing every television spot for Charlie's campaigns. From our first introduction, I liked him. He was tall and spoke in a deep, baritone voice with a distinctively East Texas accent. He had previously served in the Texas House and Senate and was heavily backed by lumber magnate Arthur Temple Jr. and his son Buddy Temple of Diboll. Buddy would be elected to the Texas House during the 1972 fall election. Arthur Temple Jr., who had been a close friend of President Lyndon B. Johnson, was anxious to have someone in Congress who was sympathetic to his views. During his time in the Texas Legislature, Wilson was employed by Temple, earning an annual salary reported to be around $14,000, reputedly the highest salary he had earned from the private sector up to that point in his career.

During that summer, there were stories about Charlie Wilson on our newscast at least once a week. His campaign was getting a lot of local coverage. One story that I especially liked had been shot in his hometown of Trinity. In it, Browning had done a man-on-the-street series of interviews that included his relatives and the people with whom Wilson had grown up in that small East Texas town. The only thing I knew about Trinity was that it was wet across the river. "Wet" in that connotation meant you could buy liquor there. When I was growing up in Lufkin, someone said they were going across the river, which usually meant they were headed to Trinity.

I didn't see Charlie again until a week after we shot that first commercial. He and Vic came by the station to see the final spot before it was to go on the air. They arrived in the evening, after the six o'clock newscast. Their day had been spent making campaign stops throughout the 2nd District. After they viewed the spot and approved it, they asked if there was someplace nearby to grab something to eat. I told them we were sending the cameraman out to pick up dinner from a small diner down the road. We added their choices from the menu, and Vic graciously picked up dinner for our whole crew. More votes!

Charlie, Vic, and I sat down to eat in the small break room just outside the studio where the news was done. I offered them a drink, to which they agreed. I knew where the Chief Engineer kept a bottle hidden, so I retrieved it and poured each of us a shot. This created a more relaxed atmosphere and gave me the opportunity to ask Charlie what it was that got him interested in politics. He told me that he was eight years old when Pearl Harbor was attacked. He said he had grown up seeing newsreels in the movie theatre and reading accounts about the progress of the war in the newspaper. He became fascinated with what was going on in Europe and the South Pacific. In particular, he developed an admiration for Winston Churchill, particularly after hearing a replay of the speech Churchill made in 1940, when he said, "We shall fight on the beaches. We shall fight on the landing grounds. We shall fight in the fields and in the streets. We shall fight in the hills. We shall never surrender!"

He said he remembered hearing that speech played over and over again many times on the radio. "It was perhaps the most stirring thing I had ever heard. It made me terribly concerned about what was happening across the ocean. I was terrified and yet curious about what real war was. You must remember, I was just a little kid growing up during the war and reading about it in newspaper articles. There were families I knew who had sons that had enlisted and were serving overseas," Charlie recalled. "It was going on far away, but it scared me as a child. I was worried about our town being attacked. As a kid, I stood watch in my backyard, protecting Trinity, keeping an eye out for any Japanese planes that might fly over our town," he paused and smiled, "I'm proud to say, not one Japanese plane ever came near Trinity."

I kept up with Charlie's career in Congress. I would see him again every two years and work on his re-election campaign commercials. At first, they were all talking heads in the studio. By about the fourth time, we started shooting on-location, making spots that had much higher production values. I remember one spot where we had him in a tank. Another was shot out on the edge of a wooded area, with deer in the background. It was the kind of location his constituency would like. There were a lot of hunters in the 2nd District. The deer we photographed was actually in a fenced-in area, but we shot it so it appeared that Charlie was walking in the woods. With clever editing, it looked like the deer were with him. One thing I learned after several years of doing his campaign commercials is that Charlie liked East Texas and the people he grew up with. It would probably surprise the people he knew in Washington to hear him when he was talking with his hometown constituents. His East Texas accent was much more pronounced than what it was when he was interviewed in Washington on the national news. That always amused me.

I was not aware of the great extent to which Charlie was involved with his covert support of the Mujahideen after the Soviet invasion of Afghanistan until I read George Crile's book *Charlie Wilson's War: The Extraordinary Story of the Largest Covert Operation in History.* I was anxious to see it when it was made into the movie Charlie Wilson's War. I thought it was well done. I thought Tom Hanks was good in the film, but I was not sure he was right for the part because I knew Charlie. I have no idea who I would have cast instead, so I suppose Hanks was the correct choice. I had also met Joanne King Herring several times, first when she hosted a local talk show in Houston and later when I was at a couple of parties that she either hosted or was also attending. I thought that Julia Roberts was a perfect casting. I thought her performance captured the essence of Joanne King Herring.

Because people don't read as much these days, I think the movie was more important in terms of making more people aware of what happened in Afghanistan from 1980 until the early 90s. I think it also made more people aware of Charlie Wilson. The one negative of the movie, for me, is that it only presents a superficial view of Charlie. He was much more complex than the portrayal in the movie. When one watches the movie, one is given the impression that the only thing Charlie did during his career was party, chase women, and develop an obsession with getting arms to the Mujahideen. His congressional career had much more substance than that. While I might not have agreed with his political stands on many issues, there is no denying that he made a huge impact in the areas of rights of the individual, in particular women's rights and the voting rights of African Americans. He worked hand-in-hand with the League of Women Voters to ensure the passage of the Safe Water Drinking Act. During his first year in office, he helped push legislation to protect The Big Thicket in Texas as a national preserve. After he was appointed to serve on the Appropriations Committee, he earned a reputation among his colleagues for his ability to negotiate votes for his bills. His support of Israel, particularly in the wake of the Yom Kippur War, led to his developing a strong personal relationship with Israeli leadership. This was an extremely important alliance during the Soviet-Afghan war when Charlie needed help in transporting man-portable anti-aircraft guns into Pakistan. He worked tirelessly to increase Medicare and Medicaid funding for the elderly, underprivileged, and veterans. Always looking out for the best interests of his constituency, he got funding passed to create a Veterans Affairs Hospital in Lufkin, Texas.

Much of the Good Time Charlie reputation is of his own doing. He lived extravagantly and made no bones about it. I personally think he relished that reputation. It fed his ego, and a public image as a flamboyant playboy was exactly how he saw himself. That other people saw him that way was fine with him. He never apologized for his excesses and never denied that he did live to excess. That is who he was, and he saw no reason to hide it from the public or to change for that matter. He had been told many times to cut down on his drinking, or it would kill him. But he continued long after such admonitions were made and made several times. Eventually, he gave up hard liquor but continued drinking wine for several years until he was forced to undergo heart transplant surgery in September 2007.

There were, of course, many allegations made that he was a user of illegal drugs. The most infamous of such allegations occurred in 1980 when he was accused of spending an evening with two strippers in a hot tub at Caesars Palace in Las Vegas. The accusations led to an investigation by the Justice Department attorney Rudy Giuliani, who ultimately had to drop the case due to a lack of evidence. Charlie never confirmed or denied the allegations. The closest he came is recorded as a quote attributed to Charlie from George Crile's book: "The girls had cocaine, and the music was loud. It was total happiness. And both of them had ten long, red fingernails with an endless supply of beautiful white powder... The feds spent a million bucks trying to figure out whether I inhale or exhale when those fingernails passed under my nose, and I ain't telling."

With regard to his reputation as a womanizer that is another reputation that Charlie enjoyed without shame. He was rarely seen without the company of a woman (or, frequently, several women). The one time it became a problem was during a trip to Pakistan in 1987, when it caused tension between Charlie and the CIA. This was during the time period when Charlie was still actively involved in getting arms to the Afghans. The agency refused to approve payments to reimburse Charlie for the travel expenses he submitted for the women he had invited along for the ride. In retaliation for the refusal to reimburse him, Charlie made certain the CIA's funding the next year was cut. There is no question that Charlie lived a party life and that he saw each day as an opportunity to play hard and live life to the fullest. He was quoted once as having said that he could take his job seriously without taking himself seriously. That was how he handled criticism when anyone accused him of allowing his lifestyle to interfere with the serious nature of his work as a sitting member of the United States Congress. To Charlie Wilson, how he lived his life was not related to the job he was doing in Congress.

I think anyone looking at the record objectively would have to agree that Charlie Wilson managed to accomplish a great deal during his twelve terms as a working member of the House of

Representatives. And it can be said that one accomplishment actually made a significant change in the world. Whether that change is good or bad remains up for debate. Looking back from a distance of thirty years, there now exists some justified criticism that perhaps the aid given to the Afghan Mujahideen went to the wrong place. Most of the money Charlie supplied ended up with Islamist hardliner Gulbuddin Hekmatyar, who has since been accused of war crimes and was later allied with the Taliban after the U. S. Armed Forces went into Afghanistan.

However, that criticism is not necessarily relevant in terms of Charlie's intentions. He was truly committed to helping the Afghan people rid themselves of the Soviet invaders. And that goal was, in fact, achieved. To the best of his ability, Charlie adopted a cause based on his moral beliefs and worked toward achieving a worthy goal. Not many people have been able to do such work on a global scale. Charlie did. I commend him for that. I was sorry when he died. I never had the opportunity to visit with him after 1988, and that is a regret because I felt we had a good relationship since the first day we met when I was at the beginning of my career. I would like to have known him after his retirement if only to see first-hand whether he still had that same exuberant lust for life as when I first knew him. Whether you agreed with his politics, one must admit that Charlie Wilson lived a full life, earning his moniker, Good Time Charlie.

Chapter 16
Willie Nelson: Saintly Outlaw

It is difficult to write anything new about Willie Nelson. He has given so many interviews and been in the spotlight for so long that there is very little about him that is not known. What I can do is share my personal impression of the man who is synonymous with the Texas brand of country music. It is a genre that Nelson practically invented, along with some help from his good friends Waylon Jennings, Jerry Jeff Walker, Kris Kristofferson, Billy Joe Shaver, David Allan Coe, Ray Wylie Hubbard, and Guy Clark. Before he was known as one of the creators of what became known as Outlaw Country Music, Willie Nelson was the writer of mainstream C&W classics such as "Family Bible," "Crazy," "Funny How Time Slips Away," "Hello Walls," "Night Life," "The Party's Over" and many others. Before he found fame as the iconic performer he is today, Willie survived in the music business as other people made hit recordings of his songs. His early songs were successful for artists such as Patsy Cline, Faron Young, George Jones, Claude Gray, Paul Buskirk, and Billy Walker. Although Willie had his "Touch Me" recording reach the Top Ten on *Billboard Magazine's* Hot Country Singles in 1962, his first Number One hit didn't happen until 1975. That was with songwriter Fred Rose's "Blue Eyes Crying in the Rain," which had been featured in the film *Red-Headed Stranger.*

I first met Willie in the 70s in Houston but did not work with him until the mid-80s, when he appeared on *Young Country*, a syndicated television show I was producing. From 1992 until the mid-2000s, I was producing and directing corporate events for clients at venues across the country, frequently in Dallas, Houston, Orlando, Phoenix, and Las Vegas. These events usually included some kind of name entertainment, and Willie and his band were

153

booked on at least ten of my projects. The only group I worked with more was The Beach Boys. Of all the performers I have worked with through the years, by far, the easiest and most comfortable to work with has been Willie Nelson. The reason comes down to Willie's laid-back style and his roadie's efficiency in setting up and striking the instruments and equipment used in their performances. Their contract had a simple rider, with very few requests, none of which were unusually demanding.

My *Young Country* television show had a simple format. It was primarily music videos, supplied by the music promoters, of the most recent releases that were charting on *Billboard*. The videos were introduced by the show's host, Alex Price, a former radio D.J. I met in Houston in the 70s. Each program also had interviews with an artist that we recorded during an appearance at various venues, like the Stockyards in Fort Worth, Billy Bob's in Dallas, The Summit in Houston, or The Oil Palace in Tyler. Segments of the interviews were interspersed throughout the program after each commercial break, with each artist acting as a co-host of the episode in which one of their music videos was played. We caught up with Willie either at a show in the DFW Metroplex or at The Oil Palace in Tyler. My memory is a little fuzzy about where it actually took place.

Before the performance, I was backstage, telling Willie about Young Country and asking if he would be willing to appear on the show. The only thing he was concerned about was that he did not want us to shoot his concert. I assured him we were going to use a video we got from his record label; he said that he was fine with that and that he would be glad to co-host an episode. We met with Willie at his bus after the show, which was parked outside the venue. He invited us in to do the interview on board The Honeysuckle Rose, the bus that he used to tour the country for each of his shows. There were only three of us involved in shooting the segment. Alex conducted the interview, I was the director, and my cameraman, Rusty Martin, shot the footage. We conducted these interviews in a style I call "run and gun." The camera was handheld and we used two wireless Lavalier mics to pick up the voices of Willie and Alex. We used a single light that bounced off the ceiling to illuminate the scene.

We had been doing these types of segments for quite some time and had the routine down pat. The first thing we did was a two-shot of Willie and Alex opening the show, some small talk between Willie and Alex about the current tour, and an introduction to the Willie Nelson music video. Then, we shot each of the commercial break segments, which were designed to play following the commercial and prior to the introduction of the next music video. We told Willie in advance whose videos were planned for the show, and he knew each of them. That made the show more interesting because Willie was able to give a brief anecdote about each of the artists slated to appear. The last segment we shot was the closing of the show, thanking Willie for co-hosting and making a plug for who would be the next week's co-host, which happened to be Waylon Jennings, who was booked the following week at Shotgun Reds, a honky-tonk just outside of Tyler. We had all the footage in the can in less than twenty minutes.

As soon as we wrapped, Willie lit a joint and invited the crew to join him, which made my cameraman happy. As we sat there, Willie began to reminisce about his career, which was an unexpected pleasure. He talked about his early childhood, which he has spoken about many times during his career. He confirmed a story I had read about his mother leaving the family soon after he was born and that his father later remarried and also moved away. That left Willie and his sister Bobbie to be raised by their grandparents in the small West Texas town of Abbott. He said the Nelson family's ancestry could be traced back to the Revolutionary

War to John Nelson, who served as a major. I asked when he first became interested in music, and he replied, "My grandmother was a singing teacher, and when I was six, my grandfather bought me a guitar."

He said that he started singing gospel songs with his sister Bobbie at a local church. His grandparents were a major force in providing their grandchildren with a strong sense of moral ethics and helped them to become heavily invested in spiritual awareness. Willie holds those values to this day. Several of his songs are grounded in his Christian beliefs. The sixth track on his 1980 album *Willie Nelson, Family Bible* is an old hymn, "Tell it to Jesus."

> "That song held a special meaning for my grandmother. When I was growing up, I believed that whatever worries you had, you could take it, Jesus. I believe that today," Willie explained.

When I questioned whether he thought his fans had any difficulty reconciling his outlaw image with his spiritual beliefs, he answered,

> "I don't know why they would. My beliefs are what they are—whether it's my opinion on political issues or in matters of faith—I don't make any attempt to force my beliefs on anybody else. People can think what they want. We don't have to agree on everything to get along. I'm certain a lot of my political opinions came out of growing up in the Depression. There were hard times in West Texas, where I grew up. All over. I grew up when the government was helping people. As I look back on those times now, I think that was a good thing."

Willie helped out the family by picking cotton, which motivated a young Willie Nelson to concentrate on music. "I didn't like working in the cotton fields," he said with a broad smile. "When I was twelve or thirteen, I found out I could make money playing and singing in honky-tonks. I liked that better than picking cotton!" His answer was not surprising when I asked who his major influences were. "Most of the country singers back then could be heard on the radio. Hank Williams, Bob Wills, Lefty Frizzell, and Ernest Tubb come to mind as first influences. Much later... much later, Frank Sinatra was a big influence. I liked the way he would sing away from the beat and make a song his own," then with a twinkle in his eye, he added, "He had style."

When you look at Willie's career in total, it is easy to see that he adopted a chameleon-like personality in the early stages of his career as a performer. It took a long time for him to develop what became his signature style.

> "Success as a performer took longer for me than songwriting. Back in the early sixties, I was working at Tootsies, and Faron Young heard me sing 'Hello Walls' and decided to record it. It was a hit for him. Then Ray Price recorded 'Night Life,' and it became a hit. After that, I got a job playing with Price's group. I was his bass player for a while."

> "Was it frustrating that other people were getting hit records from your songs," I asked. He sat there for a moment, either thinking how to answer my question or enjoying the drag he had just taken from a joint.

> "Frustrating is not the right word," he began explaining slowly. "As a songwriter, you want your songs recorded. I was really proud that Patsy had a hit with 'Crazy.' As a performer, writing my songs own songs, I thought I knew how they should be sung. It took a long time before I could click with an audience. I picked up a lot from others."

157

Willie takes his time when he is speaking informally. He speaks in a slow cadence, sometimes pausing for a moment mid-sentence before he resumes and completes his thought.

In 1961, Willie signed with Liberty Records, resulting in his first two successful singles as an artist. "Willingly" reached number ten, and "Touch Me" got as high as number seven. His first album... *And Then I Wrote*, was released in September 1962. In 1964, he was signed by Monument Records, releasing only one single, "I Never Cared For You." In the fall of 1964, Chet Atkins helped Willie get signed to RCA Victor, recording his first album on that label in 1965, *Country Willie—His Own Songs*. He also joined the Grand Ole Opry in 1965 and began what would become a lifelong friendship with Waylon Jennings.

> "I was taking whatever money I scaped up to pay for touring on the road. We barely made enough money to get by," said Willie. "While we were on the road, playing one-night stands mostly, my house in Tennessee burned down. That's when I decided to give it up, and I moved back to Texas. That was probably 1972."

In the early 70s, Austin's nightlife was just beginning to boom in the bars on Sixth Street, just down from the State Capitol. Most of the patrons were students from The University of Texas, whose parents paid most of their bills. In March, Willie played a set at the Dripping Springs Reunion, a three-day music festival that was a financial failure but served as the inspiration for Willie's Fourth of July Picnic, which he held for the first time the following year. Taking some time off gave Willie the chance to recharge, and he made the decision to get back into a studio and record again. He signed Neil Reshen to negotiate his way out of his contract with RCA, which ended up costing him $14,000 by repaying advances he had received from RCA. Atlantic Records then signed him as the label's first country artist. In February 1973, he recorded *Shotgun Willie*, which was released in May 1973 to excellent reviews.

> "That album was different from anything I had done before," Willie said. "The reviews were good, and it had a different sound that I was still developing. It didn't do too well, as far as sales, but critics took it seriously. That led to another album, *Phases and Stages*, that produced one single, 'Bloody Mary Morning,' that charted."

Those albums were the beginning of Willie's foray into Outlaw Country. But the biggest thing to come out of 1974 was the pilot for *Austin City Limits.* The program, which was produced in front of a live audience for PBS by Austin station KLRU, is now the longest-running music series in television history, having been on the air for forty-three years. The program has been honored with a Peabody Award, is a Rock & Roll Hall of Fame Landmark, and is the only television series to be honored with the Presidential Medal of Arts.

> "That label, Outlaw Country, came from the fact that in Austin, we were playing music that strayed away from the more conservative sound of the studios in Nashville," Willie says as a way to describe the genre of music better he helped make popular. "Waylon, Jessie Colter, Tompall Glaser, and I recorded *Wanted: The Outlaws* in 1976. That album made the outlaw image a permanent fixture on the music scene that was based out of Austin."

It was also the first country album to go platinum. The success of that album led to another album collaboration called *Waylon & Willie* in 1978, which included their hit single "Momma Don't Let Your Babies Grow Up to be Cowboys." Another album Willie released in 1978 was *Stardust*. He was in the studio for only ten days to make that recording, which consisted entirely of pop standards that were particular favorites of Willie's. Because of his outlaw image, most of his contemporaries did not expect much from the album. "Man, were they wrong!" Willie said defiantly.

> "Within the first year, it had reached number one on the *Billboard* Top Country Albums chart. Two cuts, 'Blue Skies' and 'All of Me' peaked at number one and three, respectively, on the *Billboard* Top Country Singles. Then, in 1979, 'Georgia on My Mind' received a Grammy for Best Male Vocalist. I'd say it did pretty well."

It was certified platinum in 1978 and would end up on the *Billboard* Top Country Albums chart for ten years. By 1988, *Stardust* was certified as quintuple platinum. In 2015, *Rolling Stone Magazine* ranked it 260 on its list of the top 500 Albums of All Time. Willie's decision to record *Stardust* was a brilliant move, and its success was like giving the finger to his critics.

More than its critical and financial success, that album showed the world that Willie had developed a style that was unique in the industry. He managed to take pop standards and turn them into country hits, something that had never been done before. His versatility, beginning with his early performances that were heavily influenced by the most popular country singers of the 1950s, to his Gospel roots and the creation of the Outlaw Genre—an incredible dichotomy—the release of *Stardust* proved that Willie Nelson was in a league of his own. Stephen Thomas Erlewine wrote in *All Music* that *Stardust* "...showcases Nelson's skills as a musician and his entire aesthetic—where there is nothing separating classic American musical forms; it can all be played together—perhaps better than any other album, which is why it was a sensation upon its release and grows stronger with each passing year." By taking a chance on the *American Songbook,* Willie covered songs that non-country singers like Frank Sinatra, Dean Martin, and Louis Armstrong made famous and then made them his own, giving them a unique and unexpected new interpretation that maintains echoes of his country and gospel roots.

Having a career beset with ups and downs, his early struggles to find his voice and an audience, during his mid-career interview, I had to ask, "Having achieved some modicum of fame, has it changed you ... as a person?"

> "Honestly, I don't think so. I like to think I've maintained the moral background I learned as a kid. When you choose a life... the life of an entertainer, you have to work hard, and sometimes there are struggles to reach your goals," he paused for a moment of thoughtful contemplation. "I had a lot of help along the way, especially early on when I watched other people have success with my songs. But eventually, I made my own mark. Hard work ... and some luck!"

He sat back and looked off into a distance only he could see. It was late at night after he had given a performance to a rowdy crowd. I thought perhaps it was time to end the interview and let Willie go. As I was about to suggest we had taken enough of his time, he began to speak.

> "The thing is this: I got lucky. There are a lot of talented people who work just as hard as I did but never had the opportunities I got. I'm thankful for my career. Every time I walk on stage, I am aware of that. If the good Lord keeps me healthy, I'll do this when I'm ninety."

When we did that interview with Willie, he had been working in the business for nearly forty years. He had worked as a successful performer for nearly twenty-five years. Within the next decade, he would achieve status as a living legend in the business. As I write this as part of my memoir, close to another forty years have passed.

Willie is still performing. He is still involved as an activist for causes he believes are important. In April 2023, just a couple of months ago, as I write this, Willie turned ninety.

> "The greatest advantage of fame is being able to use it to bring attention to things that matter," he said reflectively. "I have been fortunate to use my name for causes that I think are worthy. Live Aid and Farm Aid, for instance. It's important to give back by supporting worthy causes."

Willie has also had more than his fair share of run-ins with the law. Most of those encounters had to do with the possession of marijuana. His first arrest for marijuana possession occurred in Dallas in 1974. In 1977, he was arrested in the Bahamas after a tour with Hank Cochran. A customs official discovered a small amount of marijuana in his jeans pocket. He was arrested and jailed. After a few hours, his bail was posted, and Willie fell while jumping in celebration of being released, was injured, and had to be taken to the emergency room. Afterward, he appeared before a judge, who dropped the charges on the condition that he never return to the country. Much later, in 2010, Willie was arrested in Sierra Blanca, Texas, charged with possession of six ounces of marijuana. He was released after paying $2,500 for bail. His lawyer later reached an agreement with prosecutor Kit Bramblett to pay a $500 fine, avoiding a two-year jail sentence. Judge Becky Dean-Walker rejected the agreement on the grounds that "Due to his celebrity status, he was receiving preferential treatment." Prosecutor Bramblett declared the case would remain open "…until it was either dismissed or the judge had a change of heart." According to an article published by *Texas Monthly* in February 2012, the case has never been adjudicated and remains open—another example of how, sometimes, fame is a two-edged sword.

Willie's biggest legal battle would occur a few years after our interview, in the 90s, when the Internal Revenue Service claimed he owed back taxes. The tax debt and its accumulated interest and fees amounted to more than $32 million. In the late 70s, Willie discovered that Neil Reshen had not properly filed his tax returns. To pay off that debt, Willie made a number of bad investments after firing Reshen in 1978. These tax shelters were ultimately disallowed as deductions on his 1980, '81, and '82 tax returns. The debt continued to rise due to penalties and interest throughout the rest of the decade. In 1990, the IRS seized most of his personal assets and ordered them sold to pay off the tax lien. Friends purchased many of his items and sold them back to Willie for a nominal fee. After hiring Harvard lawyer Jay Goldberg, the attorney negotiated a settlement of $16 million with the IRS. Then, Willie recorded a double album, *The IRS Tapes: Who'll Buy My Memories,* with all profits going to pay off the debt. He then filed a lawsuit against Price Waterhouse, contending that they were responsible for investing his money in illegal tax shelters. That case was settled out-of-court for an undisclosed sum, and by 1993, Willie had satisfied all of his tax debts.

In addition to a music career, Willie debuted as a movie actor in 1979's *The Electric Horseman.* In the following years, he appeared in several films, including *The Honeysuckle Rose, Thief,* and *Barbarosa.* He played the lead role in *The Red Headed Stranger,* based on his album of the same name in 1986. Other film appearances include featured roles in *Wag the Dog, Gone Fishin',* and most recently appearing as himself in Woody' Harrelson's *Live in London.* He has also appeared in several television projects, including starring with Johnny Cash in the made-for-TV version of *Stagecoach.* He has made guest appearances on several television series, including *Miami Vice, Nash Bridges, The Simpsons, Monk, Adventures in Wonderland, Dr. Quinn Medicine Woman, King of the Hill, Swing Vote, and Space Ghost Coast to Coast.* He was particularly proud to perform in the documentary *The American*

Epic Sessions with his long-time friend Merle Haggard. In that film, the two performed two songs using original recording equipment from the 1920s, the type of equipment used for the first country songs ever recorded. The two performed a Bob Wills song, "Old Fashioned Love," and a song Haggard wrote especially for this film, "The Only Man Wilder Than Me."

Throughout his decades-long performing career, Willie embraced several musical genres. Always adding a touch of country, he has performed blues, jazz, and pop and even recorded a reggae album called *Countryman* in 2005. During the early 2000s, Willie recorded *Heroes*, duets with a number of different artists, including Ray Price, Merle Haggard, Kris Kristofferson, Snoop Dogg, Billy Joe Shaver, Sheryl Crow, and Jamey Johnson. The album reached number four on the *Billboard* Top Country Albums chart. In 2013, he released *To All the Girls...*, a collection of duets with Loretta Lynn, Dolly Parton, Rosanne Cash, Sheryl Crow, Mavis Staples, Norah Jones, Emmylou Harris, Carrie Underwood, and Miranda Lambert. It debuted at number two on the *Billboard* Top Country Album chart, scoring Willie's forty-sixth top ten album on the country charts. In 2023, a five-part documentary, *Willie Nelson and Family,* was released at the Sundance Film Festival, and Willie was inducted into the Rock & Roll Hall of Fame.

Willie Nelson has handled his fame with an adroit understanding that it is the price one pays for success. Having succeeded in so many different arenas, from performing in honky-tonks to his work in motion pictures, he is one of the few entertainers whose talents have warranted praise as a master craftsman and an artistic creator of material that will stand the test of time. Many of his compositions are already classics ("Crazy," "Always on My Mind," "Bloody Mary Morning," and "Funny How Time Slips Away," to name only a few). His songs rank among the best works of other composers whose reputations have preceded him, standing among giants such as Cole Porter, Irving Berlin, and Paul MacCartney, as well as Hank Williams, Townes Van Zandt, and Johnny Cash. His guitar skills can be favorably compared to blues greats B. B. King, Albert King, Freddie King, and Muddy Waters. What defies comparison with any other artist is Willie's singing style. His interpretation of a lyric, combined with his musical style of singing away from the beat, makes his voice one of the most unique that exists.

With talent and hard work, Willie Nelson has emerged as one of the greatest entertainers of all time—an accolade he deserves. I'm grateful to have been able to work with him several times over the years. I look forward to our next adventure together.

Allen Morris

Chapter 17
Rita Rudner: A Classy, Funny Lady

One of the most unusual encounters I ever had with a famous personality happened in 1996 or '97 (again, my fuzzy memory does not hold the exact date) when Rita Rudner was hired to entertain the Rheem-Ruud sales force during one of their annual retreats. Rita grew up in a Jewish household from Miami, Florida, the daughter of Frances and Abe Rudner. She began ballet lessons at age four. When she was thirteen, her mother died from breast cancer. After her father remarried, Rita felt an urge to become independent, and upon graduating from high school at the age of fifteen, she moved to New York to seek fame and fortune as a Broadway dancer.

Rita's first Broadway experience was a bit role in *Promises, Promises* in 1970. In 1971, she was cast in the original production of *Follies*. The now-legendary production was directed by Harold Prince and Michael Bennett, with Bennett also originating its choreography. It won seven Tony Awards in 1972 and the New York Critics' Circle Award for Best Musical. In 1974, she appeared in *Mack & Mabel,* and in 1979, she took over the role of Lily St. Regis in the long-running *Annie*, staying with the production for over a year, leaving the company in 1981.

In between gigs on Broadway, Rita noticed the lack of female standup comics during the late 70s and decided to try her hand at it. She put together an act and performed at various New York comedy clubs, honing her skills and developing her now-famous sense of timing. It was in the early 80s that Rita decided to move away from being a chorus performer and into becoming a full-time comedian. She debuted her network television in 1982 on *Late Night with David Letterman.* Many television appearances followed, including invitations to work in the UK, where she met her husband,

Martin Bergman, a British producer, writer, and director. They were married in 1988. She recorded a six-part series on BBC2 in 1990, directed by her husband. Returning to the United States led to numerous appearances on *The Tonight Show Starring Johnny Carson,* and her participation in *Rodney Dangerfield's Young Comedians Special* on HBO. In 1992, Rita appeared in the film *Peter's Friends,* which she co-wrote with her husband. The film was produced and directed by Kenneth Branagh and starred Branagh, Emma Thompson, Stephen Fry, Hugh Laurie, Alphonsia Emmanuel, and Imelda Staunton in the leading roles. The film received mixed reviews, although it won the Peter Sellers Award for Best British Film and was nominated for a Goya Award as the Best European Film. The screenplay received a WGA Best Screenplay nomination. Playing the role of Carol Benson, Rita received the Best Supporting Actress Award from the American Comedy Awards.

I met Rita when she arrived at the hotel where her performance to entertain the Rheem-Ruud sales force was to take place. Prior to the event, I sent Rita some background material on the company and brief dossiers on a couple of their lead executives so she could craft some relevant remarks to use in her performance.

Rita was to arrive by 3:30 on the afternoon of her performance, which was scheduled to begin at approximately 9:00 PM, following a dinner. Having reviewed her contract rider, I was concerned that I was about to meet the ultimate prima donna. For the uninitiated, a "rider" is part of a contract that spells out all the "extras" that must be provided to the entertainer throughout the term of their stay, expenses which are to be paid by the project producer, in addition to the entertainer's appearance fee.

Among the items that I was concerned about was the requirement that a limousine be available for Rita's use immediately after her show ended, which would be around 10:30 in the evening and available the following morning by 7:30 AM for the ride to the airport. Another item included in the rider was the requirement to have a separate dining room available near her backstage dressing room, which was to include a large tray of fresh fruits, a selection of kosher meats with sliced rye bread, and a selection of condiments, six bottles of imported champagne with fluted serving glasses, two cases of bottled water, twelve fresh face towels, and four bars of Sweetheart Soap. The only technical requirements were a follow spot (focused from the knees to above her head) and a handheld microphone, preferably a wireless Shure SM58, with a mic stand. Her dressing room requirements were a lighted makeup mirror and a full-length mirror, a clothes rack, a case of bottled water, a tray of fresh fruit, and a sofa.

Upon her slightly late arrival at 3:45, I greeted her, introducing myself as the event's producer, and had the bellman retrieve her luggage and take it to her room. I gave her the room key and escorted her to the elevator. "I would like to take a few moments this afternoon to show you where you will be performing and do a sound check if that's alright with you," I said.

"Do you want to do that now?" she asked.

"Whenever it is convenient for you. We have until 5:30 before I have to turn the room over to the hotel staff to complete laying out the dinner," I explained. "The guests arrive at 6:30 for cocktails, followed by the dinner, which is scheduled to be over by 9:00, which is when you go on."

"Let's do it now, then," Rita replied.

As I walked her down the corridor to the ballroom where the event was to take place, I casually began to broach a few of the rider items. "Your limousine will be here by 10:00 PM, although if you are doing photos with the audience members, you will most likely be tied up until 10:30."

"Why?" Rita inquired stone-faced.

"Because you agreed to pose for photos with the..." Rita interrupted before I finished the sentence.

"Not that. Why do I have a limousine at 10:00?"

"It was in your rider," I replied

"Am I going somewhere?" she asked.

"I don't know what your plans are. I just made the arrangements," I paused while I looked at the confused expression on Rita's face.

"The only place I'm going after the show is to bed," she said, laughing.

"I'll cancel the car for tonight."

By that time, we had reached the ballroom, and I told the soundman we were ready to check her mic. The room was set in rounds of ten (round tables to accommodate ten people per table) for an audience size I estimated to be around 300 people. Each table also had ten 35mm disposable cameras, one for each place setting. I escorted Rita to the platforms that had been set up as the stage and asked the lighting operator to turn on the stage wash. The A2 (assistant audio engineer) handed Rita the mic. Over the speakers hung on either side of the stage, we heard the audio engineer at the front-of-house mixing board ask Rita to give a voice level. She walked around the stage, looking toward the tables where the audience would be sitting later in the evening. She began talking into the mic: "Is this the light level? Would it be possible to bring the house lights up a little so I can see the audience. I'll just walk around talking and let you set the levels..." and she continued to chatter, obviously aware of what the engineer needed in order to adjust her microphone. At the same time, the lights were being adjusted.

"Is that level alright for you to see the audience?" I asked, taking over the mic at the front of the house.

"Oh yes, that's fine. How does it look for you?"

"You look great on the screens. It will be much brighter with the follow spot. The spot operator is not here for this sound check," I said.

"Do we need a follow spot?" Rita asked.

"Not really, but…"

Then, we both said, "It's in the rider."

"Let's forget the follow spot," Rita said.

Once the sound check was completed, I showed Rita where her dressing room was located. It was not actually a separate room. It was a space near the stage, surrounded by pipe and drape to create privacy. "This will do nicely," she commented.

"And if you will follow me, we have a dining room set up in a room off the service corridor," I said.

We walked the few steps out into the service corridor to a room next door. The hotel staff was already in the room setting it up. Hand towels were in place on a cabinet where a sink was located. There were four bars of soap still in their wrappers. The bottles of champagne were chilling in a large bowl of ice. The fruit tray was wrapped in plastic, sitting on a bed of ice. "The kosher meats and rye bread won't be brought in until 8:30," I told her. "I'm sorry, but they could not find Sweetheart Soap. I hope Camay will do."

"What is all this for?" Rita asked.

"The rider. This is your snack for before or after the show."

"I really didn't ask for any of this," she said, almost apologizing.

"It's all in the contract," I said.

"I can't believe you were told I wanted all of this. This is more food than I eat in a week."

"Have you ever read your contract?"

"I doubt I've ever seen my contract. That's all handled by the booking agent," she said.

The look on her face as she realized the extent of what her rider requirements were, was best described as an embarrassment. My expectation of meeting the world's biggest prima donna evaporated. Instead, I had just met an incredibly sweet person, someone I was certain would go out of her way to be nice to everyone she met. After this first meeting, it occurred to me that this was possibly one of her first corporate gigs. If so, it made sense that she would not be aware of the requirements her rider contained. By the time she made this booking, she had been doing the late-night television circuit and club dates. It would be five years before her stint in Las Vegas, and that would turn into a fifteen-year run. She set the record as the longest-running female solo comedy show in Las Vegas history and was the first woman to be named Comedian of the Year, an honor she had for nine years in a row.

I escorted her to her room so she could rest and prepare for her evening's performance. Then, I set about canceling the limousine for that evening and meeting with the production staff to rehearse the technical aspects of the event. We had time to run through every cue twice before we had to let the hotel staff take over. The schedule for the evening was fairly simple. At 6:30, a cocktail party began. It was scheduled to take an hour, and then the doors would be opened for the attendees to take their seats for the dinner. At 7:45, the business part of the meeting would commence. The VP of Sales was to make a brief presentation, showing charts on the two projection screens located to the left and right of the stage. He would serve as host for the evening and make all the introductions. He was followed by the National Sales Manager and Local Sales Manager, both of whom were to make awards presentations to the leading sales reps in their respective categories. Then, the CEO was introduced, who made a brief presentation about the past year's successes and introduced the plans for the coming year, saying he expected the sales force "To be like tigers during the coming year, aggressive and cunning." After his presentation, dinner was served, beginning at about 8:15. To my surprise, Rita appeared where I was sitting at my front-of-house position, calling the show as the CEO was making his presentation. When dinner started, Rita and I stepped out of the room.

> "I wanted to hear a little of the CEO in case he said something I could use," she told me.

> "I didn't hear anything particularly funny," I said.

> "I'll be funny. It's my job," she said confidently.

I sat with her outside the ballroom until 8:45, when I asked a PA to escort Rita to the backstage dressing room. At 9:00, I had the audio engineer play the pre-recorded introduction for Rita: "Rheem-Ruud proudly presents the incredibly funny Rita Rudner..."

One can never be certain how a predominately male, half-drunk room of salespeople will react to a comedian. They can be obnoxious and heckling, or they can be politely sitting there in silence. Or they can be receptive, as the audience was this night. Rita opened her performance with an adlibbed line that brought an immediate reaction from the audience,

"I was told there were a bunch of tigers in the audience. I only see men."

The audience was with her for the rest of her one hour and ten minutes onstage. They laughed at every punchline she delivered. As I listened, I was impressed with her timing and how she was able to throw out simple non sequiturs that made sense to the audience. She crafted a monologue that referenced her observations on life and somehow made those observations relevant to people who sold air conditioning and hot water equipment. She had done her homework, and it paid off in laughter. At the end of her performance, she opened the floor to questions from the audience, and again, her skill at improvising funny lines paid off as she gave answers to the audience's questions. When she was finally through for the evening, the VP of Sales told the audience, "Ms. Rudner will be available to take photographs."

She was caught in a rush of people coming to the stage, eager to have their photograph made with a "star." I admired her patience as she posed and smiled over and over again. Of the 300 people in the audience, I would bet she easily took two hundred photos before the crowd left for the lobby bar. I took her backstage to the dining room we had set up. She surveyed the room and said, "I hate to see all of this go to waste."

"We'll offer it to the strike crew. I'm sure they'll be glad to have a snack after getting all the gear loaded."

We walked out to where the strike was beginning. I found the crew chief and asked him to bring the crew together: "I'd like for you all to meet this evening's performer, Rita Rudner," I told the assembled crew.

> "I wanted to thank each of you for your part in making tonight's performance a success. Thank you for the support you gave me this evening," Rita told them. "There is a room backstage set up with refreshments and a light snack for your enjoyment when you finish striking the gear. Our producer, Allen, has kindly provided it because you have all worked so hard. Thank you."

Crew members came up to Rita, spoke with her briefly, and returned to work. I told Rita I think she made several new fans, both among the audience for the show and now with the crew. As the crew went back to work, Rita and I went back to the makeshift dining room. I popped a cork and champagne on one of the bottles and poured a glass on both of us. I toasted her on having done a successful show and asked what time her flight was the following morning. Her flight to Las Vegas was at 10:30. My flight to Dallas was at 8:30. "I need to call about the limousine and give them a time to pick you up," I said.

> "I wonder if there is an earlier flight to Las Vegas," she asked.

> "I can call and check."

When it was determined that there was an earlier flight, I had her ticket changed. "Why don't you cancel the limo, and you and I can share a cab to the airport in the morning? There's no need to spend money on a limousine," she said.

> "I have to pay for the limo anyway. But if we can both share it, that works for me," I said. We walked out through the ballroom toward the elevators as we finished our champagne. Rita grabbed one of the leftover cameras from one of the tables and said,

"Here, you and I didn't get a picture together," she said, handing me the camera.

We took a couple of selfies, and I told her I would get the film developed and send her a copy. When I got the film back, one print was good for both of us and in one, I looked bad. I sent her the one where we both looked good and kept the bad one for myself.

Rita Rudner's fame has grown since we worked together at that event back in the 90s. She has made several films, headlined HBO specials, written several books, and established herself as one of the most successful entertainers in Las Vegas history. Not bad for a Jewish girl from Miami! I admit that she was not at all what I expected. That was perhaps one of the best things about our meeting and working together. She remains one of the most ingratiating, thoughtful, and kind celebrities I ever worked with. To use an old show-biz term, she was a trouper. She checked her ego at the door and presented herself as a professional. Her main concern was to give the audience the best performance she could. She prepared well in advance to fit her material to the audience. On the day of the show, she took the extra step of watching the executives give their presentations, just so she might glean something that she could use to make her performance more relevant to the audience. That is not something I have seen many performers do.

My mother's admonition to me when I was five, "There are more important things in life than being famous. You should aspire to be a good person. Fame is fleeting. Character lasts," might have been the same as Rita's mother could have given her. It is obvious to me that Rita has lived her life and molded her career with the aspiration of being a good person, first and foremost. If that had not been the case, I don't think she would have succeeded.

Chapter 18
James Farmer III: Southern Chef, and Gentleman

I should point out that there are levels of fame derived from geography. Some people have fame only in the place where they live, in their backyard so to speak. I live in a city of just over one hundred thousand inhabitants. I know several people who are known by at least 80% of the local population but wouldn't be recognized by a single soul in Dallas, just an hour and a half away. I call that local fame (by the way, in Texas, we don't measure distance in miles; rather, in terms of how long it takes to drive somewhere). However, it is possible in the United States to have national fame, in which one is known coast-to-coast, but perhaps not necessarily known beyond the borders of our country. Johnny Carson had that kind of fame. He was known by millions for his late-night talk show, but he could walk around London in relative anonymity. Then, there is global fame. That is fame, where one is known throughout the globe. Most American presidents have global fame. I would also include some film stars and recording artists in that group, a few athletes, writers, and scientists, and John Doe.

In certain circles, James Farmer III is a household name. That is because his articles have appeared in magazines that are commonly seen in households across the nation. He has had articles published in *House Beautiful, Traditional Home, Southern Home, FLOWER,* and of course in *Southern Living Magazine.* He is also the author of ten best-selling books *A Time to Plant*; *Sip & Savor*; *Porch Living*; *Wreaths For All Seasons*; *A Time To Cook*; *Dinner on the Grounds*; *A Time to Celebrate*; *A Place to Call Home*; *Arriving Home;* and his most recent book, *Celebrating Home.* The common theme in everything he writes is "There's no place like home." As an interior designer, he brings a flair to home decorating intended to encompass all the senses, "I like for the home to reflect everything that makes living there pleasant. From the natural beauty of things brought in from the garden to the feel of a doorknob warmed by the sun and the smell of clean laundry hanging on the line, those are all things that engage the senses and enhance the experience of living in a welcoming and pleasant home," he explains.

I interviewed James Farmer III when he was the keynote speaker for the 2014 Texas Rose Festival Ladies' Luncheon. It is possible that many of the ladies in attendance that day thought they were going to hear a speech from James Farmer, the famous civil rights leader from Marshall, Texas. It is not the first time James Farmer III was confused with the late activist. It happens so often, that James Farmer III from Perry, Georgia, now delights in telling people Denzel Washington portrayed him in the movie *The Great Debaters*. It is, of course, a total fabrication, which is perfectly acceptable in the South, where adding a little color to make a good story better is expected, or as Farmer puts it, "if not considered just plain ol' good manners."

As James Famer III—author, designer, cook, and raconteur— began his presentation to an audience comprising 500 of Tyler's most sophisticated and influential women, he explained how he viewed East Texas and Georgia as the "Bookends of the South." Proving his point are the similarities between the two locations: both still honor the memory of the heroes of the War of Northern Aggression; both have annual galas requiring our young ladies to wear elaborate gowns; both consider polite conversations to be those dominated by talk about gardening and cooking and avoiding politics. Farmer's grace and charm with an audience have resulted in his growing fame as a guest speaker; in demand because he is at once entertaining and informative without any tinge of pretense or unwanted provocativeness. He is exactly as he appears; a welcome guest people feel comfortable having around, with whom they can have a pleasant conversation without any judgments or derision.

"You can put shoes on the boy, but you can't take the South out of the man!" is a phrase that Farmer the Third uses frequently, especially with those people he is meeting for the first time and, in particular, those people he meets who are not from the South. When he meets such people, he wants them to know immediately of the pride he has in being a Southerner. He does not want to embarrass those who do not have such good fortune, but he wants it made clear that his Southern roots are as important to him as having air to breathe. After all, everything that has made him who is today, is directly related to his upbringing in the South. He is a living example of what the term "Southern Heritage" embodies.

When he opens his mouth to speak, the honeysuckle tones inherited from generations of southern forebears charm his audience. Tall, handsome, and every inch a Southern Gentleman, Farmer regales his audience with stories about growing up on a farm in Georgia and the influence of his grandmother, his Mimi, who taught him to fry chicken, "It's wet, dry, fry. The beauty of southern frying is the way you can inject the season into every meal," Farmer exclaims with authority borne from years of practice, "Basil soaked in buttermilk in summer; sage in fall; rosemary in winter; and parsley in spring. I want to take the fear out of frying!" He swears one will never lack for friends if one knows how to fry chicken. In the South, frying chicken is accepted as an art form. Not everyone can fry chicken—those who can are considered to be at the top-most rank among cooks in the South.

It is the desire to preserve and honor our Southern Culture that prompted Farmer to begin writing. He published his first book, *A Time to Plant*, in 2011. This book takes the age-old rules of flower and vegetable gardening in the Deep South, and with a fresh voice, teaches a new generation of Southerners the way to incorporate the love of gardening into their daily lifestyle and entertaining. The book even includes a few favorite recipes and ideas for tablescapes and place settings. "As an author, I want to both educate and entertain. As a Southern author, I want to preserve our history, share our culture, and celebrate the eccentricities abundant throughout our heritage," says Farmer. Much of the eccentricities he shares come directly from Farmer's family forebears. Farmer believes that without the traditions handed down through the generations, much of what is most charming about Southern Culture would be lost. He wants to do whatever he can to ensure that culture thrives for generations to come.

He had penned only six books at the time of our interview, and was working on number seven. Now that he has nine, the success of his books has led to an increase in speaking engagements. "I think of myself as an author slash designer," he says with the exuberance of a six-year-old opening a birthday present, "I love speaking to crowds of people. I talk about gardening and cooking and how those of us in the South love to entertain using our Mama's silver and our Mimi's chipped Limoges." Not everyone can appreciate a fine piece of Rose Medallion (or know what that is), but James Farmer III can. More importantly, as an interior designer, he can tell you the best way to display it to share its beauty with others and enhance the overall beauty of one's home. "It is the simple things that I bring to design that make the most impact," he says.

Farmer likes to emphasize the whole concept of garden-to-table. The concept includes both the fresh foods to be eaten and the fresh flowers to adorn the table. "We eat first with our eyes," Farmer informs us, "Which is why it is perfectly acceptable to place a Mason jar filled with zinnias on the table. When guests arrive, they see those blossoms, and there is nothing like the smell of Lady Peas simmering on the stove. I think that is what heaven will smell like." The flowers available for the table reflect the seasons of the year. "Of course, I love hydrangeas anytime, and you can use plain pumpkins from October till December." The point is, according to

Farmer, when it comes to decorating the dinner table, the easiest and best solutions come straight from the garden.

Another tradition Farmer points out is how "Southerner's cling to the past by passing down family heirlooms. For instance, I have my great aunt's sideboard. It is not something I would choose, but it was my great-aunt's sideboard and it was given to me and it must be used!"

It is through his speaking engagements that Farmer made his first Tyler connections, which budded into his friendship with Betsy Ellis and Ann Brookshire. "I met Betsy in Dallas when I was speaking at Kappa Kappa Gamma Tablescapes. She bought an armful of my books to give to friends. Ann Brookshire came to Houston to hear me speak at the River Oaks Garden Club. I became friends with Ann and the result of my friendship with those two ladies was the invitation to speak at the Texas Rose Festival Ladies' Luncheon."

By sheer coincidence, when Farmer was asked to interview with *Tyler Today Magazine*, he was given several copies of the magazine, including the one from the previous winter with Frances and Ben Jackson on the cover. "That's Ben Jackson!" Farmer said recognizing his former classmate from Auburn University in Georgia. It is a small world, especially if you come from the South.

As if he did not have enough to do consulting on interior design, writing books, and speaking to garden clubs, Farmer has also served as an editor-at-large for *Southern Living Magazine*, "Can you think of a better connection for spreading Southern heritage and culture?" Farmer asks rhetorically. He and Jenna Bush (if you must name drop, drop the name of the President's daughter), who also served as an editor-at-large for *Southern Living*, have become close friends, further strengthening his Texas connection.

"I consider myself to be a recovering Baptist, so I fit in well in Texas," Farmer boasts, "Texas has always been good to me. I have done speaking engagements in Dallas, San Antonio, Austin, Houston, and Tyler. Pecan pie is now my favorite dessert." His media exposure has expanded greatly since going to work for *Southern Living*. As an unofficial Ambassador of the South, Farmer's appearances on *The Today Show; Paula Deen's Best Dishes; QVC, The Broadcast* out of Dallas; and various local programs throughout the country have provided him a platform for spreading his message about the garden-to-table lifestyle and the sheer joy of living according to the principles of Southern Hospitality!

I'm glad James Farmer III launched a campaign to promote Southern Heritage. Ever since that nasty war in the 1860s, Southerners have been given a bad rap. I don't think secession was right and would be happier if it were not part of our heritage; but it happened, it was corrected and it's over. I wish slavery had never existed. It is the single greatest blight in our nation's history, but it happened, it was corrected and it's over. It took one hundred years before the Civil Rights Act was enacted. And I'll point out that the egregious delay was primarily due to opposition from Northern legislators. It took a Southern Democrat president and support from Southern Republicans to get it passed into law. The United States is divided into four regions with the following populations and percentages within the total population:

Northeast: 57,448,898 (17.3%)

Midwest: 68,961,043 (20.8%)

West: 78,650,958 (23.7%)

South: 126,450,613 (38.1%)

In 2023, The American South is comprised of sixteen states and represents 38.1% of the nation's total population. The South has the single largest concentration of residents of any region in the country. The largest ethnic group in America represents 57.8% of the population. They are the White/Anglo-Saxon, not Hispanic or Latino group. The second largest group is the Hispanic or Latino group, representing 18.7% of the total population. The third group makes up 12.1%, and are Black or African Americans, whose forebears largely arrived as slaves. The remaining 11.4% of the population includes Native Americans, Native Hawaiians and indigenous Native Alaskans, Americans of Asian descent and Pacific Islanders, and every other ethnic group that has emigrated to America. The two states with the highest total amount of citizens, representing the diversity of backgrounds, are California and Texas. Texas is included as part of the South, as it was during the Confederacy, that makes the South the most diverse region in the country, in terms of total population. In his award-winning PBS series *Finding Your Roots,* historian Henry Louis Gates, Jr. revealed that genetic autosomal-DNA testing revealed that the average African American is of 65% Sub-Saharan African origin, and 29% European. Even more astonishing is that 35% of all average African-American males today have a White male ancestor who fathered a mixed-race child during the slavery era of American history. And here is another fact, that no doubt will upset a lot of racists. Whites, the 3 to 4 percent of all people who consider themselves all-White Americans, have some African ancestry, between .05 percent and 5 percent.

What does that have to do with James Farmer III's recipe books? Absolutely nothing, except to point out that his recipes come from a diverse cultural background, which is representative of his diverse Southern Heritage. His delight in his heritage is expressed through dishes that were essential parts of his growing up in the South. Those recipes reflect several generations of the people who handed them down to their children. The influence of many diverse cultures makes them what they are. They are culinary treasures from people who were literally living off the land. That explains his insistence on using ingredients fresh from the garden. Even in the 21st century, most people in the South still have gardens. Those who are not farming for a living, will dedicate small plots of their yards to create their gardens. And there is a proper way to make a garden: close to the front of the house is where flower gardens belong. Passersby will see the flowers and appreciate their beauty. They will immediately know that the residents are Southerners with a proper upbringing. The vegetable garden is generally in a side yard or out back. They tend to take up more space than a flower garden. Homegrown spices are generally planted closest to the kitchen for more convenience when picking them for use while preparing a midday or evening meal.

There are several dishes, common in the South today, that actually originated in Africa. During the slave era, slave owners were sent back to Africa to retrieve certain foodstuffs that were familiar to their slaves. They brought back seeds that the slaves could plant in their own gardens, so they could prepare foods they were more accustomed to eating. An example of the seeds that were imported to America from Africa is red peas. Red peas are an essential ingredient in a dish that is a favorite in Georgia called Hoppin' John. It is a rice and bean dish that originated from the slave culture. Another dish that originated in Africa is a stew made with scrap meat and okra. Okra is another plant that came from Africa and was introduced to this country during the slave era. Anyone familiar with gumbo, a New Orleans favorite, will immediately recognize that okra is frequently used to thicken the roux when making gumbo. That comes directly from a technique that originated from Senegalese tribes in Africa, and it is a dish that slave cooks prepared for themselves and for their owners. Passed down through generations, it is a dish that is now strongly identified with southern Louisiana.

Dedicating his time to preserving Southern Culture has become an obsession for Farmer. It has also brought him great fame and the financial rewards that often accompany fame. Achieving fame was never a goal for Farmer. It came to him as a byproduct of his work. He readily admits that having a name that is known helps him sell his books. But his real motivation is broader, a fortuitous circumstance that his fame allows him to indulge. His goal is to preserve the varied cultures embodied in Southern Heritage, which he explained in detail. "I spend much time on the road now making public appearances. The rest of my time is spent writing about food and décor, which is my passion. I consider myself to be very fortunate to have been born in the South and to have such a grand heritage that I can share with other people. I want our Southern Heritage to be appreciated by a new generation of Southern ladies and gentlemen. And when I use the term 'ladies and gentlemen,' I'm not talking about men and women. I'm referring to men and women who conduct themselves as 'ladies and gentlemen,' who behave the way those of us brought up in the South were taught to behave. There is a gentility among Southerners that needs to be protected and preserved, along with our rich Southern Heritage. And much of that heritage is found in the food that is influenced by many cultures, whose recipes were first handed down by word-of-mouth. We must protect and share that heritage."

Chapter 19
Dr. Emil J Freireich:
Father of Clinical Cancer Research

During a span of fifteen years, I was involved with MD Anderson Cancer Center in Houston, producing several marketing films aimed toward promoting the remarkable work of that institution, one of the leading cancer research hospitals in the world. When the Texas Legislature first authorized The University of Texas to establish a hospital for cancer research in 1941, no location was specified as to where it would be established. The Legislature authorized an expenditure of $500,000 to create a facility, and The MD Anderson Foundation offered to match that funding, provided it would be located in Houston and named for MD Anderson.

Monroe Dunaway Anderson was born on June 29, 1873, in Jackson, Tennessee, a small town roughly 70 miles northeast of Memphis. His father was a banker, and his mother was the daughter of a Cumberland Presbyterian minister, Rev. William Monroe Dunaway. Young Monroe would follow in his father's footsteps after graduating from Memphis' Southwestern Baptist University. Having grown up in the post-Civil War era, and coming from Scottish Presbyterian stock, Monroe was indoctrinated with a sense of thrift. His frugality was reflected throughout his career, which enabled him to amass a substantial fortune by 1904, when his older brother Frank, and Frank's brother-in-law, Will Clayton, invited him to invest in a partnership to buy and sell cotton.

The company they established was Anderson, Clayton and Company. Monroe left banking in 1907 when he moved to Houston to establish the partnership's presence there. Devoting his time fully to the partnership's business, Monroe would serve as chief financial officer, and after incorporation, he became treasurer and eventually president of the corporation. The company continued to flourish, becoming the single largest cotton merchant in the world. By the mid-1930s, Monroe and Will Clayton owned more than half of the company's stock. To protect heirs from enormous estate taxes should either of the two largest stockholders die, Monroe established the MD Anderson Foundation in 1936, funding it with $300,000 of his own money. After Monroe's death in 1939, the foundation received an additional $19 million from his estate. Although how the foundation's money was to be used was not specified in its charter, the trustees leaned toward health care. It was a logical move since Monroe had previously funded the establishment of the Texas Medical Center through his foundation with a gift of land and money.

The James A. Baker estate, located on Baldwin Street, served as the hospital's first temporary location when it began operation during World War II under acting director Ernst W. Bertner, M.D. In the late 40s, several war surplus Quonset huts were added for use as operating rooms and for bedding down patients. In 1946, its first full-time president was named, Randolph Lee Clark, M.D.

Lee Clark would serve in that role for thirty-two years, a tenure that marked the institution's emergence as the world's leading cancer research center. After the initial construction was completed in 1954, MD Anderson Cancer Center's original pink, marble-clad building began its operation as a treatment center and research facility. Today, the campus has been expanded into several buildings that surround the original structure. When it was completed, Clark began the arduous task of recruiting doctors to staff the new facility. Once the hospital was up and running, Clark shifted his focus to the research-side of the institution. In 1965, Clark invited Drs. Emil Frei and Emil J Freireich both working with the National Cancer Institute in Bethesda, Maryland, to launch a chemotherapy program at MD Anderson.

I first met Dr. Emil J Freireich at a luncheon at MD Anderson in 2006. The "J" in his name doesn't stand for anything; hence no period after it. We were introduced after he made a brief presentation about the progress being made at MD Anderson through incorporating PhD candidates into on-going cancer research programs. Not long after that, I was asked by Janet Cesak, who was an outside consultant handling the institution's public relations functions, to produce a documentary about Dr. Freireich's early life and his accomplishments in hematology and oncology, the work that led to his work in establishing multiple-drug therapy, which is today known as chemotherapy. Having spoken with Freireich several times since our first introduction, I was excited at the prospect of getting to know him better. He was a fascinating person to speak with, and the opportunity of spending time with him one-on-one, documenting his life's work, was an irresistible challenge.

I began work on the documentary in 2007, first reviewing footage recorded by the in-house production team at MD Anderson under the direction of Greg West, with whom I had worked previously. West's footage included a number of interviews with both colleagues and former students, providing their personal insights into Freireich's character and personality. After reviewing the existing footage that was available for use in the documentary, I began shooting interviews with several of his colleagues at MD Anderson, using a local crew consisting of Joe Vasquez on camera, Jaime Cervantes on audio, and production assistant Ben Johnson. Among the first two physicians I interviewed were Gabriel Hortobagyi, M.D., and Michael J. Keating, M.D.

Dr. Hortobagyi was born in Hungary in 1947 when the country was under communist control. During the 1956 uprising, his family was able to escape, crossing the border into Austria. The Colombian ambassador helped arrange political refugee status for the family, and they emigrated to Bogota, Colombia, where young Hortobagyi completed his education, earning a medical degree from the Universidad Nacional de Colombia, graduating at the top of his class. He was sent to the small village of Pacho, located on the western slope of the Andes. There, he served as the only doctor in the region, working in every medical capacity, ranging from surgeon to gynecologist to emergency services, and even as pathologist conducting autopsies. At the age of twenty-four, he left Colombia for the United States, where he was accepted at Cleveland's St. Luke's Hospital for his internal medicine residency. It was at a one-day American Cancer Society Symposium in Ohio that he first heard Dr. Emil J Freireich speak. "When most people spoke about cancer, it was in dire, pessimistic, hushed tones," Hortobagyi said, "But when Freireich spoke, he was optimistic and upbeat about the inroads being made in cancer treatment. It was an inspiring talk!" It was so inspiring that Hortobagyi immediately applied to join the MD Anderson Cancer Center.

When I interviewed Dr. Hortobagyi, he spoke with reverence, saying, "Freireich was a part of your entire life because you spent your entire waking day in the institution. Freireich was the heart and soul of the department and was constantly involved in everything that we did." During the interview with Dr. Keating, he expanded on that definition of Freireich, stating, "I think the thing that sets Jay apart is that he has no boundaries in his thinking, no preconceived ideas. He doesn't lock into a particular point of view. He'll say, 'The prevailing point of view is X, so I'm going to look at it from the point of view of Y.'" Keating received his medical degree in 1966 from the University of Melbourne in his native Australia, completing his residency in Medicine Surgery at St. Vincent's Hospital in Fitzroy. He was appointed Fellow at the Royal Australasian College of Physicians in Sydney in 1970. From 1974 to 1975, he was a fellow at the University of Texas System Cancer Center, MD Anderson Hospital, and Tumor Institute in Houston, Texas. Today, he serves as a Clinical Professor in the Department of Leukemia, Division of Cancer Medicine at The University of Texas MD Anderson Cancer Center.

Keating spoke affectionately about the relationship between Dr. Freireich and his wife, Deanie. "Deanie and Jay obviously fell in love. There were elements of the man that were easy to love. There were elements of the man that were really difficult to get along with at different times," said Keating. Speaking about Freireich's work ethic, Keating mentioned that he would arrive around seven-thirty every morning and work a full day, frequently leaving during the early evening hours. One of the major contributions Keating attributes to Freireich is the lecture series known as Grand Rounds. "Before he took over Grand Rounds, it was really a very barren area that people were not attending. So, he developed a new format, that he could take a theme and find three people who were working on different aspects of the theme; and to do that on every area of cancer in a comprehensive cancer center meant that he actually had to study who was here and what they were doing, and how to marry all these things together."

Despite Freireich's occasional impatience and irascible nature, Dr. Hortobagyi said that once one got used to his style, Freireich was always teaching, leading his colleagues to look further into everything they were working on. "The more he challenged you, the more the message was, 'There's something here... there's some gold hidden in this, we just need to find it.' But underneath that, there was this teddy bear. And he had this incredible connection with patients. Staring you down was no longer there when he related to patients. That was the real Freireich." When I asked whether Dr. Freireich achieved a balance between his professional life and his private life, Hortobagyi replied, "Probably not." Dr. Keating said, "The imbalance, where he was giving so much energy to figuring out the ways of curing leukemia and other cancers, has been the great gift. But it hasn't been a gift that was given without any cost."

When I was finally able to meet with Dr. Freireich and his wife, Deanie, at their home, she described exactly what that cost was. "I think the family lost a lot of his time in absentia. Especially when the kids were teenagers, it was pretty difficult. I felt like a single mom, actually." As she spoke those words, Dr. Freireich looked lovingly toward his wife, glancing down to the floor at one point, in effect acknowledging his guilt. He then reached over and patted her hands, saying, "This is the one who made my career possible. Because she kept me sane, doing this kind of stuff takes very long hours, and when you get involved in something, it's a total commitment. So, family time is something you treasure. I could have some time with my family, but there was no question about the priorities. My wife knew it. My kids knew it. My work was my first priority," he said without reservation or apology.

Emil J Freireich was born in Chicago on March 16, 1927. His parents, Mary Klein and David Freireich, were Jewish immigrants from Hungary. "I don't have any memory of it, but from conversations with my sister and my mother, I learned that my father died suddenly in 1929, at the height of [the stock market] crash, presumably related in some way," Freireich explained. "My mother and father both spoke English poorly. They ran a little Hungarian restaurant, and when my father died, he left my mother with two children, two and five, no money, and no job. My mother ended up working in a sweatshop. And she did the only thing she knew how to do, which was to make hats. And she worked for something like two cents an hour, and she worked all hours. We never saw her."

Growing up poor during the Depression had an impact on Freireich as a young boy. He spent much of his time alone, but he remembered an incident that would affect his direction in life. "When I was about ten years old, I got tonsilitis. Everybody did... And in those days, there were no antibiotics... Fortunately, we had a family physician who lived in our community and was a 'tree grows in Brooklyn' type, Doctor Rosenblum. When I got tonsilitis, he said, 'The treatment is ice cream.' Now, how can you beat that? I loved Dr. Rosenblum, and I spent the next ten years dreaming of being the most famous doctor in the world ... But when I was a senior in high school, there was another 'tree grows in Brooklyn' guy; he was a PhD in physics. He told me that if I could get twenty-five dollars, I could probably get into medical school. This was in 1944, and my mother said, 'Okay.' Now, she had never seen twenty-five dollars, but she went around the ladies that she circulated with, and she found a lady who had inherited some money from her husband's death and was doing good deeds. And she gave my mother twenty-five dollars so I could go to college."

As it happened, Freireich was able to enroll at the University of Illinois in Champaign at the age of sixteen. He took a job waiting tables at a sorority house, for which he was paid in meals. To earn spending money and buy cigarettes, he talked the ladies of the sorority house into letting him wash the floors every weekend, for which he earned six dollars. As his first semester in college was coming to an end, he was concerned about how he would be able to pay for the next semester. "I had become friends with another student, whose name I can't remember, who had polio. He and I were talking and he asked me what I wanted to do, and I told him I wanted to go to medical school, but I didn't have any money."

> "I have the deal for you," my friend said. "The man from the Illinois Rehabilitation Institute is coming by to see me, and because I have polio, they pay for my books and tuition. Is there anything wrong with you?"

> "Well, I broke my leg when I was playing basketball in high school," Freireich said.

> "I'll have him come by and see you," said his friend.

"So, the guy from the Illinois Rehabilitation Institute came to see me, and he looked at my leg, and authorized my fees for tuition and books. I got my undergraduate education paid for by the taxpayers of the State of Illinois."

The Second World War was still raging when Freireich completed his first year of college. He was eighteen and received his draft notice. "So, I stopped doing any school work since I was certain I would be inducted into the military. I went to Chicago and reported to the induction center," he remembers. The recruits were all told to strip down and then walked in line through a phalanx of doctors, one looking into their ears, another looking at throats, another checking reflexes, and so forth. Toward the end of the examination, Freireich recalled being examined by a disheveled, angry doctor. "He had on a lab coat, with a cigarette hanging out of his mouth, ashes all over the front of his coat, and he bellowed out, 'Has anybody here ever broken a leg?' I raised my hand, and he told me to step out of line. He asked how I broke my leg, and as I answered, he began a tirade about the war. He was obviously opposed to our country's involvement in a war that we had no business being involved in and how war is such a waste." The exam was over, and the recruits all got dressed and lined up at a table, where their paperwork was stamped. Freireich's was stamped 4F. "That doctor, who was so opposed to the war, was marking as many recruits as he could justify as 4F to keep them out of the war. I went back to Champaign and back to school."

By the time he received his bachelor's degree, he was working on a medical degree and graduated in 1949 from the University of Illinois College of Medicine at the age of twenty-two. He did his internship and residency in internal medicine at two Chicago-area hospitals, one of which was Cook County Hospital, where most of the patients were indigent. At the time, Freireich's goal was still to become a family practice physician like Dr. Rosenblum. "There were very few doctors working there that had any experience. The interns and the residents were all taking care of the patients. So, it was a community of young physicians who were learning to be doctors. You had enormous responsibility," Freireich remembered. "It was great training because I learned about a broad range of disciplines, from working ENT to cardiology to surgery to medicine to orthopedics. I did everything. It was everything I needed to become a family doctor."

He remembers that the interns were working thirty-six hours on and twelve hours off. One patient showed up, and it was a cardiac patient. "It was an interesting case; I knew I could save his life and worked on the man for over an hour. Later, when I was doing rounds, I couldn't find him. I asked the nurse where he was, and she told me not to worry about him. He was too sick to make it, and they had sent him to the death room. The policy at Cook County was that once a patient left the exam, the nurses took over, and they decided where the patients went. I told her I was the doctor and wanted him back on the ward. She said that wasn't how it was done, that interns didn't make those decisions. I was adamant and insisted he be brought back to the ward. They brought him back, and I was able to treat him, and he made it and was discharged. Shortly after that, I was called into the director's office, who told me I was a troublemaker and, that I couldn't just ignore the hospital rules, and that I should leave. I got fired from my internship at Cook County."

There was another hospital just across from Cook County, Presbyterian Hospital, where all the rich people went. "It had a lot of fine doctors, and I went over there and told them I wanted to complete my internship and residency with them," Freireich recalls. "They had just recruited a new Chief of Medicine, Dr. Howard Armstrong, who was a well-known Boston doctor who had recently been discharged from the army. I had heard him speak a few times, and he was a brilliant man who knew a great deal about medicine.

And that was an area I needed to get more experience in. Surgery was easy, and orthopedics was easy, but medicine was very complicated. You have all these different drugs and patients who fail, so I wanted to learn more about medicine." Freireich recalls that Presbyterian Hospital was a completely different world. They had paying patients and rich doctors who were among the best in their fields and could teach young interns what they needed to learn. "It was just what I needed. I learned a tremendous amount about medicine," said Freireich.

Another major event that occurred while he was in residency at Presbyterian was meeting Haroldine Lee Cunningham, the beautiful nurse who would become his wife and lifelong soulmate. Deanie, as she was known by her friends, remembered her first impression of the young Dr. Freireich, whom she called Jay, which thereafter was how everyone he knew referred to him. "He called me up for a date first, and I wouldn't go out with him. He was pretty young," she said while laughing. "I was in my last year of nursing school, and then I was the head nurse in the outpatient department at Presbyterian Hospital, and he came through as the resident."

> "She would tell me, do this or do that…" Jay said, interrupting Deanie.
>
> "The reason I did that was because he was always late coming in."
>
> "I knew immediately that she was the boss," Jay laughs.
>
> "And the patients were all sitting out there, and ol' party boy was out late the night before," she laughed. "But he was a good doctor when he showed up."

Upon completion of his residency, Dr. Armstrong asked Freireich what area he felt deficient in his training. "I told him that I didn't want to offend him but that the guy who taught hematology was an absolute jerk. He didn't know anything, and that was an area where I felt my training was lacking," Jay explained. Armstrong told him the best hematologists in the field were all in Boston, at Harvard, Tufts, and Massachusetts. Armstrong wrote him three letters of recommendation, and Freireich loaded his '46 Pontiac with all of his worldly possessions and took off for Boston. On his arrival, because Armstrong was so well respected, Jay was able to get interviews with all three of the world's finest hematologists. All three offered him a position in their respective programs, but Dr. Joe Ross at Massachusetts Memorial was particularly interested. He had just received a grant to do research and offered Jay a position in his research program, offering to pay $3,000 a year. "That was a lot of money! The decision was easy to make, and I accepted Memorial's offer of a fellowship in hematology. Once there, my assignment was to do research on anemia in patients. I wrote and published a paper on the original study I conducted on anemia, and that was the beginning of my interest in doing research while treating patients, using the clinic as a laboratory."

In the meantime, Deanie quit her job at Presbyterian in Chicago and headed to the East Coast. She visited her cousin in New York and then flew to Boston. "After all the time we had spent together in Chicago, I figured that Jay was either interested in getting married or he wasn't. It was Valentine's Day, and I sent Jay a telegram letting him know I was coming to Boston," Deanie related how she intended to issue an ultimatum. If he was not interested in taking their relationship to the next level, then she would go to Colorado, where she had another friend who could help her get a nursing position there. "I got in my car and drove to the airport to meet Deanie," Jay said.

"He was late," said Deanie.

"I was late… I grabbed her luggage, threw it all in the

backseat and asked if she would like to see my lab. I had been working twenty-hour days and was really proud of the work I was doing and the paper I was writing. I was going to be this famous scientist... anyway, we got to the lab, which was in a rough part of town. We parked the car, and I took her into the lab and told her all about the project I was working on," Jay remembered.

"When we left to go find a place for me to stay, we got to the car, and it had been broken into," Deanie remembers.

"Her luggage was gone. So, now she had no place to stay and no luggage," Jay recalled, smiling as he remembered the incident, which was just one of the cherished memories from the early days of their courtship.

Jay was on his way to becoming famous for his ability to combine patient treatment with research in the clinic, and Deanie got a room at the YWCA, called the American Nurses Association, and found a job that was scheduled to last for six weeks at Massachusetts General.

"That was good for me because I figured in six weeks I would know what Jay's intentions were..." Deanie said.

"But she didn't say that to me. I didn't know the plot," Jay laughs. "She had a master battle plan."

"No, you had a choice..." Deanie said defiantly.

"As she said, she gave me an ultimatum. And we got married," said Jay.

"We were married by a Justice of the Peace on Beacon Street. We knew two people, both doctors, and one was a Canadian, and he was my maid of honor," Deanie laughs at the memory.

As newlyweds, Jay continued his work in hematology, and Deanie found another nursing position. However, they also started a family together. "The military was still drafting doctors, and by then, the war in Korea was on. One doctor had been drafted because he was a doctor and filed a case in the Supreme Court. The court ruled it unconstitutional. However, the military was desperate for physicians and began drafting every physician who was eligible. You could either accept a commission as an officer, or you would be drafted as a private if you turned that down. So, I accepted my commission as a captain in the army."

The man who ran the medical school at Boston University was Dr. Chester Scott Keefer. When the Eisenhower Administration created the Department of Health, Education, and Welfare, the publisher of the Houston Post, Oveta Culp Hobby, was named as head of the new department. In turn, Mrs. Hobby appointed Dr. Keefer as the first Assistant Director of Health, Education, and Welfare. At the time, Keefer, eighty years old, was well-known as an educator and highly respected for his administrative skills. His first assignment in this new role was to staff the National Institute of Health in Washington, D.C., which had been created eight months earlier in 1954. Jay was summoned to Keefer's office. "I thought, okay, I'm about to get fired again," Jay laughs.

> "Have you heard of the National Institute of Health in Washington?" Keefer asked.

> "No," Jay replied.

> "I want you to report to the National Cancer Institute in Bethesda, Maryland, at 8:00 a.m., Monday. Tell Dr. Zubrod I sent you," Keefer commanded.

By this time, the Freireichs had an eight-month-old daughter, and Deanie was pregnant with their second child. "I was a captain in the army, and this was an order. I had no choice but to drop everything and move to Bethesda." Jay drove to Bethesda and immediately reported to Dr. Gordon Zubrod, who was the medical director of the National Cancer Institute. Zubrod was an established physician who was beginning to make great strides in cancer research. He was known for his decisiveness and his concise evaluations of situations, resulting in unemotional interactions with colleagues and subordinates and a decidedly direct tone in making assignments.

> "I introduced myself to Dr. Zubrod, and he asked what my field was. I told him I was working in hematology. He sat back, thinking for a moment, and then he leaned forward and, shaking his finger toward me, spoke quietly."

> "Why don't you cure Leukemia?"

> "I was told I had an office on the twelfth floor, so I left Zubrod and got in the elevator to find my office," Jay recalls. "As I was walking down the hallway, I saw a sign at one office that read 'Emil Frei III.' I thought to myself, 'That's just like the military; can't even spell my name!' So, I walked into the office, and there was this tall skinny guy with no hair, and I said, 'You're in my office.'"

> "No, your office is next door. I am Emil Frei III," said Dr. Frei.

> "That was the beginning of a friendship that has lasted since that day. Tom Frei has been my superior, my teacher, my colleague, and my best friend. A giant of an intellect and a giant of a person."

One of the greatest problems facing doctors who were treating pediatric cancer patients was the nonstop bleeding that was common among leukemia patients. Early chemotherapy drugs had been used by Dr. Zubrod in treating cancer patients, but most of the patients were dying before they could undergo drug treatment. "Most of the children lived only eight weeks after being diagnosed. The disease was essentially a death sentence. We had to find out how to stop the bleeding before we could develop a cure," according to Jay. There were two great strides that made it possible to develop a cure.

Dr. Freireich contended that the bleeding was caused by not enough platelets necessary for clotting the blood as it circulated throughout the body. It had been known since the end of World War II that the blood platelets in atom bomb victims had been wiped out by the radiation, which caused those victims to die from massive hemorrhaging. Freireich's research proved that insufficient platelets in pediatric cancer patients caused those patients to hemorrhage. Through his research, he also suspected that replacing the platelets was useless unless the platelets were obtained from fresh blood. "The protocol from blood banks was that the oldest blood on hand was to be used first. Platelets in donated blood can only last about a maximum of forty-eight hours. The blood that was being given to these children was too dated to contain any useful blood platelets."

Based on his assumptions, Freireich developed an idea to build a machine that could separate the components of blood. He shared his idea with an IBM engineer, George Hudson, and with Edmund A. Gehan, PhD, whose work in biostatistics was instrumental in predicting outcomes based on collecting empirical laboratory data. Based on Gehan's mathematical computations, he agreed with Freireich that, provided enough platelets could be infused into patients, it would be possible to arrest the hemorrhaging, which would then allow for the use of drugs to attack the cancer itself. This left two major issues to be solved: 1) Develop a method for collecting platelets to be given to the patients immediately; 2) Determine which drugs would be most effective.

Freireich developed his idea further, and working with Hudson, he built a prototype machine that could collect blood platelets. The original purpose of the machine was for leukapheresis therapy of chronic lymphocytic leukemia (childhood leukemia), although once the machine was proven to be viable, the Continuous Flow Blood Separator Machine uses were expanded to harvest red blood cells, white blood cells, leucocyte-rich or platelet-rich layers, plasma; essentially, the machine makes it possible to separate all of the components in the blood to individual parts that can be used in various ways to treat any blood-related condition. It is an understatement to say that the machine created a revolution in medical treatment. Freireich invented and held the patent on the machine.

Once the machine was used with patients, their hemorrhaging stopped, and it was possible to begin treating the cancer cells directly. Again, working with the clinic as the laboratory, Freireich took the unprecedented step of treating his patients directly, collecting and evaluating the data, and immediately tried another method if something was not working. Dr. Sydney Farber had developed a drug that appeared to arrest the cancer for a time, but it did not produce a complete remission. Freireich logically concluded that a combination of drugs would produce better results. This had been proven in the treatment of tuberculosis through trial and error. Freireich believed that the best results would be achieved when the drugs were administered simultaneously. The cocktail of drugs became known as VAMP: an anachronym for the individual drugs used, which included vincristine sulfate, doxorubicin hydrochloride (Adriamycin), methotrexate, and prednisone. This methodology was devised first using only three drugs by Dr. Emil J Freireich, Dr. Emil "Tom" Frei III, Dr. James F. Holland, and Dr. Charles Gordon Zubrod. In 1961, a fourth drug was added, with much of the medical establishment speaking out against such a trial in fear of killing the children. "Instead, 90% of the children went into remission," said

Freireich. "It was magical. We began this process in 1955 when the mortality rate of leukemia in children was nearly 98%. By 1965, we had succeeded in curing acute lymphocytic leukemia in children. Today, the survival rate is 90% overall."

Having achieved the success they did in 1965, the National Cancer Institute received a visit from Dr. R. Lee Clark. Clark had been watching from the sidelines and kept abreast of the progress that the National Cancer Institute was making in every area of cancer research. Clark's goal, however, was to build the biggest and best cancer research center in the world—in Houston at MD Anderson. First, he visited with Dr. Tom Frei, telling him he would pay whatever he needed to get his life in order if he came to Houston. He further enticed Frei by telling him they could build a bigger and better program than what they had accomplished in Bethesda by coming to Houston. Then, Clark showed up at Deanie and Jay Freireich's home. "I came home, and Lee Clark was sitting with my kids in his lap. He had dinner with us. He charmed my wife out of her shoes. And when he left, we were going to Texas!"

Upon arriving in Houston, Frei and Freireich were given free rein to immediately begin the work necessary to transform the fledging MD Anderson Hospital into the most prestigious, well-respected cancer research center in the world. "We had to start from scratch. We had to recruit patients, and we had to build laboratories. Clark brought a temporary building from his ranch and had it set up in a parking lot. That became our first lab. Other war surplus Quonset huts were used as classrooms and offices. We created bed wards and leased beds from Hermann Hospital in a few of those huts until the construction of proper buildings was completed. And we had to get money," Jay remembers. "Because we had come from NIH, and NIH had developed a successful fundraising program, we had an inside track into donors. From 1965 until Developmental Therapeutics ended in 1983, we had a positive balance of dollars with the institution. In other words, the overhead on our grant money exceeded our state budget."

There is no question that Dr. Freireich made an indelible mark on MD Anderson. In fact, an argument can be made that he was an instrumental catalyst in its development into what it is today. The best source for commentary regarding the impact Dr. Freireich made during his first twenty years at MD Anderson comes from his colleagues, those people who shared those years with him:

> "On his eightieth birthday, let's salute the man, who in one decade, created the Big Bang in clinical Cancer research" - Dr. Jordan U. Gutterman

> "His expertise was in bringing together people with various qualities, who, working together, made a very solid team. He recognizes excellence in people." -Dr. Edmund A. Gehan

> "Another contribution is making clinical research and clinical investigation important. The old academic style was that you taught your medical students, you took care of your patients, you served on a committee, and you had a little lab project you worked on so you could call yourself a scientist. Freireich did work in the lab, but more importantly, the lab was the clinic." -Dr. Evan M. Hersh

> "I hope when the history of oncology is written, Dr. Freireich will be remembered as one of the giants in the field, a true pioneer in the field, one of the positive leaders in the field," -Dr. Gabriel Hortobagyi

> "I remember him telling us that progress will be made if you don't spend your time thinking about getting credit for it." -Dr. Gerald P. Bodey

"MD Anderson went through several phases of development," according to Dr. Keating. "The first was when it was purely a surgical hospital. And then, radiation therapy came along and became an important element of local treatment. But, the treatment of widespread disease was struggling until Drs. Frei and Freireich came along in 1965. So, the whole thing of taking it from a potentially curable local cancer to saying we can take a go at eradicating widespread cancers is where Frei, Freireich, and their whole team of colleagues elevated the whole process."

Adding on to Keating's attitude about the importance of the direction Freireich and his colleagues took MD Anderson, Dr. Evan Hersh, a Fellow at NIH who first met Freireich in 1960, said, "I would say that Dr. Freireich dealt with obstacles, of which he faced many, by persistence, by never giving up; in terms of professional setbacks, when every promotion he felt (and we felt) was appropriate for him, but didn't happen—for one reason or another—he never gave up. He never turned his back on MD Anderson, even though MD Anderson didn't always deal properly with Freireich." Dr. Gerald P. Bodey, with whom Freireich worked at MD Anderson for nearly fifty years, watched Freireich in his dealings with the administration many times,

> "He was very enthusiastic about anything he thought was important, so if an obstacle got in the way, he didn't give in easily."

At the same time that Freireich was making an impact on MD Anderson, the institution was making an impact on Freireich. "My years working at NIH, when we were discovering that it was possible to change cancer outcomes (something we were able to prove with our work in childhood leukemia), at that time, I considered those years the most satisfying of my career. Looking back on that, I realize now that they were just the beginning years. So much more has happened in the field since then that we now have a realistic vision of what the future of cancer can be—that we will be able to control cancer in the future. There was a time when polio was a terrible scourge. The Salk vaccine changed all that to the point that polio almost does not exist anymore. I truly believe we can have that same outcome with solid tumors and other forms of cancer. What we have learned from the work done at MD Anderson is that everything we develop that provides treatment for leukemia can immediately be applied to other cancers. It is just a matter of time until we discover the common connection and develop a universal treatment that can eradicate cancer altogether. I truly believe that."

During more than fifty years at MD Anderson, Dr. Freireich trained thousands of oncologists, from all over the globe. He is one of the most highly respected doctors in the world and is considered to possess one of the greatest intellects of any practicing physician—anywhere. Despite his many accomplishments, his greatest legacy to the world is embodied in the generations of doctors he has trained. Few individuals in any field have made the impact on their chosen profession that Dr. Emil J Freireich has.

> "I have been fortunate to live in a time in America where things got better every day. I go to work every day, and I do things no one else can do. And what I do saves human beings' lives," Freireich boasts. "I saved lots of lives in my career, and I've got more to do!"

Editor's note: When Dr. Freireich retired in 2015, he visited MD Anderson on a daily basis. His advice and counsel were still sought after by his students and colleagues. Dr. Freireich passed away at the age of ninety-three on February 1, 2021.

Chapter 20
Mercy Ships:
Delivering Medical Care Around the Globe

There is a group of medical professionals who have not achieved the level of fame that Dr. Freireich did during his career. In fact, achieving fame is not one of their goals. Improving the lives of patients is their goal. However, their work is just as important as that of Dr. Freireich and has affected thousands of lives across the globe. They are the professionals who sail in the Mercy Ships, providing medical care to patients in remote locations, where such care might not be possible were it not for the determination and dedication of these selfless individuals who saw a need and then set about fulfilling that need.

Don Stephens was living in Lausanne, Switzerland, when he put together a team that surveyed a number of ocean liners, searching for a suitable craft to convert into a hospital ship that could serve the world's poor. His dream became a reality in 1978 with the purchase of the *Victoria*, an Italian cruise ship built in 1953. Purchased at its scrap value cost of $1 million, the vessel was renamed the *Anastasis,* Greek for "resurrection," and underwent a four-year conversion from passenger liner to floating hospital, becoming the first of the Mercy Ships. The 522-foot ship was outfitted with three operating rooms, a dental clinic, an X-ray machine, a laboratory, and 40 patient beds. It began its operations as a hospital ship in 1983 in Central America and the South Pacific with a crew of 350, including Don Stephens, his wife Deyon, and their four children.

The Stephens family lived on board for ten years. During that time, the ship sailed from ports-of-call in the islands of the South Pacific to Central America, the Caribbean Sea, and ultimately to the continent of Africa in 1991. "Living onboard the first Mercy Ship was a privilege for us as a family. Though not always easy, we wouldn't change a thing," said Don Stephens. "The education my children received, their classmates from around the world, and the opportunity to provide tangible help more than made up for the inconvenience of a small cabin! Living where I worked provided an opportunity to design and implement an organizational structure that blended thousands of years of maritime history, the risk management of modern medicine, and the heart of God. And all this while raising my family onboard!"

Today, Mercy Ships is a global charity with its International Operations Center located at Garden Valley, Texas, just outside of Tyler. According to Stephens, locating in East Texas was an inviting location for Mercy Ships to establish its International Operations Center, "With access to two intercontinental airports, strong family values and plenty of good schools and churches, our staff thoroughly enjoys the Tyler area. It is a location where they raise their families and are involved in community life."

Mercy Ships provides free specialized surgeries for patients in Africa, health care training and mentoring programs for African medical professionals, renovation of health care facilities, dental clinics, mental health programs, agriculture projects, and palliative care for terminally ill patients. In addition to its USA office in Texas, there are international offices located in Australia, Belgium, Canada, Denmark, France, Germany, Holland, Norway, New Zealand, Spain, South Africa, South Korea, Sweden, Switzerland, and The United Kingdom.

The organization has operated four hospital ships since its inception. Currently, the *Africa Mercy* is the only ship in operation, although another purpose-built ship is on the drawing board. The *Africa Mercy* has greater capacity than all three of its predecessors combined. This 16,500-ton ship was acquired in 1999 through a donation from the Balcraig Foundation. The $62 million refit was funded by donations from the Oak Foundation and continuing support from the Balcraig Foundation and other trusts, corporate gifts-in-kind, and individual contributors. Originally a Danish rail ferry called the *Dronning Ingrid*, the vessel was renamed the *Africa Mercy,* and the conversion was completed at the A & P Shipyard, Newcastle-upon-Tyne. A comparable new vessel with five operating rooms and 82 patient bed capacities would cost more than double that price.

The ship's maiden voyage was in 2007 to the West African port of Monrovia, Liberia. There, supplies, equipment, and crew from the *Anastasis* were transferred from the oldest Mercy Ship to the newest. The volunteer crew of the *Africa Mercy* provides free medical services and surgical procedures on board, including cataract removal/lens implants, tumor removal, cleft lip and palate reconstruction, orthopedics, and obstetric fistula repair. The hospital is equipped with a CT scanner as well as X-ray, laboratory services and a Nikon Coolscope, allowing remote diagnosis almost instantaneously. An onboard satellite communication system allows doctors from the ship to confer with doctors in developed countries across the globe. Using modern diagnostic techniques and computer imaging, doctors from the ship can share images and patient information with colleagues around the world in mere seconds.

Mercy Ships has some 1,600 volunteers working in locations across the globe every year. There are 900 volunteers in Africa each year. At any given time, 400 hundred volunteers from 45 nations are on the ship. A most remarkable fact is that volunteers will pay their own costs associated with their service to Mercy Ships. This includes crew fees, travel expenses, passports, immunizations, insurance, and personal expenses. This commitment from volunteers allows Mercy Ships to use direct contributions from its supporters to bring medical treatment to the poorest of the world's poor. Volunteers are also frequent blood donors to surgical patients due to the need for blood and the ship's limited space for maintaining an onboard blood bank.

From the beginning, Don Stephens knew it would take special types of people to be involved with the Mercy Ships mission. "Volunteer professionals are critical to our mission of bringing hope and healing to Africa," Stephens says, adding, "We have doctors, surgeons, nurses, cooks, mariners, accountants, and others who give selflessly of their time and skills. Together, they are transforming nations, one life at a time." A couple from Tyler, Texas, has that special sense of commitment. Dr. Jerry Putman and his wife Marty began volunteering with Mercy Ships in the early 2000s. For both of them, their service is a calling.

Jerry grew up in West Texas, near Lubbock. He graduated from West Texas State University in 1975 with a Bachelor of Science degree. Then, he attended The University of Texas Medical Branch in Galveston, where he received his medical degree in 1979. "For me, going into medicine was a clear path to take. I did not have much perspective on what that meant; I just knew it was something I was supposed to do," Putman explains. After serving an internship and residency at John Peter Smith Hospital in Fort Worth, Putman was board-certified in family practice and spent three years as a family practitioner before starting a second residency in obstetrics and gynecology at Baylor College of Medicine in Houston. Upon completion of his training in 1988, he moved to Tyler and began private practice.

Jerry's wife, Marty, grew up in Arkansas. She studied Business Education and English at Southwestern Baptist University in Bolivar, Missouri. Through the encouragement of friends who worked at Pine Cove, Marty moved to Tyler after college and joined the Pine Cove staff. Jerry and Marty met in Tyler, where Jerry became one of the founding members of Tyler Obstetrics and Gynecology LLP.

In the late 90s, Jerry read Bob Buford's book *Halftime*. "I think reading Buford's book, which is about finding purpose for the second half of one's life, had a profound effect on me. It changed my attitude about what I was doing and the direction my life was taking," Jerry recalls. In the early 2000s, Jerry learned about the Mercy Ships program and its mission to serve the poorest of the poor with badly needed medical attention. He heard about their need for doctors to help women who had suffered injuries from childbirth. "What happens is that many of these ladies don't have access to operative care while they are in labor. If they cannot pass the baby normally, they can be in labor for days, up to a week or more," Putman explains, "Usually, the baby will die in utero, and the women suffer injuries inside the birth canal." The injury to the bladder and birth canal, known as a fistula, causes severe incontinence. The women then experience constant wetness from being soaked in urine 24/7. This creates horrible social issues, in which these young women are shunned by the people in the communities where they live.

At one time, obstetric fistulas were a worldwide scourge. In the late 1800s, doctors learned how to prevent and treat the problem. And by the 1930s, the last fistula hospital in America had closed. Today, most doctors in Europe, and in particular those in the United States, have never seen the problem. However, across the African Continent, where so many women live in remote locations, far from any type of health care facility, the problem remains a constant issue. "I wanted to learn about this surgery. So, we took a trip to Sierra Leone aboard the *Anastasis* to see firsthand what the conditions were," Putman said. "After returning, we sold the house, resigned from the practice, joined Mercy Ships, and moved to Sierra Leone."

That was in 2004. At the time, their older boys were in college, and their daughter Emily was in grade school. They moved to Africa, where Jerry learned how to repair fistulas and began working in a hospital in Freetown that was operated by Mercy Ships. He continued that mission for three years, until 2008. "Living in America, it is hard to imagine the level of poverty that exists in other parts of the world," Jerry explains the satisfaction derived from his work in Africa. "These ladies have been outcasts in the villages where they live. Some of them have been wet for years, living without dignity, without comfort. The surgery changes them. I get to see that transformation and how it changes their lives. These women return to their villages dry. She regains her place as a Human Being. It's pretty powerful to watch."

Mercy Ships has a dress ceremony for the women who undergo the surgery. Each patient receives a new dress before they return home. Before surgery, unaware that there was any hope for them, they envisioned that they would live with the shame and discomfort for a lifetime. Mercy Ships has given these women a new life. The dress symbolizes the change that results because of the access to medical care Mercy Ships provides.

After three years, the Putman's returned to East Texas and Jerry rejoined the practice at Tyler Obstetrics and Gynecology in 2008. The family resumed attending Bethel Bible Church, their church home since the late 80s. In 2014, the Putman's once again renewed their commitment to Mercy Ships as volunteers. "While Jerry works on the ship repairing fistulas, I work with the programming department. Last year, they had me design and conduct a class on translating medical language from English to Malagasy (the language of the Malagasy people of Madagascar). I worked with a translator, and we conducted the class together, teaching the ship personnel how to speak simple medical phrases," Marty said.

According to Putman, the *Africa Mercy* brings first-world medicine to the developing world. The two greatest impediments to medical care access are cost and transportation. Most of the population is living at a subsistence level. They can barely afford to feed their families, let alone have anything available for medical care. The high-quality surgeries that Mercy Ships provides are life-changing, and they are provided free of charge to the patient.

When the ship is to be docked in a particular location, an advance team from the ship goes into the country to announce the ship is coming. They advertise the fact that free medical help is on its way, and they make the local populace aware of the services that will be available. Screening teams set up meetings with the locals to evaluate their medical needs. They create medical charts that provide valuable background information on the patients that help prepare the doctors once the ship arrives. The advance team also schedules transportation times to pick up individuals who are scheduled to receive specific treatments, such as maxillofacial reconstruction, fistula repair, and other major surgical procedures.

Another service provided is the training of surgeons, anesthetists, nurses, biomedical technicians, and support staff in surgical best practices, infection control, water sanitation, and waste incineration—affecting the entire health care system. Some of this training takes place onboard the hospital ship. Mercy Ship teams also travel to local hospitals to train health care professionals on safer operating room procedures and give other courses to increase their level of capacity for safer surgical and general medical care.

Basic first aid and proper nutrition classes are taught based on the resources readily available in that specific geographic location. Local citizens can also receive instructions on personal hygiene and how to maintain a clean environment. There has also been an effort made to educate the populace about methods to reduce the spread of communicable diseases. Mercy Ships works with local partners to renovate existing facilities and build new centers to help improve the local health care infrastructure. This includes training programs to enhance the standards of care within the local population in partner hospitals or other health care institutions. The goal is to strengthen technical skills, develop the abilities among local resources, and contribute towards improved working conditions.

Beginning in August 2016, the *Africa Mercy* was docked in Cotonou, Benin, a small country in West Africa. During the *Africa Mercy's* 10-month stay in the Republic of Benin, Mercy Ships provided over 1,700 life-changing surgeries for adult and child patients onboard, treated over 8,000 at a land-based dental clinic, and provided holistic health care training to Beninese health care professionals. Mercy Ships Medical Capacity Building Programs are designed to foster transformational development within the health care structure of the host nation. These projects have been specifically developed to impart knowledge and skills while modeling and encouraging compassion and a professional work ethic. These projects incorporate one-on-one mentoring opportunities, internationally recognized courses for groups, and structured observation in the *Africa Mercy* hospital. Since its founding in 1978, Mercy Ships has provided services valued at more than $1.2 billion, including:

- Performed more than 81,000 life-changing or life-saving operations, such as cleft lip and palate repair, cataract removal, orthopedic procedures, facial reconstruction, and obstetric fistula repair
- Treated over 143,000 dental patients, including over 377,000 dental procedures

- Trained more than 5,900 local professionals (including surgeons) who have, in turn, trained many others
- Trained over 37,400 local professionals in their area of expertise: anesthesiology, midwifery, sterilization, orthopedic and reconstructive surgery leadership
- Taught over 193,000 local people in basic health care
- Completed over 1,100 community development projects focusing on water and sanitation, education, infrastructure development, and agriculture

For more information on volunteering or donating to Mercy Ships, visit www.mercyships.org

Allen Morris

Chapter 21
Historic Precedence – Television in the Courtroom

Nearly a decade before, I went to work for the Buford-owned television station in Lufkin, its parent station, KLTV Channel 7 in Tyler and was responsible for broadcasting the first-ever courtroom trial on live television in the United States. That historic precedence was in the making and was not lost on the management or the engineers at KLTV. Every effort was made to ensure the coverage was technically perfect. Amid controversy, the resulting trial set a precedence for allowing broadcast coverage of future trials and made a lasting change in the American Judicial process.

As television became a bigger influence on American culture in the 1950s, its impact nearly derailed the movie industry. For the first time in history, people could sit in the comfort of their living rooms and be entertained with both the sound and the sight of programs ranging from situation comedies to musical revues to dramas to live coverage of major sporting events. With coverage of the communist witch-hunt hearings conducted by Senator Joe McCarthy, it became obvious that virtually any subject could find an audience through television.

The first trial ever televised was that of Adolf Eichmann. Israeli Prime Minister David Ben Gurion insisted on televising the trial as a way to educate the generation that had come of age after World War II about the atrocities of the Holocaust. For his protection, Eichmann was housed in a bullet-proof glass booth during the sixteen-week trial, becoming known forever after as "The Man in the Glass Booth." Extraordinarily, most viewers knew little about the Holocaust when the trial began. Holocaust survivors did not speak about their ordeals at the hands of the Nazis until that trial. This trial, in which more than 100 witnesses testified to the atrocities they suffered at the hands of the Nazis, led other survivors to realize the cathartic benefit of telling their personal stories.

It was the following year that an American courtroom televised a criminal case. Not nearly as dramatic as the Eichmann case, the trial of Billie Sol Estes, a one-time associate of then Vice President Lyndon Johnson, was granted a change of venue from Reeves County in West Texas to Smith County and the District Court for the Seventh Judicial District at Tyler. Massive pre-trial publicity, including the defendant's association with the Vice President, gave the case national notoriety. A pre-trial hearing took two days, beginning on September 24, 1962. The purpose of the hearing was to get a ruling on two defense motions: the first to prevent telecasting, broadcasting by radio, and news photography, and the second, a motion for a continuance. After the second day of the hearing, the judge denied the first motion and granted the continuance. The trial was set to resume on October 22, 1962.

The initial hearing took place in an atmosphere of confusion and considerable disruption. At least twelve cameramen were in the courtroom shooting motion picture film stills and broadcasting the proceedings live. Microphone and video cables snaked across the floor, and there were at least three microphones on the judge's bench, with others positioned at the jury box and counsel tables. After granting the continuance, the judge ruled further that a booth be constructed at the back of the courtroom to conceal the cameras when the trial resumed the following month.

After sixty-one years, many people living in Tyler today may not know that it fell to the engineers from KLTV to construct the booth and install the cables necessary to capture the proceedings, both live and on videotape. Butch Adair, retired as Chief Engineer at KLTV, recalls what he remembers about the coverage of that trial, "That trial was six years before I started working at Channel 7, but

I heard about it from people who were there. Herschel Knight was the camera operator, and Hudson Collins was the Chief Engineer. Hudson told me about building the booth in the back of the courtroom, with a small opening for the camera lens. He said they had to match the paneling of the room so the booth hiding the camera would blend in with the rest of the room. The judge insisted that it be as unobtrusive as possible."

At the end of the trial, the court found Billie Sol Estes guilty in a 5/4 decision. However, the defense team used the television coverage of the trial as the basis for their appeal to the United States Supreme Court on April 1, 1965. The high court announced its ruling the following June 5, 1965, in a decision written by Justice Tom Clark:

> "The question presented here is whether the petitioner, who stands convicted in the District Court for the Seventh Judicial District of Texas at Tyler for swindling, was deprived of his right under the Fourteenth Amendment to due process by the televising and broadcasting of his trial. Both the trial court and the Texas Court of Criminal Appeals found against the petitioner. We hold to the contrary and reverse his conviction."

Justice Harlan said: "In a 'highly publicized and highly sensational affair,' such as a 'criminal trial of great notoriety,' there is a probability that prejudice against the defendant will result, and therefore, televising hearings and proceedings from such a trial is 'inherently lacking in due process.'"

Elaborating further, the five justices voting to overturn the conviction based their final opinion on the notion that the presence of television cameras, in this particular instance, created an atmosphere in which the mere fact that television cameras were being admitted to the court proceedings, in and of itself, lent credence that due process was denied the petitioner on the basis of the notoriety that was attached to the trial by the mere presence of the cameras:

> "From the moment the trial judge announces that a case will be televised, it becomes a cause célèbre. The whole community, including prospective jurors, becomes interested in all the morbid details surrounding it. The approaching trial immediately assumes an important status in the public press, and the accused is highly publicized along with the offense with which he is charged... The conscious or unconscious effect that this may have on the juror's judgment cannot be evaluated, but experience indicates that it is not only possible but highly probable that it will have a direct bearing on his vote as to guilt or innocence. Where pretrial publicity of all kinds has created intense public feeling, which is aggravated by the telecasting or picturing of the trial, the televised jurors cannot help but feel the pressures of knowing that friends and neighbors have their eyes upon them. If the community is hostile to an accused, a televised juror, realizing that he must return to neighbors who saw the trial themselves, may well be led 'not to hold the balance nice, clear and true between the State and the accused.'"

As it turned out, the high court ruling overturning the conviction was based on the pre-trial hearing, not the actual trial. The court ruled in the case of Texas vs. Billie Sol Estes the pre-trial hearing created an atmosphere in which more importance was attached to the status of the trial and its defendant than was expected. As a result, the public and potential jurors were likely to assume the defendant must be guilty; otherwise, there would be no interest in televising the proceedings.

At the same time, the court stated that future technology could change the circumstances, and the rulings made at a future date could be radically different:

> "The theory of our system is that 'the conclusions to be reached in a case will be induced only by evidence and argument in open court, and not by any outside influence, whether of private talk or public print.' It is said that the ever-advancing techniques of public communication and the adjustment of the public to its presence may bring about a change in the effect of telecasting upon the fairness of criminal trials. But we are not dealing here with future developments in the field of electronics. Our judgment cannot be rested on the hypothesis of tomorrow but must take the facts as they are presented today. The judgment is therefore reversed."

It can be logically argued that all the trials that have been televised since the trial of Billie Sol Estes are directly as a result of the reversal of the judgment in the Estes case. Today, it is felt that televising a trial is the only way to protect "the public's right to know."

One of the most famous trials that supports the notion that the presence of cameras in the courtroom affects the trial's outcome is the trial of O.J. Simpson that took place in the 90s. Simpson's celebrity status alone helped create immediate interest in the case. Giving the public access to view the proceedings helped create the circus-like atmosphere that followed. Simpson was charged for the murders of his ex-wife Nicole Brown and her friend Ron Goldman. The trial was the first in American history in which broadcast coverage was allowed for the entirety of the proceedings. And while the prosecution's case was based primarily on circumstantial evidence, the public's interest in the proceedings was dramatically increased when DNA evidence was introduced. It was the first instance in a U.S. courtroom in which the veracity of DNA evidence being tested in the court. However, the DNA evidence, that should have been of extreme value in establishing the prosecution's case, was overshadowed by the theatrics that took place in the courtroom. The most dramatic of which was when the lead attorney for the trial, Marcia Clark, allowed her colleagues to have O.J. Simpson put on the gloves he was alleged to have worn while committing the murders. There is a basic rule-of-thumb taught to every law student: never ask a question to which you do not already know the answer. When the prosecution had Simpson try on the gloves, it was a tactic that backfired, as the jury watched Simpson struggle at putting on the gloves, which obviously did not fit. Defense attorney Johnny Cochran's famous closing statement line, "If it doesn't fit, you must acquit," was taken to heart by the members of the jury who declared Simpson innocent on all charges. Nearly three decades later, people are still debating whether Simpson was actually guilty or not.

The proliferation of cases where television coverage was being allowed led to the participants in the cases becoming famous, not only the defendants in such trials, but in many instances, the lawyers who pled the cases either as prosecutors or defense attorneys. The sensational nature of televised trials titillates the public. Unfortunately, the public's interest in following the progress of trials has developed into a lucrative part of the entertainment industry. The genie is out of the bottle and the serious subject matter, particularly in murder cases, is beginning to be homogenized to the point that the viewing public is no longer horrified by the details surrounding such crimes. Instead, they are mesmerized by the gory details and follow the trials as they would a Playhouse 90 drama. Court TV was established in 1991 as a cable channel rapidly growing to three million subscribers. It soon acquired additional programing, *Homicide: Life on the Streets*, and *Forensic Files*. Through several ownership changes, it was relaunched as truTV in 2008, expanding to coverage beyond its concentration on true crime. Live courtroom coverage is now available over multiple streaming services, including YouTube, Roku, Tubi, Pluto TV, Amazon Fire TV, Apple TV and many others. A competitive network is called Law & Crime, the Live Trial Network that provides gavel-to-gavel coverage of trials across the nation. There are no less than twenty-two programs named after judges who preside over court cases: Judge Judy, Judge Jerry, Judge Jeanine Piro and so forth. There are more than one-hundred distinct program titles referencing criminal courtroom proceedings, presented live, and replayed 24/7 on live broadcast, cable and streaming services. It is big business, generating billions of dollars annually.

And to think, it all began at a small television station located in the piney woods of East Texas. It is an interesting footnote in history that a town, whose initial fame came from its rose bushes, would become known as the originator of the first trial ever televised in the United States. When William Wayne Justice made the ruling desegregating public schools in the United States, he made that ruling in a Federal Courthouse in Tyler. Playing host to Federal Courts has given Tyler yet another distinction. And during the sixty-plus-years since momentous decisions have come out of those courthouses, Tyler has grown from a town of 51,000 residents into a city of more than 109,000 residents. With that population growth, Tyler's fame has also grown. In addition to the seat of justice, Tyler is now known as an educational center, a medical center, a retirement haven, a tourist destination, a transportation center, and the largest retail center in East Texas.

Allen Morris

Chapter 22
Judge Bill Bass: The Man from Martins Mill

Two of the best pieces advice I ever received from my father were: 1) Always get to know the local District Attorney; and 2) It never hurts to be friends with a Federal Judge. Despite not being a member of the legal profession, I have been friends with Judge Bass and his wife Patsy for more than forty-five years. They were frequent guests at parties held at my house. We were part of a group who hosted an unofficial parade during the Azalea and Spring Flower Trail every year from 1980 until the mid-90s. He was also inducted as a member of our "super-secret" Order of the Blossom, the group of men who hosted the annual Azalea Ball, also held at my house in the older part of the historic Azalea District in Tyler. When Bass was presented with the Justinian Award, I was asked to write a profile about him. I learned many things I did not already know during that interview.

The Justinian Award for Professional Excellence is named after the Emperor Justinian I of the Roman Empire. He commanded ten of the wisest men in his realm to draw up a collection of Roman laws known as the Corpus Juris Civilis, which means "body of civil law." The Justinian Award was presented on April 26, 2017, to Judge Bill Bass in recognition of his years of service on the bench at the 12th Court of Appeals in Tyler, acknowledging his integrity, service to the community, service to the legal profession and for his warmth, friendliness and camaraderie with his fellow legal professionals.

Judge Bass's father was in the Southwest Pacific for three years and ten months during World War II. While he was away, Bass' mother decided the place for a ten-year-old boy was the Bass family farm in Martins Mill. "That move was a life-changing experience for me. Nobody had running water. Rural electrification didn't reach

225

our farm until the winter of '46, so, I had the experience of doing my school work by the light of a kerosene lamp. I had a horse, a beagle hound, and on my eleventh birthday, I received a 16-shot .22 rifle. What else could a boy want?"

The family moved back to Dallas a year after the war ended where young Bill's father had returned to his pre-war job as Director of Public Health. However, young Bill continued to spend his summers working on the family farm. "I always knew I was going to come back to Martins Mill," he recalls.

Bass graduated from North Dallas High School and entered Texas A&M when it was still an all-male military school. He took part in student government and was a member of the Ross Volunteer honor company. Upon graduation, Bass was commissioned as a 2nd Lieutenant of Field Artillery in the U. S. Army. Shortly after, he entered active duty; but not before he met his future wife at the Esquire Theatre in Dallas. They dated for about six weeks and decided to get married. Bass went to Fort Sill, Oklahoma, for five months. He and Patsy married immediately before Lt. Bass left for an eighteen-month tour of duty in Germany. Patsy followed three months later.

The Hungarian Revolution broke out in 1956. The Cold War was heating up, "I spent most of my time guarding the border," Bass recalls. Patsy was nineteen, had a new Austin Healy convertible and a German maid. She had plenty of time to travel and a husband who had to be gone half the time. "She was having such a good time, she wanted me to stay in the army," remembers Judge Bass. Their first child, James, was born in Wiesbaden, Germany.

After his discharge from the army, Bill and Patsy made it back to the farm in Martins Mill. They had a cow/calf operation and raised about one hundred acres of corn. "It was a great time. Patsy loved it, too. To be your own boss and go to work on your own place and eat every meal with the family—that's a natural way to live," says Bass. But nature did not cooperate. 1963 and 1964 were the two driest years in Texas history up until that time. The drought devastated crop production and drove cattle prices down. During this period, the Bass family added three daughters. "I could see I wasn't going to be able to support a wife and four children as a farmer. Farming is a great life, but not a great way to make money."

Bill was active in Van Zandt County politics. He was a precinct chairman of Martins Mill and county campaign chairman for the presidential election. Several of the local lawyers encouraged him to go to law school. Bill entered SMU Law School in September 1965. In his second semester of law school, he was called out of class to answer a phone call from Canton attorney Clyde Elliott, Jr., who told him to get back to Van Zandt County and file for election as State Representative in a newly created open district that included Henderson, Kaufman and Van Zandt Counties. "I had always wanted to be in the legislature, but I don't think I would have run without that push from Clyde."

There were three opponents in the race and Bill won the runoff election in June. He returned to law school before the legislative session began. Early in his legislative service, Bass met kindred, rebellious spirit, John Hannah, who became a lifelong friend. "Hannah was from Lufkin. He replaced Charlie Wilson in the House of Representatives when Charlie was elected to the State Senate. We became office mates and served the same three terms." In those days, only the most tenured representatives had private offices.

Bass and Hannah were never part of the "Speaker's Team." They styled themselves as the "Mildly Progressive Agrarian Front." They were more notable for bills they co-authored that were ahead of their time (like utility regulation) rather than for bills they actually got passed. In their final session, they became part of a bipartisan ethics reform coalition that came to be known as the "Dirty Thirty."

The Dirty Thirty sought a House investigation of the Sharpstown Scandal. The scandal resulted from the discovery by the Securities and Exchange Commission of loans made to the Governor, the Speaker of the House, and other state officials by the bank controlled by Frank Sharp. The loans coincided with the passage of a bill submitted to a special session by the Governor that would benefit Sharp's bank. Speaker Gus Mutscher's attempts to suppress an investigation were typically heavy-handed. Mutscher's eventual indictment and conviction resulted in his resignation as Speaker of the House. In the next election, over half of the incumbent members of the state legislature were defeated or chose not to run. It was the largest turnover in the state legislature of the 20th Century.

Mutscher's resignation paved the way for Price Daniel Jr. to be elected to the Speaker's post. Molly Ivins reported in the *Texas Observer* that Price Daniel's candidacy was born "...not in a smoke-filled room, but in a Baskin-Robbins, where those present (Bass and Hannah) were eating ice cream cones, the flavors of which were unrecorded." Price Daniel Jr. promised to serve only one term. In that one term, he pushed through reforms that weakened the, until then, dictatorial power of the Speaker. Other reforms forced candidates to make public more details about their campaign finances, imposed more disclosure requirements on lobbyists, and passed or strengthened open records and open meetings laws.

In 1967, Representative Billy Williamson of Tyler introduced a bill to create a two-year upper-level college in Tyler. He reintroduced the bill in the 1969 session and finally secured its passage in 1971. "I'm proud that I co-authored the bill in all three sessions, but I can take no credit for its final passage. Billy did that," says Bass, "We owe Billy Williamson for the creation of the institution that, after its incorporation into the UT System (sponsored by Senator Peyton McKnight), became The University of Texas at Tyler."

After leaving the legislature, Bass was elected to the Constitutional Revision Commission, a thirty-seven-member body charged with rewriting the Texas Constitution. "We drafted a shorter, better document, I believe. But, after the Sharpstown and Watergate scandals, the public became suspicious of change and government, in general, so our efforts bore no fruit." However, Bass said it was a great experience to serve on a group that included Chief Justice Robert Calvert, Senator Ralph Yarborough, Dean Page Keeton of the UT Law School, and future Watergate Prosecutor, Leon Jaworski. "I had the opportunity to debate the selection of judges with Jaworski just before he left to become Watergate Prosecutor. We gave him two blank tapes as a going away present."

Bass completed law school during his first term in the legislature. Clyde Elliott, Jr., the lawyer who encouraged him to go to law school and who pushed him into running for the legislature, offered Bill a job in his office in Canton. They practiced law together for sixteen years as the firm of Elliott and Bass. It was a general practice – both civil and criminal. "Clyde had gained a statewide reputation as a condemnation attorney representing landowners. A substantial part of our income came from condemnation cases. Clyde was a great lawyer, an honest man, and generous to a fault. I don't recall a cross word between us during the years we were together."

They remained partners until Governor Mark White appointed Bass to replace retiring Judge Connally McKay on the 12th Court of Appeals in Tyler in 1985. The 12th Court of Appeals hears the appeals from the district and county courts in eighteen counties between Dallas and Louisiana. Three Appellate Judges hear and decide each appeal by majority vote. Every losing party in a civil case, or defendant in a criminal case, has a constitutional right to one appeal. Death penalty cases go directly to the Court of Criminal Appeals in Austin. In almost all other cases, the appeal is to the Court of Appeals. "We must deliver a written opinion in each case addressing each issue raised by the appellant. That means we spend most of our time reading and writing." After the governor's appointment, Bass was twice re-elected to the Court of Appeals, without opposition. Upon his retirement from the Court in 1995, Judge Bass and his wife Patsy went to live for six months in Korcula, a Croatian island in the Adriatic Sea. During the next three years, they traveled. Judge Bass studied Spanish in Mexico, Costa Rica and Argentina and German in Vienna and Berlin.

In 1999, Judge Bass was named to the Texas Supreme Court's Appellate Task Force. Since 2003, he sits as a Senior Appellate Judge with the 12th Court of Appeals. "I don't need a computer or a briefing attorney. For the last ten years, it has been possible to do most legal research using the Internet." However, Judge Bass still uses real books from the library and writes his opinions in longhand using a Number 2 pencil.

A significant adventure in Judge Bass' career grew out of a sailing trip he and John Hannah made to Croatia. On June 26, 1991, Slovenia and Croatia voted for free enterprise and independence from Yugoslavia. At that time, Yugoslavia was still a communist state. Fighting broke out between the Slovenians and the Yugoslav National Army. "I called John, who was then the Texas Secretary of State, and asked, 'When do you think we will ever again have the chance to see a war in Central Europe with *Sound of Music* scenery?' He immediately said, 'Get the tickets!'"

Bass and Hannah flew together to Zagreb, where they met with the Speakers of the House of both the Croatian and Slovenian parliaments and visited with politicians and university professors in both countries. One month later, fighting broke out in earnest in Croatia. "John and I resolved to go back, but he hurt his back floating down the Rio Grande two days before we were due to leave; so, I went on alone."

Bass wanted to go to Croatia's third largest city, Osijek, which was under attack by the Yugoslav army and surrounded on three sides. He met a freelance journalist who had a car and a driver on his first day in Zagreb. They drove to Osijek and toured the town to see the devastation. They returned to an underground shopping mall under the main square that served as a refugee shelter and headquarters for journalists. "We had just gotten underground when a 120mm mortar shell hit next to the shelter's entrance. The reporter rushed up and shouted down the stairs, 'The old man who just left to check on his house looks like he's dead and a little girl is wounded.' Reluctantly, I followed her up the stairs," Bass recalls the events of that day, "An ambulance arrived in a minute. Croatia is not a third-world country. We went back underground into the shelter. There was a direct dial telephone on a makeshift desk. I was angry after seeing a man killed by an artillery shell that had no military purpose. I had the phone number of my friend, Congressman Charlie Wilson, who had helped the Afghans against the Russians. I dialed Charlie's number, and sure enough, my call went through. I delivered a tirade – 'Croatia has voted for free enterprise, democracy and independence. They are fighting the last communist army in Europe. Do something! We have a dog in this fight!' I hung up the phone and turned around. The reporters who had been sitting on their packing cases were standing and applauding after overhearing my call. Some had tears in their eyes. It was an emotional experience."

Later that week, Bass had the opportunity to have a private interview with the man who became president of Croatia. "I left the

Presidential Palace where I had the interview. The square outside was empty because of the air raid alarms. I paid no attention to them because Zagreb had never been bombed. As I crossed the square, a bomb hit the palace I had just left, turning its red tile roof into a huge terra cotta cloud. I set the land speed record getting to the nearest bomb shelter!"

The call Bass made to Charlie Wilson from Osijek was the subject of an article that ran in many newspapers across the United States—Dallas, Dayton, Phoenix, Atlanta, to name a few. A few months later, Bass was the only non-Croatian board member of the Croatian American Association. He spoke at their annual convention and was part of a four-person delegation that met with Vice President Quayle to plead for recognition of Croatia. In January 1993, Bass accompanied Charlie Wilson back to Croatia. "We met with the president, generals from the military, religious leaders, and refugees just released from captivity. Charlie was a big help in getting the United States recognition of Croatia as an independent country. He also secured a $60 million appropriation earmarked for Croatian refugee relief."

Judge Bass has enjoyed an exceptionally interesting life. Among his greatest joys is the family he and Patsy reared together. Their son James is a doctor in Oklahoma. Their oldest daughter, Suzanne, recently retired as a lawyer with the U. S. Department of Commerce. Their middle daughter, Julia, was a longtime Journal Clerk of the Texas House of Representatives, before her untimely death in 2014. Elizabeth, the youngest daughter, is a novelist who lives in Victoria, Canada. Asked which of his careers brought him the most satisfaction, Judge Bass simply replied, "I can't tell. I loved farming. I was fortunate enough to serve in the legislature at a watershed time. I practiced law with a great partner at a great time to be a lawyer while still living on our farm. It was a great privilege to be present at the rebirth of a nation. And I cannot think of a better job than to be a judge on the Court of Appeals."

Aside from my long friendship with Judge Bass, and my respect for him on so many levels, is the fact that many of the people who were part of his life became part of my life. I developed relationships with almost everyone he mentioned as he was recounting the story of his life to me. I knew John Hannah in Lufkin when he was first elected to the Texas House. Later, Hannah lived two houses down from mine in Tyler when he was appointed to the Federal Bench. His younger brother James was friends with me and my brother. Of course, I knew Charlie Wilson, Judge Connally McKay, Senator Peyton McKnight, and Representative Billy Williamson. I met Vice President Dan Quayle, Senator Ralph Yarborough, Governor Mark White, Texas House Speaker Gus Mutscher and later his successor, Price Daniel, Jr. I also met the irrepressible Molly Ivins, whose writing I admired. It was also interesting to hear about Charlie Wilson's Afghan intervention from a different perspective. Bass and I were also both good friends with Rush McGinty, who was involved in the infamous Sharpstown Scandal, that Bass mentioned briefly in the article. I suppose the biggest thrill about getting to know people like Judge Bass, is being able to stand on the sidelines of history-in-the-making. I have always enjoyed watching how people who have the ability to wield a certain amount of power do it. Some do it ruthlessly. Others, like Bass, do it with honor and great respect for the rule of law. I wish there were more people like Bill Bass.

Allen Morris

Chapter 23
Earl Campbell and Gary Baxter: Project Rose

I first met Earl Campbell when he was drafted by the Houston Oilers in 1978, the first pick in the first round of the draft. Before the NFL draft, Campbell had an outstanding college career, as a running back for The University of Texas Longhorns from 1974 until 1977. During his senior year in college, he won the Heisman Trophy and earned unanimous All-America Honors. He was the first recipient of the Davey O'Brien Memorial Trophy as the most outstanding player in the Southwest Conference. He ended his college career with 4,443 rushing yards and 40 rushing touchdowns in 40 games in four seasons.

His entrance into the Houston community was met with constant offers to appear in television commercials. His agent wisely limited his participation to two clients, Ford Motor Company, as a national client working through the J. Walter Thompson advertising agency, and Fingers Furniture, a local furniture retailer. As part of his compensation for appearing in their commercials, Finger's Furniture furnished the new house Earl built for his mother Ann. I was working as an editor with KDOG-TV and edited most of the commercials that Earl appeared in during his first year in Houston.

Earl's first year playing in the NFL saw him named as NFL Offensive Rookie of the Year, Offensive Player of the Year, and NFL Most Valuable Player—titles he earned in each of his first three seasons playing with the Oilers under the leadership of Coach Bum Phillips. During those first three seasons, Earl rushed for 5,081 yards, scored 45 touchdowns and led the Oilers to three straight playoff appearances. His style as a running back was reported in the press as "aggressive and punishing with the ability to break tackles through sheer force." Earl did not run around defenders; he ran over them. During his time with the Oilers, there was only one play: "Hike the ball, give it to Earl."

However, that aggressiveness was not the way to have a long career in the NFL. Constantly running powerplays against NFL professionals was as punishing on Earl as it was on the opposing players. Earl retired from professional football during the 1986 preseason, after two-seasons with the New Orleans Saints. Recognizing that the beating he had taken throughout his career was too much, Earl rationalized his decision, saying, "I'm a man; not a little boy. I believe this is the best thing—not only for myself, but for the Saints." Earl Campbell is recognized as one of the greatest running backs in the history of the game, finishing his career with 2,197 carries, 9,407 rushing yards, and 74 touchdowns. Earl was inducted into the College Football Hall of Fame in 1990 and the Pro Football Hall of Fame in 1991.

After taking a much-needed rest, Earl began his post-NFL career at his alma mater, The University of Texas at Austin, as a valued consultant to the football program. In 2003, his youngest son, Tyler, was diagnosed with Multiple Sclerosis. Earl now spends a great deal of his time helping Tyler spread the message about how to live with MS. It is just one of the many ways Earl believes he can give back to the community. Another way to give back came about through his relationship with Gary Baxter, a former NFL player, who is also from Tyler.

Gary Baxter was a standout Corner Back from 2001-2008. He played first with the Baltimore Ravens, and later with the Cleveland Browns. Baxter was drafted out of Baylor University in the second round when the Ravens were the defending Super Bowl Champions. The Ravens used Gary as a situational player during his rookie year, and then he started for the next three seasons as Corner Back, Nickle Back, and Safety, proving himself to be a solid member of the best defense in NFL football during those seasons. He was traded to Cleveland, where he sustained a career-ending injury. It was while recovering from that injury that Gary began researching health care facilities and discovered that a sports medicine facility, combining research and treatment, didn't exist. He decided to create one, but realized it was not something he could do alone. That's when he took his idea to fellow Tylerite Earl Campbell.

That is how the Project Rose Research Institute for Sports Science came into existence. The goal of the institute is for the research of combat injuries, treatment, prevention, rehabilitation and care in primarily sports, and health and wellness, although the facility will be able to treat any type of trauma-caused injury. According to Tony Wahl, CEO of Texas Spine & Joint Hospital, a major emphasis of the Project Rose Research Center will include performance training, in addition to both surgical and non-surgical treatment of injuries, "What will make this new facility stand out from anything that currently exists in this market is its clinical approach to research, whereby data from patients will be collected and analyzed. This will eventually provide valuable data that can be shared worldwide to develop not only treatments, but more importantly, to help establish measures and practices that will prevent traumatic injuries from occurring," Wahl says.

Another unique aspect about Project Rose is the two people whose passion is behind its development. Earl Campbell and Gary Baxter, both former NFL players who have personal experience with sports injuries and the subsequent treatment of those injuries are the passion and drive behind Project Rose. "Gary and I are both from Tyler, and we both have an interest in developments that will help our hometown community. That's why we decided to make Tyler the home base for the Project Rose Research Institute for Sports Science. We approached Tony Wahl with the idea about two years ago because we knew what he was doing at Texas Spine & Joint

Hospital and it just seemed like a good fit," Campbell says.

"When I was a kid growing up in Tyler, I always knew I wanted to make it to the NFL. I went to John Tyler High, and naturally Earl Campbell was a major inspiration for me when I was playing at the same school where he had led the team to the state championship a generation ahead of me," Baxter remembers, "I made it to the NFL when the Baltimore Ravens drafted me out of Baylor." After his rookie year, he started in forty-six games over the next three seasons, recording six interceptions, thirty-six passes defended, three sacks, two forced fumbles and two-hundred fifty-three tackles.

In March 2005, Baxter signed a free agent contract with the Cleveland Browns. He tore a pectoral muscle that caused him to miss eleven games in the 2005 season. The next season, on October 22, 2006, his career was dealt a blow when he tore the patella tendons in both knees during a game against the Denver Broncos. "I was lucky to be in Cleveland where I could be treated at The Cleveland Clinic, one of the best places in the country for sports medicine," says Baxter. "As a professional athlete, I had the very best medical care available, which is a big advantage most people don't have. I tell people that I always knew I would play in the NFL. What I didn't know was how I would leave it."

By suffering a catastrophic injury, Baxter realized a lot of things he had not previously considered, not the least of which was awakening him to the fact that he was not invincible. "I was in a hospital bed for two months and could not move my legs. I had no range of motion, and I could not exercise. It made me think about the future for perhaps the first time in my life." It also made him realize that most people do not have access to a professional athlete's medical care. This became the source for an idea that began forming in his mind about what he could do to help ordinary people gain access to better health care.

Another of the realizations about the future was the fact that a young athlete's conditioning changes as the body ages. The types of exercise, and the focus of those exercises, are different throughout the different stages of one's life. "As I thought about building a sports science research center, I decided to tour different facilities around the world, and to see what was available across the country in America. One thing I learned was that there were several facilities that specialized in one or two types of injuries. It was a very fragmented industry. What the market was lacking was a facility that provided all-encompassing care. The vision that evolved was to create a facility that engaged in the treatment of the body at all stages of life, from youth through adulthood and middle age and to elder care," Baxter says.

The types of injuries that the Project Rose researchers plan to study come from a wide range of sources, which includes sports injuries. The facility is available to professional athletes as well as student athletes from throughout our region. "An important aspect of the service we intend to provide is taking care of children who play sports—from the earliest age possible," says Baxter. Many sports injuries come from a variety of causes. Some may result from physical contact between athletes, such as football players hitting one another while blocking or tackling, to sprains caused by twisting an ankle while running. Most people don't associate the game of golf with major injuries; however, golfing is associated with many tissue injuries. A typical golf tissue injury is caused by the strain placed on the body at various stages of the golf swing.

Although the primary impetus for creating a research center was the result of his personal experience as an athlete, Baxter quickly realized that a significant number of injuries suffered by the average person are related to occupational hazards and accidents around the home or in traffic. To create an all-encompassing facility meant that those classes of injuries needed to be included as part of the total service offering. Tracking data on those injuries is equally as important as creating a database on sport injuries.

An obvious source of traumatic injuries is those suffered by soldiers in combat. Combat injuries are prime examples of the severe trauma that a body can be subjected to by bullet wounds or through the powerful force of an improvised explosive device. Such injuries frequently require a long time to heal completely, measured in years instead of months. Those injuries are also among the ones requiring extensive rounds of physical therapy or training in the proper use of artificial limbs and prosthetics. Injuries to muscles, connective tissues and bone injuries are a primary service line of Texas Spine & Joint Hospital, which was further justification for approaching Tony Wahl with the idea to house Project Rose.

The study and treatment of traumatic brain injury (TBI), primarily concussions, was already on the radar screen for TSJH according to Tony Wahl, "We intend to use innovative testing and baseline measurements for school-age athletes to build our database. Gary Baxter has solicited help from multiple leading companies and institutions, such as The Center for Brain Health, a noted software and application developer, and an eyewear company. In addition, the hospital has formed a local multi-specialty concussion treatment team. We want to assure that all post-concussive signs and symptoms are assessed and treated."

"When I was an active player, not much existed in the realm of preventive care for injuries," Campbell says, "The science behind motion and body kinetics was not something anybody ever discussed with me. I just grabbed the ball and muscled my way through the line and ran as hard as I could down the field. What we hope to do with Project Rose is change that. We want to get these young kids and train them how to take care of themselves. Show them the proper way to exercise the different parts of the body to get maximum benefit without causing unnecessary injuries."

One of the ways Project Rose addresses this particular issue is through the biomechanics laboratory, which is designed to study human motion. The lab uses a series of motion capture cameras that encircle the patient to create a 360-degree view. The cameras are able to detect abnormal movements that may make a player or person prone to injury or may identify what caused an injury, after-the-fact.

By viewing body movements from every possible angle, it is possible to analyze exactly how the patient's body is moving, and how various parts of the body are interacting with other parts of the body. This method will identify movements the patient makes that could be identified as a possible cause for injury. Once identified, it is possible for researches to work with the patient to correct the abnormal movement. Viewing the images that the cameras capture allows the researcher to show the patient exactly what movements are causing problems. Then, by employing training techniques to employ the proper movement mechanics, the patient is able to modify movement to correct bad habits and drastically reduce the possibility for injuries.

A turnkey approach to implementing the programs employed by Project Rose is a key element leading to the success of those treatments. Following an injury, a typical patient receives either surgical or non-surgical intervention, which is then followed by an intensive physical therapy regimen, during which research data is collected. Analyzing that data, and comparing with results from similar cases, researchers are able to recommend the most appropriate rehabilitation program, which will eventually lead to performance training and a healthier life. That completes the total treatment program, all of which will be available under one roof through Texas Spine & Joint Hospital and Project Rose.

Baxter says a major part of the program's success is through the collection of data. "By studying different injuries from different people, we can compare and contrast the treatments. That research is going to change how we look at exercise and body mechanics. We learn how range of motion works and how to determine the limitations inherent for the whole body under specific circumstances."

Although certain programs will be developed over time, which is the nature of developing a clinical research program, many programs that have already been developed enable Project Rose to implement treatments immediately to the community. This is made possible through a cooperative that has been established between Project Rose and research organizations including The University of Texas at Tyler Department of Kinesiology; these organizations provide the research and pending studies and Texas Spine & Joint Hospital and Project Rose provide the facility.

Another area to be a major Project Rose focus deals with sleep studies. What does it mean to get plenty of rest? How do you know if you are getting plenty of rest? The answer is you don't. "But you can know through sleep study. We are setting up a sleep study program for that very reason," Baxter adds, "Getting proper rest, uninterrupted rest, is one of the most important factors of good health. When we are asleep is the time that our bodies repair themselves. Rest is important for the physical being and also for the sake of the mind. Many neurological problems are directly related to a person's nightly sleep patterns."

Sleep is one of the main keys to optimum health. Sleep studies may be performed overnight in the Project Rose Sleep Program or in a patient's home by using a home sleep study kit that has been developed by some of the finest experts in the industry. Both options are offered. While sleep studies provide significant amounts of useful data, the most important pertains to tissue oxygenation. Without adequate tissue oxygenation during sleep, proper healing cannot occur. For example, a patient with sleep apnea may stop breathing several times each minute. When that happens, the patient maintains a below-normal oxygen saturation level. A patient with severe sleep apnea is likely to experience slower or incomplete healing of an injury. Sleep apnea can also cause delayed recovery from surgery.

When people sustain a critical injury, they frequently have no idea where to start. The Project Rose Research Center is a facility that helps them figure that out. Since no two people have exactly the same needs, each program is tailored to the individual. By sharing research data, scientists and doctors the world over will begin to have the knowledge needed to develop more effective treatments. "In the era when Earl Campbell became the Tyler Rose, an ACL injury was a career-ending injury. Today, with proper treatment, a player can be back on the field as soon as nine months," Baxter says, "The Project Rose Research Institute for Sports Science changes the paradigm for not only athletes of all ages but for soldiers returning from combat as well as the average person from the community."

"One thing I want to make people aware of is how Tony Wahl from Texas Spine & Joint Hospital shares the passion that Gary and I have for Project Rose. The way he recognized the vision behind Project Rose, and how he embraced its goals, is what helped make this dream a reality," Campbell emphasizes. Baxter observes, "Tony Wahl's leadership helped Texas Spine & Joint Hospital become one of the premier medical facilities in East Texas. His business acumen is responsible for creating their partnership with Baylor, Scott & White, which is one of the finest research facilities in the country. Because of that, Project Rose Research Center for Sports Science has access to a staff of award-winning scientists, medical researchers and doctors who are responsible for over 2,000 research protocols annually, spanning more than fifty-eight medical specialties. These are elements that will guarantee the success of the research programs we will initiate through Project Rose!"

"What impressed me most about Project Rose was the passion that Earl and Gary had when they first introduced me to their idea," says Wahl. "It did not take much for me to develop that same passion. I knew the personal experiences that they both had in dealing with sports injuries. I understood their individual commitment to using their celebrity for helping others. More importantly, I had faith that the goals of Project Rose are attainable. I am proud to be able to play a role in getting this project off the ground. I have no doubt the work that will be done by the researchers of Project Rose will benefit the world of Sports Science for generations to come!"

Since the inception of the Earl Campbell Tyler Rose Award in 2012, I have had an annual reunion with Earl Campbell. The evening is a dinner held at the Willow Brook Country Club in Tyler. The award recognizes the top offensive player in NCAA Division 1 football who also exhibits, "the enduring characteristics that define Earl Campbell: integrity, performance, teamwork, sportsmanship, drive, community and tenacity; specifically, tenacity to persist and determination to overcome adversity and injury in pursuit of reaching goals." The award is limited to players who were born in Texas, attended a Texas high school, or attended a Texas junior college or university and is presented by SPORTyler, Inc., in conjunction with the City of Tyler, The Tyler Convention & Visitors Bureau and the Tyler Area Chamber of Commerce. Earl Campbell, and members of his family are always present. The evening is hosted by Earl's two sons, Christian and Tyler, with Earl making the actual presentation to the award recipient. One of the things that makes the honor more endearing is how the Campbell family embraces the recipient as a member of the Campbell family.

Through the years the award has been presented, I noticed how the years of taking the physical punishment of playing football had taken a toll on Earl. In the early years, he was using a cane; then, he progressed to a walker. In the last couple of years, he was driving around in a motorized cart. Although his physical abilities have been affected, his spirit has not been dampened. He displays the same kindness and concern toward other people that he did when I first met him in 1977. Fame has not changed the man he is at his core. If anything, what fame has done is to provide an easier path for Earl to achieve the things he believes are important in life. He uses his fame to do good for others, living his life according to the Golden Rule, as he was taught from early his childhood growing up as the sixth of eleven children in poverty.

Earl would never characterize his childhood as having been poor. He would tell you of the riches he was surrounded with; the guidance of his beloved mother Ann and the love of his many aunts, uncles, siblings and cousins. Earl is philosophical about where he came from, that which brought him fame and to where he is today, "If it weren't for the dark days, we wouldn't know what it is to walk in the light."

Allen Morris

Chapter 24
Michael Morton:
The Nightmare Case of Wrongful Conviction

Not everyone wants to be famous. In fact, most people don't. As mentioned earlier, fame can be a two-edged sword. This is an example of becoming famous for a bad reason. In this instance, fame came through news coverage of a murder trial. The defendant in the case was caught-up in a legal system where he was never presumed innocent until proven guilty. From the first moment he was accused, everyone—from family members to people who had once been friends—assumed he was guilty. He was presented in the press as a monster, who committed a horrible crime and had no remorse. For Michael Morton, becoming famous was a nightmare.

Most people would think the nightmare began the moment the judge announced the verdict. Michael Morton says it was earlier than that, when the police showed up and arrested him. "I can understand how most people would consider it a nightmare, but I never thought of it like that," Michael contradicts, "After what happened I was overwhelmed. I tried to compartmentalize everything. Life became a series of small chores: going to work, cleaning the house, doing the shopping, and taking care of Eric."

On August 13, 1986, Michael was thirty-two years old. He was married to Christine and together they were parents of a three-year-old son named Eric, who had recently recovered from open-heart surgery to correct a congenital defect. Before leaving for his job as a supermarket department manager that morning, Michael wrote a note to Christine that he left on the bathroom vanity. The note mentioned Michael's disappointment on his wife not being intimate with him the night before, which happened to have been his birthday. The note ended with the words, "I love you." At 5:30 that morning, Michael left for work. He never saw Christine alive again.

Sometime later that morning, police found Christine's bludgeoned body. After six-weeks of investigation, police arrested Michael Morton and charged him with murdering his wife. His conviction for murder came on February 17, 1987. The judge sentenced Michael Morton to life in prison. During the trial, the prosecution presented no witnesses and no physical evidence tying Michael directly to the crime. The only theory of the case presented by the Williamson County DA's office came from the note found on the vanity. According to the prosecution, Christine was beaten to death because she refused to be intimate with her husband on his birthday.

> "The verdict was a big surprise. I never expected a conviction. At first, it was difficult to reconcile in my mind. As time goes by, you adapt. You never like it, but there comes a point when you become accustomed to it," Michael explains. He says the first day in prison is like drinking water from a fire hose. "For the first few months, you just react to things going on around you. You respond to the situation because you cannot plan. It's loud. The food is bad. Clothes don't fit. There is absolutely no privacy. I was lucky, in one way; I spent a couple of weeks in county jail with a bunch of other guys waiting to be transferred to the prison. There, I met an old con who was in his late forties. He had been there before, many times. He gave me some good advice, 'Keep your mouth shut and your eyes open.'"

The Court awarded custody of the toddler Eric to Christine Morton's sister, Marilee Kirkpatrick of Houston. A provision of the custody agreement was that Kirkpatrick was to ensure that Eric visited his father twice each year. Throughout his childhood, Eric's aunt took him to the Wynne Unit at the prison in Huntsville, where they sat together at a table in the prison yard visiting the man Eric knew only as the person who had murdered his mother.

> "Looking forward to seeing my son is what kept me going. Although it had been ordered immediately, it was over a year before the visitation actually started. Eric was four and half years old by the time he came for the first visit," Michael remembers. "I recognized I was losing things in my life: my wife, my assets, my friends, my reputation, everything. That is all part of incarceration. My son was my hope. He was the light at the end of the tunnel, the one thing I could hold on to."

By the time Eric was a teenager, he decided he no longer wanted to make the twice-yearly visits to the prison. He felt no emotional connection to the man wearing prison whites that he visited twice a year. He wrote a letter to his father telling him so. Not long after Eric stopped visiting, Marilee Kirkpatrick met Paul Olson. After they were married, Eric considered them his mom and dad. Making matters worse for Michael Morton, Eric had his last name changed to Olson when he turned eighteen.

> "I got a letter, not from Eric but from someone else, telling me he was being adopted and changing his name. After all the bad things that had happened to me, this is what finally broke me!" Michael recalls that he called out to God, uncharacteristically.

About ten nights later, as Michael was going through his usual nightly routine of putting on headsets and tuning in radio stations from Houston, without any warning, he happened on a station playing harp music. He listened for a moment and was suddenly bathed in a golden light. He could feel warmth from the light and an exhilarating feeling. At the same time, calmness surrounded him and he was certain he felt God's presence, and a divine, limitless and very personal love. His alarm went off, and Michael sat up. He wondered why he had been visited, and was certain it meant life was about to change. He craved worthiness for this intervention in his life. He would spend another decade in prison before anything happened.

During the investigation into Christine's murder, a mountain of evidence indicated the likelihood of a break-in, which was what Michael Morton had told police he believed occurred. Michael's brother-in-law found a bandana, covered with blood, at a construction site just behind the Morton's home the day after the murder. A few days after the funeral for Christine, her mother reported a conversation she had with her grandson Eric. Police recorded what she told them. Eric had been present during the murder and had told her that a monster had beat up his mother. She went on to say that she specifically asked the child whether his father was present, and that Eric had responded that, "Daddy was not home."

Neighbors told police investigators that a green van had been parked several times on the street behind the Morton's home. A man had been seen getting out of that van and walking off into a nearby wooded area. Police records also included that Christine Morton's credit card had been presented at a San Antonio jewelry store, where an officer stated that he could identify the woman who had attempted to use the card.

During his trial in 1987, the prosecution did not call Sergeant Don Woods to testify. It seemed odd to the defense team that Woods, who had been the chief investigating officer of Christine's murder, would not be called. The only reasonable explanation the defense team could surmise for not taking his testimony was that the prosecution was possibly hiding evidence. They raised this concern with the judge, who immediately ordered that all of the reports and investigation notes compiled by Sergeant Woods be turned over for his review. Absent from Woods's materials were evidence concerning Eric's eyewitness statements to his grandmother, any mention of the green van as reported by the neighbors, and any mention regarding Christine Morton's credit card found in San Antonio.

> "My original lawyers from White and Allison in Austin exhausted all appeals. I heard about an organization in New York that specialized in DNA, and I wrote a letter, and my parents, my aunt, cousins and my sister all wrote letters to the Innocence Project. In a fluke, it turned out one of the attorneys on my defense team knew Barry Scheck of the Innocence Project. Scheck said they would take the case, and added it to the pile of pending cases," says Michael. It took several years for the case to work its way to the top of the list.

In 2005, John Raley of the Houston law firm Raley & Bowick, along with Nina Morrison of the Innocence Project in New York, filed a motion requesting additional DNA testing on items of evidence from the crime scene. The court granted permission to test some of the items. The ruling excluded testing the bloody bandana found near the Morton's' house. The results of these tests were declared inconclusive because they did not completely rule out Michael Morton as the source of the DNA found on the bed he shared with Christine.

Another five years passed before the Morton Case Team was allowed to conduct tests on the bandana and hair from the bandana. After these tests, the lab reported finding both Christine Morton's DNA and the DNA of an unknown male. When the test DNA results were run through the CODIS databank (a DNA database system), it matched that of Mark Norwood, a felon from California, who had lived in Texas at the time of Christine Morton's murder. Morton's lawyers and the Travis County District Attorney discovered that a hair from Norwood was also found at the scene of the murder of Debra Masters Baker in Travis County. Baker had been bludgeoned to death in her bed, two years after Christine's death.

After nearly twenty-five years, Michael Morton was released on October 4, 2011. He was officially exonerated on December 19, 2011. Today, Michael Morton lives at Hideaway Lake just outside of Tyler. He divides his time speaking to various law groups and church groups. Occasionally, he helps The Innocence Project by lobbying some politicians or assisting in fundraisers. Sometimes, they ask him to speak in Washington, D.C., and in Austin.

> "When I was first released, I went home to East Texas and my parent's house in Liberty City. I started going to my mother's church, First Baptist of Liberty City, where hundreds of that congregation had been praying for my release for so many years," Michael recalls. It was there that he met Cynthia Chessman, a friend of Michael's sister. She was among those who had been praying for his release all those years. "She asked me to go for a coffee date. We went out to some coffee shop in Kilgore and talked for hours. We saw each other practically every day for the next fourteen months. We were married on March 9, 2013."

Michael is one of at least eighty-six defendants in Texas whose convictions have been overturned between 1989 and 2011. In a quarter of those cases, a total of twenty-one, including Michael's, the courts have ruled that prosecutorial errors usually contribute to wrongful convictions. Michael's attorneys filed a Texas Open Records Act request as part of the post-conviction DNA litigation. When they finally obtained the other documents showing his innocence, Raley and the Innocence Project filed a brief on his behalf. The Texas Supreme Court then ordered a Court of Inquiry to determine whether Ken Anderson, the former prosecutor who went on to become a judge, had committed misconduct.

When the Court found probable cause that Anderson had violated criminal laws by concealing evidence, they charged him with criminal contempt. At the same time, the State Bar of Texas brought ethics charges, and in November 2013, the former DA entered a plea to criminal contempt and agreed to serve a 10-day jail sentence. He resigned from his position as a district court judge and permanently surrendered his law license.

It is likely that most people would feel that Ken Anderson got off with a wrist slap, especially in light of what Michael Morton lost because of his wrongful conviction. Michael is extremely philosophical on the subject,

> "The biggest lesson I learned from all of this is 'forgiveness.' I hold no animosity toward anyone. There is nothing we can do now to change anything. The first time I actually forgave anybody who was connected with this ordeal, I felt cleansed. John Raley reminded me that keeping animosity in your heart is akin to drinking poison and hoping the other guy dies from it—it is counter-productive. It is to our benefit to forgive. The first one is tough. It gets easier each time."

Despite all the time lost when denied the ability to rear his own child, Michael is grateful his son is back in his life. He says he realizes that people cannot make up for lost time, and he strives to make the most out of the present and to look toward the future with hope. Today, Eric lives in Houston with his wife and his three children.

"To his credit," Michael says with conviction of a proud father, "Eric was able to completely reinterpret what he had believed for his entire life. He is wonderful now! Our relationship," he stammers for a moment, searching for the right words to describe his feelings, "we have an average father/son relationship... it is very good," he pauses for a moment and then announces, "This summer we are going to Ireland with a group of guys. I am looking forward to it. It should be a really good time!"

Michael Morton cannot get back the time he lost serving those years in prison. He will never recover completely from the nightmare of losing his wife and having his child taken away. However, he has come to terms with that and is ready to settle back into living what is left of his life, only now, without the intrusion of fame. He is happy to slip back into relative anonymity.

Chapter 25
Patrick Mahomes: Greatest of All Time?

When Patrick Mahomes was a senior at Whitehouse High School, he was given a choice that few young athletes faced. That choice was to continue his education or to go straight into the world of professional sports, complete with a lucrative signing bonus offered to him by the Detroit Tigers to play baseball. His decision was to go after an education first and concentrate on a professional career in sports later.

Today, Patrick Mahomes is arguably the most famous football player on the planet. A two-time Super Bowl MVP, his current contract with the Kansas City Chiefs pays him $45 million a year. It is estimated that he earned an additional $40 million for endorsements in 2021. If he can avoid serious injury, Mahomes is destined for a long and distinguished career, one that could eclipse that of Tom Brady. Mahomes and Brady have faced one another six times, and each time, the games were high-stakes, high-scoring battles. Currently, they are tied 3-3 against each other. As for their regular season records, Brady is 58-20, and Mahomes is 64-16.

My first meeting with Patrick Mahomes was on the occasion of his announcement that he had chosen to attend Texas Tech. My son, Noah Collins Morris, was there to photograph the event. It was Noah's first paying gig as a professional photographer. On this evening, Patrick was only known for his athletic skills as a high school player. What many local sports fans knew, and what may not have been known by others across the state, was how well Mahomes played other sports. He lettered as a four-year varsity athlete in baseball and basketball. He helped lead the Whitehouse basketball team to a 28-7 record in his senior year, averaging 19 points and eight rebounds a game. His impressive personal performance during the playoffs included 37 points and 49 points during the postseason.

His performance on the baseball field is just as impressive, if not more so. Mahomes played all three outfield positions, shortstop and pitcher. He batted .400 as a senior with three home runs. He was a two-time all-state selection and four-time all-district pick. He pitched a no-hitter over Mount Pleasant as a senior with 16 strikeouts and went three for four, nearly hitting for the cycle in the nightcap of the doubleheader. He helped lead Whitehouse High School to the state semifinals during his senior year. It was Mahomes' outstanding performance in baseball that led to his being the 37th round draft pick by the Detroit Tigers in the 2014 Major League Baseball First-Year Player Draft, and that lucrative signing bonus mentioned earlier.

As a junior at Whitehouse High School, just a few short years ago, Patrick Mahomes received heavy recruiting overtures from Kliff Kingsbury, who was with Texas A&M University at that time. Mahomes was an outstanding high school football player who was well-known throughout East Texas. Lettering three years playing varsity football, Mahomes earned the 2013 Texas Association Press Sports Editors High School Football Player of the Year. He was named the Associated Press Class 4A Offensive Player of the Year; All-East Texas Most Valuable Player; Rivals Texas Top 100 and; Blue-Grey All-American; and as a senior Mahomes helped his team to its first-ever football district title, going 12-1 while passing for 4,619 yards (287-of-495) and 50 touchdowns. He rushed 157 times for 948 yards and 15 touchdowns.

Kingsbury eventually became the head football coach at Texas Tech. He remained interested in getting Mahomes to sign with him, only to play as a Red Raider, not an Aggie. The number of offers Mahomes received from various schools, including Oklahoma State and Rice, surprised no one. Kliff Kingsbury's recruiting efforts to convince Mahomes to join his team in Lubbock faced not only competition from other collegiate football programs, but the lure of big money from Major League Baseball. Two things can be credited for enabling Kingsbury to succeed in getting Patrick Mahomes on the Texas Tech football-playing roster. One was an agreement with the Texas Tech Head Baseball Coach Tim Tadlock that allowed Mahomes to play both football and baseball. The other, and most likely the stronger factor on the decision, was the influence of Randi Mahomes, Patrick's mother.

"I wanted it to be his decision," remembers Randi Mahomes, "I did not want to encourage the wrong decision, one he might regret later in life; however, there is no secret that I always wanted Patrick to get an education. His father and I both missed out on college, and I did not want that to happen to Patrick."

Many in East Texas remember Pat Mahomes, a native of Lindale and Patrick's father. He spent eleven years playing major league ball for the Twins, the Red Sox, the Rangers, and the Pirates, and he played for two seasons in Yokohama, Japan. When Patrick was five years old, his dad was playing for the Mets against the Yankees in the World Series. "When he was young, I would play catch with Patrick in the hotel rooms during spring training," Pat recalls, "but it was in 2000, when I was playing in the World Series, that I noticed he had real talent. He was five then, and during batting practice, he was out on the field shagging balls."

Although Pat and Randi divorced when Patrick was six, Pat has remained close to his son and his younger brother, Jackson. "His mom and I are still best friends," Pat says, "I retired from pro ball his freshman year and was able to be there for most of his high school games. When offered the opportunity to go pro right out of high school, which is what I did, I told him to follow his dreams. I told him, 'You'll figure it all out along the way. You can play football or baseball, you might go into the pros, or you get an education and be whatever you want.' Whatever he does, I am proud of him."

For Patrick, the decision was not as daunting as it appeared to those who were waiting for him to make up his mind. Education was always a priority. While the lure of a professional contract was appealing, Patrick felt his education was more important in the long term. He was hopeful that the opportunity to play professionally would present itself, but if not, then he planned to have a business career in sports management. With a degree in hand, Patrick figured he won either way.

As the Texas Tech Red Raiders began their 2015 season, Mahomes was the starting quarterback, hoping to improve on an already stellar record. In his first year, he played in seven games, starting the final four games of the season. His record includes throwing for 1,547 yards with 16 touchdown passes on 105-of-185 passing with four interceptions. He posted a 56.8 completion percentage, 151.22 passing efficiency, and averaged 221 passing yards/game, which ranked second among all NCAA freshmen in passing efficiency, fourth in passing TDs, and ninth in passing yardage. Patrick set a Big 12 freshman record with 598 passing yards against No. 5 Baylor. He tied a Big 12 freshman record with six touchdown passes against Baylor and broke three freshman school records in standout performances, including passing yards, yards of total offense, and passing touchdowns.

Randi is also proud of the way her eldest child relates to his brother Jackson and their baby sister, four-year-old Mia Randall. "He misses Mia, and is very protective of her," Randi says. "Jackson is totally different from Patrick. He is good at other things, like basketball. He is aggressive and wants to be in charge. I told Patrick that it is hard to be his brother. I think he is sensitive that his younger brother sometimes gets the short end of the stick. That is a characteristic I am proud Patrick developed. For Patrick, winning is not everything. He is humble, and when he brags, he brags on the whole team, not himself. His Little League coaches remarked about that, and now his college coaches have noticed that same quality."

Both of his parents expressed their pride in the 3.91 GPA Patrick has achieved at Texas Tech. "He started getting college credits at Tyler Junior College while he was still in high school," Randi recalls. His head start in college meant he would be eligible for the football draft after his third year. By then, he would have his bachelor's degree in Finance and Sports Management. If not drafted into the NFL at that time, Patrick planned to begin work on a master's degree and play another year of college football. "I admit I am a proud mom. I am very proud of his athletic achievements," Randi says, "However, I am prouder of his scholastic accomplishments."

As far as the Kansas City Chiefs were concerned, the 2017 NFL Draft was one of the most surprising in years, primarily because of their first-round pick of Texas Tech quarterback Patrick Mahomes II. Once again, my son Noah was there to photograph Patrick's reaction the moment it was announced that he was drafted by the Chiefs. The last time the Chiefs drafted a quarterback in the first round was back in 1983. According to B. J. Kissel, an online reporter with the Chiefs organization, "John Dorsey was so aggressive in that he traded up so many different times. A lot is going to be made of Patrick Mahomes and the history of the first-round quarterback, but the fact is he (Dorsey) traded up three times in this draft, all for offensive players … In four previous drafts, John Dorsey had only traded up twice … Patrick Mahomes led the nation in passing, moving up seventeen spots from twenty-seven to ten … Down the road, whenever he gets on the field, whatever Mahomes does is really going to be one of the things that people take away from this draft."

In his last season at Texas Tech, Mahomes led the nation by racking up 5,052 yards passing, 41 touchdowns, and throwing only ten interceptions. He is only the third college quarterback to throw more than 5,000 yards in more than one season. Mahomes also had a good running game during his college career, rushing for 845 yards and scoring 22 touchdowns. During his first press conference with the Chiefs, Mahomes credited Coach Kliff Kingsbury at Texas Tech with allowing him to control the offense during the game, "I could change the play, change the route the runners would take ... It was my decision to call a running play or to pass," Mahomes explained, "I felt that helped me a ton, especially as I transition into the NFL. I know I have a lot to learn and a lot that I have to work on, but at the same time, I felt that helped a lot more [in preparing for the NFL]."

What makes Mahomes' success all the more interesting to the casual observer is the fact that he has only played football for five years now. He did not start until his sophomore year at Whitehouse High School. Prior to that, he played baseball. It was only natural since his father, Pat, was a major league relief pitcher for eleven years. In his senior year, the younger Mahomes threw a 95-mile-per-hour fastball and once pitched a no-hitter and struck out sixteen batters in a single game. He began preparing for the MLB draft, looking for the opportunity to play professional baseball and accept a million-dollar signing bonus. He was offered a contract by the Detroit Tigers but turned it down in favor of attending Texas Tech and playing both football and baseball.

His parents were both happy with his decision to attend college instead of beginning a professional sports career. "When offered the opportunity to go pro right out of high school, which is what I did, I told him to follow his dreams," his father, Patrick Sr., said. "I told him, 'You'll figure it all out along the way. You can play football or

260

baseball, you might go into the pros, or you get an education and be whatever you want.'" His mother, Randi, had that same attitude. She wanted him to go to college, but she wanted it to be Patrick's decision, "His father and I both missed out on college... I did not want that to happen to Patrick," Randi says.

Despite having the agreement to play football and baseball, Mahomes played baseball for only one season at Tech. His mother says he was ready to quit baseball in favor of trying for the starting quarterback position in his sophomore year. "His father and I both told him he needed to honor the commitment he had made and play baseball that year. I reminded him that he had an opportunity many kids never get and that I did not raise a quitter." He played baseball that spring. Ultimately, football won out over baseball. As a sophomore at Tech, Mahomes threw for 4,200 yards, 36 touchdowns, and only 15 interceptions.

Mahomes is known as an "air-raid" quarterback, a moniker not necessarily considered to be an advantage in the NFL. When asked why he thought he could make the transition into the NFL successfully when other players with a similar style and background have failed, Mahomes replied, "First off, because of how much control I had of the offense there [at Texas Tech]. A lot of air raid quarterbacks haven't had that before... That's definitely going to help the transition a little bit... The coaching that the Chiefs have, Coach Reid and Coach Nagy, those guys will help me a lot. They will push me to be the best quarterback I can be, which will really help." Asked what he looks forward most about playing quarterback for Kansan City, Mahomes replied, "Just the opportunity to throw the ball down the field and score is always awesome!"

One thing Mahomes wants people to know is that he plans to take Whitehouse and Texas Tech with him to Kansas City. He is proud of his roots and of his family. He is especially grateful for the coaching he received from Coach Chad Parker in Little League, Coach Adam Cook at Whitehouse, and Coach Kliff Kingsbury at Tech. He included them all at his watch party held at Lago del Pino. He might have attended the draft in Philadelphia but chose instead to stay in Tyler so as many of his family and friends who wanted to share the moment could. In addition to his former coaches, the group assembled on the evening of the draft, which included his parents, Randi and Pat Mahomes, his brother Jackson, and little sister Mia. His grandparents, his girlfriend, Brittany Matthews, and several of his former Whitehouse High School teammates were also present.

With a bright future facing Patrick Mahomes II, the likelihood was that he would compete with Tyler Bray for the position of Chiefs' backup quarterback. Bray has worked with QB Alex Smith for the past four seasons. His rifle-accurate arm will be tough competition for the rookie Mahomes, who would only have four preseason games in which to demonstrate his ability. GM John Dorsey and Head Coach Andy Reid were both anxious to see how quickly Mahomes could learn the Chiefs playbook and how quickly he could assimilate into the NFL style of playing the game. As for Mahomes himself, confident in his abilities, he was looking forward to the challenge of proving himself at the professional level.

Patrick Mahomes joined the Kansas City Chiefs in 2017. In his second year with the Chiefs, Mahomes was named the NFL's Most Valuable Player. Two seasons later he led the chiefs to victory in Super Bowl LIV in 2020, and was named Super Bowl MVP. He played in his second Super Bowl in 2021 against the Tampa Bay Buccaneers, who won the game 31-9. Tom Brady was the opposing quarterback. In 2022, he was once again named the NFL's Most Valuable Player. In 2023, he led the Chiefs to a second victory in Super Bowl LVII, and again was named Super Bowl MVP. At the age of twenty-seven, he has established himself as the best quarterback currently playing in the NFL. Regarding the success he has had, Mahomes says, "The best thing about it is you're showing kids that no matter where you grow up, what race you are, that you can achieve your dream."

As impressive as his work on the field is, his work off the field is even more so. He is using his fame and wealth to support initiatives that focus on health, wellness, communities in need of resources, and other charitable causes. *15 and the Mahomies* is the foundation Mahomes created in 2019 to facilitate that support. Among the foundation's programs are "Read for 15" aimed at encouraging children to read; "15 for 15" provides support for 15 youth-oriented charities centered on academics, science, the arts, classroom supplies, athletics, children with disabilities, after-school programs, and more; "Volunteer for 15" is a partnership with The Youth Volunteer Corps to encourage youth ages 11-18 to make a pledge to volunteer 15 hours during the summer; these programs are in addition to helping fundraising efforts for other nonprofits, ranging from Boys & Girls Club, Make-A-Wish, Variety Clubs International, Special Olympics, children's Advocacy Centers, and more than four dozen others.

While much of *15 and the Mahomies'* initial work centered on charities in the Kansas City area, Mahomes is also involved with organizations throughout East Texas, as well as supporting nonprofits in Lubbock, where he lived while attending Texas Tech. To date, with the support of his high school sweetheart and now wife Brittany, Mahomes has raised nearly $100 million for nonprofits operating in every place he has lived. The couple have personally guaranteed financing for a new stadium in Kansas City and donated more than $5 million of their own money. "Since before I joined the league, it has been a goal of mine to make a lasting impact on the communities that have given so much to me," says Mahomes. "Together, we are making a lasting impact on kids in underserved communities."

Patrick Mahomes has taken his fame in stride. He uses it as a tool to do other things, the things that he believes are more important than being regarded as one of the greatest quarterbacks to ever play the game. Sure, he wants to become the greatest quarterback of all time. He wants everything that his career can provide to ensure financial security for his family. But when you earn more than enough to take care of everything at home, there is a responsibility to use the rest to give others a hand-up. For Mahomes, raising money to support nonprofits, which in turn support the kids throughout the community, is what is important. Being successful, and famous, is a great path to follow to accomplish what Patrick Mahomes believes to be important. Mahomes is a prime example of how one man's fame can be used for the greater good of others!

Chapter 26
Ben Vereen: Variety Club International

Getting a phone call from Suzy Bergner always means one of two things: she wants you to go for a drink and some socializing, or she needs your help for some worthy cause she is working on. Either way, it is always worth taking the call. Suzy is an anti-socialite socialite. She is outgoing, seems to know literally everybody, and lives to party.

In the mid-nineties, I was commuting from the Dallas/Ft. Worth metroplex to Houston as a producer for Richard Kidd Productions, which was later bought out by Caribiner Communications. Rather than staying in a hotel, I bought an apartment on Taft Street, not far from our offices in the Texaco Building, which served as my Houston residence during the week. Most weekends, I would go home, but sometimes my wife Nina would bring our son Noah to Houston for the weekend. There were plenty of things for us to do on those weekends to entertain our four-year-old. One of his favorite places was the Children's Museum on Binz Street, just south of the downtown area. Another favorite place was the Natural Museum of History. They had a dinosaur exhibit and an atrium filled with thousands of varieties of butterflies. Little kids loved that place. When we spent our weekends in Houston, our time was strictly just the three of us; none of my Houston friends had met my wife.

Nina's actual existence became something of a joke among my friends in Houston. Since none of them had ever met her, they believed she was a myth, a name I made up. They referred to Nina as "Phantom." Sometime, in June of 1998, Holly O'Dell, Stephanie Hart, and I saw the writing on the wall as Caribiner stock took a nosedive. We decided it was time to bail, and formed our own company, Extreme Corporate Communications. With our new company located in Houston, I convinced Nina it was time to relocate our family to Houston. Nina did not want to live in the city, and we found a house she liked in Kingwood, a bedroom community northeast of downtown where many of my clients working in the energy sector lived. When we couldn't sell our house in Arlington, we rented it to a player on the Texas Rangers.

One of my best friends from Houston is Myra Jolivet. She had been an anchor at the CBS affiliate KHOU and left broadcasting for the greener pastures of Shell Oil Company, working in Marketing and Public Relations. Shell Oil was the biggest client we had at ECC, and when Myra and I first met, we clicked right away. We remain close friends to this day. It was Myra who introduced me to Suzy Ferrett Bergner, who was then married to Houston attorney Dick Bergner.

I had casually mentioned to Myra that Nina would be joining me in Houston and during a cocktail hour at a cigar bar on Kirby Street that included me, Myra, Suzy, and talk radio host Michael Berry. Myra blurted out, "I have news. Phantom is coming to Houston!" Without missing a beat, Suzy shifted into her party-host mode, "When will she be here? We'll have to plan a dinner party. I'll host it at our condo. I need a target date. How soon can you let me know something definite?"

Within two weeks, we gathered at the Bergner's condo. Present were Suzy and Dick Bergner, Myra Jolivet, Marlene McClinton (before her infamous on-air resignation as anchor at KHOU), Arthel Neville (stopping to visit Houston friends on her way to a new position she was starting with Fox News), Gail Brown (who worked in media, ran an after-school pick-up service, was a house-sitter, and eventually worked at Parks & Recreation in Houston). It was a fun evening and a nice welcome to Houston for Nina.

Fast forward to 2002. Suzy had a new fund-raising project; this time for Variety International, the children's charity that was begun by eleven theatre owners and showmen in Pittsburgh, Pennsylvania, in 1927 as a social club. "The Variety Club" did charitable acts. In December 1928, those eleven impresarios were playing cards backstage after a matinee at the Sheridan Square Theatre when they heard whimpering coming from the auditorium. When they went to investigate, they found an infant and a note:

> "Please take care of my baby. Her name is Catherine. I can no longer take care of her. I have eight others. My husband is out of work. She was born on Thanksgiving Day. I have always heard of the goodness of show business, and I pray to God that you will look out for her. — A Heart-Broken Mother"

Unsuccessful in locating the child's mother, the men decided to act as her Godfathers and dedicated themselves to providing for her support and education. They named her Catherine Variety Sheridan (their organization's middle name and the restaurant's surname where she was found). As word spread, more clothing, food, and toys than were needed were donated to help other disadvantaged children. Thus, was born the mission for Variety Club:

> Focusing on multiple unmet needs of children who are sick, disadvantaged, or live with disabilities and other special needs at a local, national, and international level. Our aim is to maximize the real, long-term positive social impact for all children. Variety welcomes the support of any person who shares our ideals and objectives.

Local chapters of Variety Club hold fundraisers within their respective communities every year. These are frequently multiple-day events, culminating in a performance featuring a headline entertainer and local entertainers from the community. From 2002-2004, Broadway star Ben Vereen was the star entertainer in

Houston. I received a phone call from Suzy asking if I would produce promotional materials, including broadcast commercials promoting Vereen's appearance. I made arrangements for a makeshift crew to meet us at our studio located near the Houston Astrodome late on a Saturday afternoon, just a few weeks before his 2002 scheduled appearance.

By the time Suzy arrived with Ben, the crew was ready for the shoot. The crew included a camera operator, an audio engineer, and a TelePrompTer operator. Myra Jolivet came with me to handle the makeup. Once introductions were made, Ben said we didn't need the TelePrompTer because he already knew the copy we were recording. Myra dusted Ben with face powder and he took his mark in front of the camera. I asked the camera to roll, and called action. Ben recited his lines and I called "Cut." I asked for a playback and we reviewed what Ben had recorded. It was perfect. I then suggested that we make three versions of the same spot, specific to each day they would be running, adding lines, "Saturday night, I'll see you at the Hobby Center..." and "Tomorrow, I'll be at..." and so forth. Once we had those versions in the can, I asked for Ben to adlib another spot, explaining the purpose of Variety, The Children's Charity.

> "I'm Ben Vereen. I'm proud to be part of Variety International, the Children's Charity that has been helping children with special needs since 1929. These children don't need pity. What they need is understanding and the support of people who recognize their ability to lead as normal lives as possible, despite the disabilities they may have. Your support for Variety International ensures that these children have the resources they need to overcome obstacles. Won't you join me by making a donation so these children can achieve their full potential in life?"

I found Ben Vereen to be a real professional. He came to do a job, for an organization he believes in and supports without reservation. He was as charming as I imagined him to be when I first saw him perform in *Pippin*. I count that afternoon as one of the highlights of my career. I was especially pleased when Nina and I were invited to one of the private events held for committee members who were working behind the scenes to make the 2002 Variety Fundraiser a success. A couple of weeks after we had filmed the spots, Ben Vereen was back in town for his concert. He was involved in many of the special events held during those few days, one of which was at the former Ritz Carlton Hotel, which had been converted to the St. Regis Houston.

This particular event was a private party held in one of the smaller meeting rooms. This room had been a Cigar Bar when it was the Ritz Carlton. It was lined in dark wood paneling, and a small stage had been installed on one side. We were seated at a front-row, centerstage table; members of an audience numbering about one hundred volunteers and their significant others. Ben Vereen took the stage after half an hour and thanked everyone for their hard work. He then explained his commitment to Variety and the work the organization does in cities across the country, helping children regardless of their parent's ability to pay. He then addressed the audience,

> "I cannot let this evening go without giving you a taste of Broadway." And with that, he launched into an a 'Capella version of "Magic to Do" from *Pippin*.

As he began his second selection, a woman from the audience rose from her seat, sat down at a piano on the stage, and began to accompany him. He had not noticed her joining him. And he was not happy about it. He immediately stopped singing and turned toward the woman,

"Would you please stop that."

The startled woman began to explain her presence, "I thought you needed some accompaniment…"

"I don't. Now, please go back to your seat," he said firmly.

Obviously mortified with embarrassment, the woman returned to her seat, gathered her belongings, and she and her husband left.

"That was a first. I've never had someone from the audience interrupt a performance like that," Ben said.

The audience sat in stunned silence, not knowing exactly how to react. Ben then picked up where he left off, starting his second selection. It was obvious that he was as shaken by the interruption as the audience was by his reaction. Both the audience and the performer were now uncomfortable. What began as a charming performance had turned into a disaster. His timing was off, and the audience, who had been previously warm and receptive, only gave polite applause when he finished the number. He cut his performance short. He briefly referenced his upcoming performance at the Hobby Center, apologized to the audience for cutting the evening short, and left the stage.

The audience had no way of knowing how many songs Ben was planning to sing before he cut his performance short. For the majority of the audience, he had done what he was supposed to do and the evening was over. However, there were some members who expressed concern while having after-dinner drinks. Of the group that went to the bar for drinks afterward, I would say their opinions were fifty-fifty—half the group agreeing with Vereen that the woman was wrong to get on stage with him; and the other half holding the belief that Ben had over-reacted. I personally felt his reaction was normal for a professional performer. The woman had no business getting on the stage, regardless of how good her intentions may have been. Was Ben's reaction to her harsh? Perhaps. Was he wrong? I don't think so. He was donating his time, just as members of the audience had donated their time for the cause. He deserved to be able to give his performance without interruption.

I expressed my opinion to those gathered in the bar. It had no effect in terms of swaying anyone to change their opinion. The group remained split, and that was that. Most agreed that the incident was unfortunate, although each side remained adamant in their point-of-view. Some expressed their disappointment toward Vereen's reaction, which I thought was unfair. Having been a performer myself, I understood his reaction. Those who did not have never been performers. That lack of reference was reflected in their opinions. It made me think about how quickly human beings are to make judgments without giving consideration to opposing viewpoints. I find that sad.

Allen Morris

Chapter 27
Brig. Gen. John C. Thomson:
Marking Military Milestones

People who make a career in the military are not usually looking for fame and fortune. That was certainly true for John C. Thomson III. His motivation was to make a difference for his country, which came from his deeply-rooted patriotism. His fame was derived from news reports about the war in which he was engaged, not necessarily about him personally. He became famous because of his role as a leader of the men and women who were on the front lines.

After his junior year at Tyler's Robert E. Lee High School, John Charles Thomson III decided he wanted a career in the military. His father was an Army Noncommissioned Officer (NCO) for twenty-two years, retiring in 1979, as a Master Sergeant. The elder Thomson served overseas tours in both Korea and Germany and saw combat duty in Vietnam. He understood and supported his son's decision, but advised that he should get a college education and go in as an officer.

"Being an army brat, I always thought joining the Army would be something I would want to do someday," says Thomson, "Going to West Point never seriously occurred to me until my dad brought it up and told me to write a letter to our congressman, Ralph Hall." Ralph Hall from Rockwall became a member of the House of Representatives in 1980. As the congressional representative for District 4, which included Tyler at the time, Hall had the privilege of nominating up to five candidates for an appointment to each of the service academies. As Thomson began his senior year at Lee, he wrote a letter to Hall.

"I received an answer from Hall's office stating interviews with cadet candidates were scheduled in Rockwall the following January," Thomson recalls. "My parents had to sign a permission slip because I was only seventeen. A panel of several retired generals conducted the interviews. I remember it was a cold Saturday. Because my name was last in the alphabet, my interview was the last of the day. A week later I found out I was chosen and would start basic training at West Point on the first of July 1982, about a month after our high school graduation."

The Continental Congress established The United States Army on June 14, 1775. It is the nation's oldest military branch, with some 1.1 million Soldiers among the active, National Guard, and Reserve components, the Army is also the largest branch of military service. The other branches of military service are the Navy, the Air Force, the Marines and the Coast Guard. There are three general categories of rank: Enlisted Personnel, Warrant Officers, and Commissioned Officers. Certain grades of enlisted personnel in the Army, Air Force, and Marine Corps have the status of Noncommissioned Officer (NCO). In the Navy and Coast Guard, the equivalent is Petty Officers. Warrant Officers, although not required to have college degrees, are highly trained specialists who remain in their primary specialty throughout their careers. Warrant Officers outrank Enlisted Personnel. Commissioned Officers are the "Top Brass," whose primary function is providing overall management and leadership in their area of responsibility. To become a Commissioned Officer, an individual must have at least a four-year bachelor's degree. Promotion to a higher rank requires demonstrating outstanding potential to serve at the next grade and also generally means completing a master's degree. Since the beginning, designations of rank mark career milestones for individuals serving in the Armed Services.

Memorial Day, May 27, 2013, marked the 27th anniversary of Thomson's commission as a 2nd Lieutenant in the United States

Army. Exactly one month later, on June 27, 2013, John C. Thomson III became a Brigadier General at a ceremony held at Fort Carson in Colorado Springs. He received his star from General Ray Odierno, the operational commander of the "surge" in Iraq and later the 38th and Chief of Staff of the Army. Thomson previously served as Odierno's Executive Officer in Iraq from April until July 2009, while Odierno was Commanding Officer of the Multi-National Forces-Iraq. After that assignment, as a Colonel, Thomson commanded the 41st Fires Brigade, 1st Cavalry Division at Fort Hood, Texas, from October 2009 until July 2011. Following that command, he went to the Pentagon and became the Director of the Chief's Coordination Group (CCG), serving once again under General Odierno. In April 2013, Thomson assumed the duties of Deputy Commanding General for the 4th Infantry Division at Fort Carson, Colorado.

During his promotion ceremony, Thomson made the following remarks:

> "I stand here with a great sense of humility, for we all know that the Army Profession is not about self. Any single promotion pales in comparison to the 187 streamers that adorn the Army colors. Those colors of courage represent campaigns that American Soldiers fought for, bled for, and died for since 1775. They are why we enjoy freedom and liberty today. To me, there is no greater honor than supporting and defending our Constitution. To do so as part of a team of professionals, all sworn to the same cause, is an incredible privilege.
>
> I'd like to thank my family. They are my strength and I know that they'll still be by my side after an inevitable retirement ceremony someday down the road.
>
> To Holly, Tyler, and Parker—I am standing where I am

today because of you. You are my rock, and I love you. Thank you for allowing me to be a Soldier.

Since 1775, the U.S. Army has fought and won our Nation's wars, successfully defending freedom around the globe. It is because of our Soldiers' sacrifices and that of their families that we enjoy our American way of life. The Army is the greatest institution on the face of the earth, and I am honored to serve in its ranks. Steadfast & Loyal, Army Strong!"

"The several opportunities to command over the course of the last two decades have been an incredible honor and privilege," Thomson confides his feelings about achieving the rank of Brigadier General. "It is the pinnacle of leadership. Commanders are responsible for the training and readiness of their soldiers, the welfare of their families, the accountability and maintenance of their equipment— everything. You are trusted with our Nation's sons and daughters. It is a tremendous responsibility."

Never one to shirk a responsibility, Thomson did four combat tours of duty before his latest promotion. There are two types of commissioned officers, Line and Non-line. A Non-line officer is a non-combat specialist, which includes lawyers, chaplains and medical officers. A Non-line officer cannot command combat troops. Thomson is a line officer. He deployed to Kandahar, Afghanistan, with the 4th Infantry Division Headquarters to serve as the deputy commander for Regional Command – South (RC-S) as part of the International Security Assistance Force (ISAF). His career experience and training prepared him for the role he played in Afghanistan.

"We were reducing our presence in Afghanistan during that time. We were transferring responsibility for security over

to the Afghan National Security Forces (ANSF),"
Brigadier General Thomson explained. "Our primary
function was to train, advise, and assist all elements of the
ANSF in southern Afghanistan—the army, the police, the
border security forces. It was part of the Inteqal process,
the Dari and Pashtu word for transition. The aim was for
Afghan forces to secure their national elections the
following spring and effect full security transition across
the country by the end of 2014."

Thomson's deployment to Afghanistan was for one year, until
July 2014. During that time, his family remained in the United
States. Family includes his wife Holly and their two sons, Tyler and
Parker. Tyler was born March 3, 1997 (the same day Thomson
achieved the rank of Major). Parker came along on April 26, 2002.
"The boys have grown up in a military family, they understand that
Dad gets deployed and cannot be with us all the time," Holly
explains using her dutiful-military-wife voice. Holly Davis knew
John Thomson in high school, although they were not close. Holly
remembers, "He was on the football team and sacked groceries at
Brookshire's."

Both Holly and John Thomson have strong ties to Tyler. John's
parents, Theresia and John, although divorced, both live in Tyler.
Holly's parents, Barbara and Charles Davis lived in Bullard. Her
father retired after forty-years with Brookshire's as EVP and COO.
He also sat on the board of directors. Holly was teaching sixth
graders at Bullard when she and John became acquainted again in
1991.

John recalls, "Desert Shield was underway and I was at Field
Artillery School in Fort Sill, Oklahoma. When Desert Storm started,
twenty of the twenty-two members of my class were informed we
were to ship out to Saudi Arabia the following Monday, as

replacements for expected casualties to liberate Kuwait. We had the weekend to go home. I made the five-hour drive to Tyler to see my parents and some high school buddies." That Saturday night, John and his buddies went to Bennigan's. Holly was there, too, with a group of friends. Holly remembers getting into a conversation with John, "He mentioned he was leaving for Saudi Arabia on Monday, and I asked him for his address so my students could send letters."

The Desert Storm action was over almost as soon as it started. Holly's students sent letters, and John wrote back. As soon as he learned he was being reassigned, John wrote that he was coming home to Texas for a couple of weeks before shipping back out to Germany. Holly invited him to speak to her class in Bullard.

> "I showed up wearing desert camouflage gear and ended up speaking to the whole school instead of just one class," John says. "After my presentation, I took questions from the kids. Most of the questions were the normal stuff that you get from eleven- and twelve-year-olds, 'What did you eat? Did you get shot at?' and then one little girl asked, 'Are you and Miss Davis getting married?' That was pretty funny."

> "We were married at Tyler's Marvin Methodist Church in the summer of 1992," Holly recalls. "We had a short honeymoon and I went to Germany with John."

> "As soon as we got back to Germany, I left for a four-week training exercise," John remembers how he made certain Holly got an international driver's license and settled into off-base housing before leaving her alone. "One thing that was helpful for Holly is that military families are a tight-knit community. They tend to be extroverted and are eager to help newcomers get oriented to a new situation."

"My life changed. I became an Army wife," Holly says. "It helped that I was able to teach at the Department of Defense Schools. Throughout our marriage, I tried to be supportive of John and his career, but at the same time, depending on the assignments and the location, I always managed to find opportunities to work and teach."

Any marriage takes work to make it last. Military marriages take more effort. Holly views her marriage and the efforts she and her husband both make as a team effort.

"We don't have limitless amounts of time together, so we are protective of the time we have and try to make the most of every moment. Whether it's time with the boys or time shared between just the two of us, I think John and I both do a pretty good job of being appreciative and respectful of each other."

John and Holly both agree that communication is important to the success of their relationship. When John is deployed or traveling, they stay connected through letters, email and Facebook.

"In all honesty," Holly confesses, "the letters and emails we've exchanged during his deployments are among the things I treasure the most. I think they are great reminders of the bond we share and the commitment we have to each other."

John is keenly aware of the sacrifices required of his family because of his career in the military. He does not take their support for granted.

"Whenever we have time together, we make every moment count. I want my family to have great memories of being together, but for the same reason, I want my boys to understand and appreciate the privilege of serving our country. The freedoms we enjoy come at a cost. I never want them to forget that," John says.

A military career appealed to John, in part, because he thought it would be a job where he did not have to wear a tie and sit in an office. Assignment to the Pentagon required wearing a tie and sitting in an office.

"What is different about my job, compared to civilians who work in offices, is that time in the Pentagon has a direct impact on the national security of our country. But it was a relatively small percentage of my overall time in the service," John rationalizes, "some people spend thirty years behind a desk. Deploying to Afghanistan puts me back with a tactical unit, with soldiers, at the tip of the spear. How many careers provide a person with such a variety of experiences, to travel to places all over the globe, to be part of an organization where you know what you do makes a tangible difference, where you get to be part of something greater than yourself?"

Brig. Gen. John C. Thomson III sums up his feelings about his life as an officer in the United States Army this way,

"I am a soldier. I work hard to serve my country and do my duty. I leave the policy decisions to the politicians. We must never forget that our country was attacked on 9/11. We need to do whatever is necessary to keep our country safe and recognized as the beacon of liberty throughout the world. I love our country. I love our freedoms. I want my kids, and their kids, to enjoy the same freedoms we had. It is an honor for me to serve our Nation. The Lord has blessed me and my family. The Army owes me nothing— I owe it. I will stay in the Army as long as my country needs me."

Holly and John agreed that when the time came to retire, Tyler would be the place where they would make their home. They both love Tyler and East Texas. They loved the city enough to name their first-born Tyler. Tyler is the place that means family to them. It is the place where their relationship started. Holly was a teacher. John was a soldier. It is fitting that their respective careers complemented one another. As the old saying goes, "If you can read this, thank a teacher. If you can read this in English, thank a soldier."

Ten days after his previous promotion, Thomson was deployed to Kandahar Province in Afghanistan. Serving in Afghanistan from July 2013 until July 2014 provided John with another opportunity of working in a complex, operational environment, among soldiers who share his commitment of service to our nation. At the time, he said being deployed put him back with a "tactical unit of soldiers, at the tip of the spear. How many careers provide a person with such a variety of experiences—where you get to be part of something greater than yourself?"

Following his deployment to Afghanistan, Thomson was assigned as the 75th Commandant of Cadets at his Alma Mater, the U.S. Military Academy at West Point. There, Thomson was responsible for the administration, discipline, and military training of cadets at the academy. A commandant candidate must be "a leader of character, competence, and commitment with the ability to educate, train, and inspire cadets to a lifetime of service to the Nation." During his time as commandant, Thomson was frequently seen in the company of cadets, leading them as they participated in company runs while training and on the sidelines at athletic competitions such as the annual Army-Navy football game, cheering the team on toward victory. His background of service in combat zones and working on the Joint Chiefs in Washington, DC staff, coupled with his affable personality and friendly demeanor, endeared him to the cadets. When his service at West Point ended,

Thomson turned his command over to Brig. Gen. Diana M. Holland was the first female to assume the role of commandant of cadets. Thomson was a true role model for aspiring officers.

> "No one asked me where I wanted to go; however, if anyone ever did ask, I would say, 'Texas!'"

Thomson explained that he was assigned to Fort Hood, Texas, in December. He was promoted to the rank of major general on October 2, 2015, and on January 7, 2016, he assumed command of the almost 25,000 soldiers that comprise the 1st Cavalry, a unit that was originally formed on September 13, 1921 at Fort Bliss, Texas.

> "Taking command of America's First Team is a great honor, and an even greater responsibility. The opportunity to command an operational formation is what every officer trains for, and dreams of fulfilling," Thomson states, his voice filled with confidence and determination. "There is no greater duty than to ensure our troops are ready to deploy at a moment's notice. Job number one is readiness. When the phone rings, it must be answered on the first ring; and we must be ready to respond to any contingency at that moment."

He was taking charge of a division that has an illustrious history. The unit was nicknamed "First Team" by Major General William C. Chase because they were "First in Manila," in February 1945. Later, they were "First in Tokyo," leading the U.S. Occupational forces into that city. The Division further distinguished itself with the first amphibious landing of the Korean War, and later they were the "First in Pyongyang," closing in the North Korean capital city. During the Vietnam War, the First Team flew in to relieve the besieged Marine base at Khe Sahn, and later they were the "First in Cambodia," in May 1970. First Team staged elaborate deceptions in support of the main ground forces in January

1991, as part of Operation Desert Storm. In 1998, the Division assumed the mission of Task Force Eagle, providing peace support operations in Bosnia-Herzegovina. From the beginning of the Global War on Terror, the 1st Cavalry Division has been deployed four times to Iraq in support of Operations Iraqi Freedom and New Dawn, and two times to Afghanistan in support of Operations Enduring Freedom and Operation Freedom Sentinel.

> "Taking command of the 1st Cavalry Division was a tremendous privilege, but came with significant duties and obligations. The higher you go in rank, the more people under your charge," Thomson explains the role of a commanding general in philosophical terms, "The mission always comes first, it is our Warrior Ethos. But the Army is about people, an intrinsically human endeavor. There are constant challenges on your time. You must be at the right place at the right time, and you must use time to its best advantage. It is imperative to take care of your family." When he says *family*, he means the troops under his command. "The decisions commanders make can affect the lives of thousands of other people. I have to always keep that in mind."

By 2016, Thomson had been serving his country for thirty-four years, four years as a West Point cadet and thirty years as an officer.

> "When you ask what the greatest highlight of my career is, the answer is very difficult for me to define," he said. He stops to think for a moment. Years of training prompts him to be as precise as possible, even when answering a personal question. "The highlights would be those few times when I had the privilege to lead our nation's sons and daughters. The opportunity to actually command is a small portion of a total career," Thomson said. "For most of us,

the first time was as a lieutenant. Then, with each change in rank, sometimes there would be an assignment that included a command opportunity. Out of the thirty years I have been an officer, I would estimate that only eight years offered a command opportunity."

While being a commander is the highlight, it is not what motivates John C. Thomson III. His motivation comes from deeper meaning, a part of his family heritage. As the son of a master sergeant, he grew up as an army brat and the value of service to one's country was instilled at an early age. The opportunity to serve the Nation, in whatever capacity needed, *that* is his motivation.

"I think of this assignment as my fifth time to be called to Fort Hood. The first was when I was in the second grade until the seventh grade when my dad was stationed there. I was the bat boy for the 1st Cav's baseball team one summer," Thomson recalls.

His second assignment to Fort Hood was in 1984 as a Cadet at West Point. He went through cadet troop leader training one summer with the 1st Cav, learning the basics of how to lead soldiers—his third time at Fort Hood was from 1998 to 2003 when he was a major and lieutenant colonel in the 4th Infantry Division. By that time, he was married with one child. He and Holly celebrated the birth of their second son, Parker, in 2002. His fourth time was from 2009 to 2011 as the commander of the 41st Fires Brigade, part of the 1st Cavalry Division. That unit is still there; it has only been re-designated as the Division Artillery Brigade. Now, his fifth time to be called to Fort Hood, he comes as Pegasus 6, the commander's call sign for the 1st Cavalry Division.

"I was especially honored to have so many people who played important roles in my past attend the change of command ceremony," Thomson says, acknowledging five separate groups who attended.

First were the members of his immediate family, wife Holly and his sons, Tyler and Parker. His mother Terry and his in-laws, Barbara and Charles Davis, all from Tyler were there. Next was a group of friends from his high school days. Ten in all made the trip, including a few with whom he played football at Robert E. Lee High School. Another group was some of his classmates from West Point. Most of them are no longer in the military, although a few continue to serve in uniform. He was especially pleased to see a group who were lieutenants in Germany together, their first assignment after graduating West Point.

> "None of us were married then, and we spent a lot of time together during the three years we were stationed in Germany. Several of us, including me, never went home during that time," Thomson remembers. Finally, there was a group of mentors, retired generals and senior non-commissioned officers, "All people who invested time in me when I was a young officer growing up. What success I achieved, is due to them. I owe them all a debt of gratitude. I am extremely humbled that they came to the ceremony," Thomson remarked.

One thing every person serving in the military has in common is how this choice affects their entire family.

> "When you sign up, you have to understand the impacts to your spouse and your children. They sacrifice as much as you do," Thomson says.

That means missed birthdays, missed vacations, missed athletic competitions, and more. Even if it is an assignment stateside, that means relocating to a new base. The children leave the friends they made in one location, and have to make new ones. They have to change schools.

> "My assignment to West Point meant my eldest son had to move during his senior year. That is a tough thing to ask a teenager," said Thomson.

Holly Thomson understood the sacrifices she would have to make when she and John were first married. At the time, John was assigned to duty in Germany. So, Holly's introduction to the military also involved a distant move, a foreign country, a different language, and a new culture.

> "It was a rewarding experience and I was quick to learn that a military marriage is a team effort," Holly says. Not long after arriving in Germany, the couple was separated when John went on a four-week training exercise. "Fortunately, I was able to teach at the Department of Defense School, so I had a job that kept me busy," Holly recalls.

> "One thing that helps is that military families are a tightly knit community," John remembers, "They tend to be inclusive and are eager to help newcomers get oriented to new situations."

> "Our lives changed again once we started a family. Since then, we have moved around a lot. Every time John got a new assignment, we moved," says Holly.

That includes ten moves for Holly, eight moves for Tyler, and six moves for Parker. Tyler attended six different schools by the time he graduated from high school, and by 2016, Parker was already in his fifth different school in eighth grade. On top of those moves, the family has also endured several lengthy separations when John deployed to combat zones.

> "The family cannot follow when you are in a combat zone,"

286

Thomson explains, "The key to a successful family life is making every moment count. Whatever time we have to spend together, we make the most of it. I want my family to have great memories of being together. I want them to know how much I appreciate the sacrifices they make. Without my family's support, I could not have the career I have."

Despite the sacrifices, John Thomson has no regrets about his career choice.

"I love what I am doing, and not because of the pay or the easy workload," Thomson said, then laughed, "I love my country. I love being around young men and women who want to serve their country and be part of something bigger than themselves."

What message would you want to give to the young men and women just leaving high school who are considering a military career?

"The first thing I would do is thank them for considering service to their country as an option. It is not for everybody," Thomson pauses a moment in thought. "Today we have an all-volunteer military. It takes a special breed of people to volunteer for a job that demands so many sacrifices. However, there is great reward in being part of a group of people that all take an oath to support and defend the Constitution of the United States, against all enemies, foreign and domestic. Words like teamwork, dedication and commitment have a special meaning for those individuals. The training they receive will teach them things about themselves, about how they have much more endurance than they ever imagined. They will learn the value of being on time, of hard work, of discipline. More than anything, they learn to live the seven Army Values—loyalty, duty, respect, selfless service, honor, integrity, and personal courage."

It has been said that the true measure of a man is calculated by how much he is willing to give in service of others. Major General John C. Thomson III has demonstrated his measure, time and again. I salute his passion and his patriotism. I applaud his dedication. I thank him for his service to our nation.

Chapter 28
Larry Hagman, Larry Dierker & Joel Grey:
The Highlight of My Season with the Astros

In the spring of 1979, I was under contract to Metromedia, traveling with the Astros Baseball team producing their out-of-town baseball games for broadcast on KRIV-TV 26 in Houston. My dad was proud when he heard I was working with a professional baseball team, since I was never athletic as a kid. My brother played all sports, but I was never any good at it. My talents were as a performer. My dad was always supportive of whatever I did, but my being with a professional sports team was something he could brag about with his buddies.

Shortly after I got the assignment to go on the road with the team, I met with Larry Dierker, who had recently retired as a baseball player and was hired to be the color announcer for our broadcasts. It was his first year in the broadcast booth, and he was a little nervous. I told him I would help him with being an announcer, and he could help me learn about baseball. We hit it off immediately and spent a great deal of time together on the road. During one of our many late-night outings while on the road, Larry told me about an idea he had for a book he wanted to write about baseball played in the Dominican Republic, Cuba, Puerto Rico, and other Caribbean locations during the off-season. The premise of his book, based on his own life experiences as a young pitcher, was that a pitcher had been sent to play ball during the winter break so a seasoned catcher could work with him to help improve his pitching. I thought it was a great premise for a movie. I kept that idea in the back of my mind throughout my time with the Astros.

I first met Dierker when he was a player with the Astros. For a couple of seasons when I was first working in television, Kenny Boles and I would go to Houston to film interviews with players. Kenny and I went to Lufkin High School together, and both of us were working at KTRE in Lufkin as sophomores. By 1971, Kenny was the sports anchor and I was directing the nightly newscasts. We shot the interviews on an old Auricon 16mm film camera that used mag-striped film. Although Kenny had given me instructions on how to load the film, he never let me do it, preferring to load it himself. He was afraid I might not do it right and we would return to the station with no stories! We would arrive at the Astrodome a couple of hours before gametime, so we could get the camera set up on the field at Homeplate. I would stay with the camera while Kenny went up to players and asked for the interviews. One of the first baseball interviews I ever filmed was with Dierker.

Dierker had been drafted by the Houston Colt 45s in 1964 at the age of seventeen. He had been scouted by none other than Tommy Lasorda, the Hall of Famer who managed the Dodgers from 1976-1996, winning two World Series Championships and twice being named Manager of the Year in the National League. In his scouting report during Dierker's senior year at William Howard Taft Charter High School, Lasorda stated that he "saw ideal mechanics and arm action that seemed right for the majors." Dierker's debut in the major league occurred on his eighteenth birthday, and he struck out Willie Mays in the first inning. He only played in three games that first season with the Colt 45s. The next year, the team became the Astros with the opening of Astrodome. Dierker made twenty-six mound appearances during the Astrodome's inaugural year, earning a 7–8 record, a 3.50 ERA, and 109 strikeouts in 146.2 innings. In 1968, he pitched the opening game of the season against the Pittsburgh Pirates, a complete game in which he allowed four runs on six hits. The Astros managed a 5-4 win. The next year, Dierker was the first Astro pitcher to win twenty games in a season, when he was only twenty-three. That year he compiled a 2.33 earned run average and threw 232 strikeouts over 350 innings, which landed him a spot on the National League All-Star Team. In 1971, Dierker was once again selected for the All-Star Team. On July 9, 1976, Dierker pitched a no-hitter against the Montreal Expos before a home crowd at the Astrodome. He was traded to the St. Louis Cardinals on November 23rd that year and played his final eleven games as a pitcher in 1977, before he was released on March 28, 1978. From 1979 until 1996, he would serve the Astros as their color commentator in the broadcast booth. On October 4, 1996, Dierker would be named as the twelfth manager of the Houston Astros, replacing Terry Collins. Houston finished in first place in four of the five years Dierker managed the team, winning the Division title in 1997, giving Dierker the distinction of being the sixth rookie manager to win a division title. The team set a club record 102 wins in 1998, a record not broken for twenty years. The team's 1998 performance resulted in Dierker being named NL Manager of the Year. The following season, the Astros won 97 games and their third consecutive NL Division title, the team's first division three-peat. The 1999 season was marred during a game against the San Diego Padres when Dierker suffered a grand mal seizure, requiring emergency surgery and five weeks of convalescence before he could return to helm the team for the duration of the season.

Much of Kenny's 1971 interview was about Dierker's appearance in the upcoming All-Star game, about which Dierker remarked, "It's a great honor, but I'm focused on how we're doing [the Astros] this season. We're on track to make the Divisional Playoffs, and that's what I'm looking forward to." The Astros would end the season tied for fourth place in the NL West; Dierker's season ended in August due to a rotator cuff injury. The team played 75 games that season, which was decided by a one-run margin. It was an all-time NL record that stood for twenty years.

The first game I worked with Dierker as a producer was during spring training, which took place in March 1979 at Cocoa Beach, Florida. I spent the first few days getting to know who the players were and what positions they each played. I read in The Sporting News that the Astros were considered one of the best rosters of pitchers in the National League. Since Dierker had been a pitcher, I was naturally interested in hearing his thoughts about the pitching roster:

> "There is no question that J.R. Richard dominates with his fastball and slider. You can't miss him, he's 6'8" and probably the most feared pitcher in baseball right now. Two reasons: he is hard to hit, and a batter getting hit by a wild pitch can get injured. He is phenomenal on the mound, but he doesn't have great control. Joaquin Andujar is also consistently good. He's a good starter and also good in the bullpen. He works well under pressure and has good control over the ball. [Joe] Niekro throws a mean knuckleball. It's a tough pitch to hit, and he controls it well, placing it in the strike zone wherever he wants it. His older brother is Phil Niekro, who plays for Atlanta. Ken Forsch is another pitcher to watch this season. [Joe] Sambito is one of the best closers in the National League. He had eleven saves in eighty-eight innings pitched last year, and collected ninety-six strikeouts."

The 1979 season would be a watershed year for the Astros. Ken Forsch threw a no-hitter in the Astrodome against the Atlanta Braves, winning the game 6-0 on April 7th. His brother Bob threw two no-hitters while pitching for the St. Louis cardinals, making the Forsch brothers the only set of brothers to throw no-hitters in MLB history. That same year saw the Niekro brothers, Phil and Joe, tie for the most wins—with 21 each—the only time in MLB history that brothers shared that statistic. This would be the first season that the Astros came the close to a divisional title. The following season, 1980, they would win their first post-season playoff berth.

It was just before the 1979 All-Star break when I moved my family to Tyler. My friend Frank Melton was the general manager at KLTV, at the time the only television station in the Tyler market. He wanted me to set up a creative services and production department for his station when my contract with the Astros was over. Since my wife was a small-town girl who didn't like living in Houston, especially alone with two small children while I was on the road, she liked the idea of moving. I was not involved with the All-Star Game, and I went home to Tyler and began the process of getting to know the people at the TV station, where I would be working after the baseball season was over. Linda Hagman was working at the television station at that time. She was interested in knowing what I was doing with the Astros and thought it was an interesting job. During a casual conversation, I mentioned that I was working on a treatment for a baseball movie. I told her the basic storyline and she said, "You should talk to my husband Gary. His brother is Larry Hagman. I bet Larry could hook you up with some movie people in California." I finished the treatment and had it bound with a cover that had the title emblazoned across the front in gold lettering: *Winter Ball*.

When I got back with the team after the All-Star Break, I showed my treatment to Dierker and told him an idea I had to invite Larry Hagman to sit with us in the broadcast booth during the one of the final three games on our schedule, which just happened to be against the Dodgers, September 28th, 29th, and 30th. I managed to get hold of Gary Hagman, and he called his brother and confirmed arrangements for Larry to join us in the broadcast booth for the first game of the series. Larry showed up wearing a cowboy hat, looking every bit like the character he was then playing in the hit series

Dallas. He also brought along his own "refreshments," which he mixed continually throughout the game.

In the broadcast booth that day were Gene Elston, doing the play-by-play, with Larry Dierker handling the color commentary, while Dwayne Staats was handling the radio broadcast with engineer Bob Green in the adjoining booth. Gene Elston began calling play-by-play for the Houston Colt 45s in their inaugural season of 1962, and continued calling for the Astros until late 1986. He was inducted into the Texas Baseball Hall of Fame in 1993, the Texas Radio Hall of Fame in 2002, and in 2006 was honored with the Ford C. Frick Award and inducted into the MLB Hall of Fame for his contributions as an announcer. Staats was with the Astros from 1977-1984, doing color with Elston and calling play-by-play on radio. He has been the Tampa Bay Rays play-by-play announcer since the team's inception in 1998.

During the September 28th 1979 game against the Dodgers, Larry Hagman was announced as a guest in the booth that day, and was on camera before the first pitch was thrown out. Although he was a Dodger fan, Larry Hagman would occasionally make on-air comments about the game as it progressed, especially during plays that favored the Dodgers.

When the game was over, with a win by the Dodgers, which eliminated the possibility of the Astros going into the post-season Divisional Playoffs, we left for Hagman's beach house in Malibu. Gary Hagman drove Larry Dierker in our rental car, and I rode with Larry Hagman in his recently purchased Mercedes. As we were walking through the parking lot, not surprisingly, Larry was swamped by a few autograph seekers. After signing autographs, he asked one of the group of girls if they wanted my autograph, too. They immediately looked at me, naturally registering no sign of recognition, but then smiled and thrust their autograph books at me

… just in case I was *somebody*. I signed, and wished them all luck, and we continued toward Larry's car. As we were making our way to the car, he leaned over to me and said, "That's kind of fun, isn't it?" referring to signing autographs.

As soon as we got in the car and started making our way out of the parking lot, Larry asked me to mix him another drink. I suggested that I could drive, not feeling especially safe with him driving. "Oh, nonsense. You don't know the way to Malibu," he said. "Now, let's talk about this movie idea you have."

As he drove, I explained that *Winter Ball* was about how major league baseball teams use the winter leagues, located in close proximity to the Caribbean, for their players to gain more experience. Especially with pitchers, this experience allows them to work on the basics of their role in learning how to read the game as it progresses. It also gives them time to develop more control over various types of pitches they can deliver and helps them learn what situations require which pitch to move their strategy of the game forward. For some of the older players, working out during the off-season can extend their playing careers, at least for another year or two. I added that much of the drama of the film comes out of the relationships developed between the characters as they express their desires and ambitions; one is just beginning a career with starry-eyed hope, and the other is trying to hang on to a career without admitting he knows his prime was passed long ago.

> "There is a role for you. You could play the world-weary manager of one of the clubs who takes an interest in a particular young pitcher," I said, in an awkward attempt to pique his interest.

> "That might be interesting," he replied as he exited at a sign pointing toward Malibu.

"I'll tell you who might be a good producer for a film like that," he finished the drink he had and handed me the cup, signaling me to make another. "Jerome Hellman. He won an Oscar for *Midnight Cowboy*. He does a lot of films that deal with a person's internal conflict. He did *Coming Home* and *The Day of the Locust.*"

"Do you know him?" I asked naively, and he looked at me and held out his hand for the drink.

"Yes, of course."

"Does he like baseball?"

"I don't know. He likes a good story," Larry said, laughing, taking a swig from the cup.

When we arrived at Malibu Colony, Hagman explained to me that he had bought his ocean-front house when he was starring in *I Dream of Jeannie* with Barbara Eden. He was one of the first residents of the exclusive beach community and was often referred to as "The Mad Monk of Malibu," the "unofficial mayor" of Malibu Colony. When one entered the street where his house was located, there were nothing but garages facing outward. It was like driving into an alley. There was a walkway leading from the driveway to the back entrance of the home. Walking into the house from the rear entrance, I first noticed a photograph hanging on a wall, just at the doorway leading to a powder room. The photo was of a television screen, with the image of Hagman's mother, Mary Martin, in her role as Peter Pan during a live presentation on NBC. Standing there looking at that photograph, I remembered watching that performance as a child. What made the photograph more memorable was a child standing in front of the television, reaching out to touch the screen. The child was Heidi Kristina Hagman, Mary Martin's granddaughter, who was probably about two years old when the photo was taken on December 8, 1960, the night the show was broadcast. As we walked further into the house, Hagman pointed out paintings hanging on the walls that had been done by his mother.

Mary Martin was one of the biggest stars on the Broadway stage, beginning in 1938 when she starred in Cole Porter's *Leave it to Me.* In the second act, she sang "My Heart Belongs to Daddy" and became an overnight sensation. That song was reprised in the film *Night and Day,* a biography of Cole Porter (played by Cary Grant), in which Martin played herself in a scene where she auditioned for Porter. It was one of her few movie appearances, and her rendition of "My Heart Belongs to Daddy" was established as her theme-song from that moment on. In 1949, she starred in *South Pacific,* a tremendous success that made her the toast of Broadway and for which she won a Tony Award. She toured with the play and opened in London's West End production in November 1951. Her next big success came in 1954 when she starred in *Peter Pan* and received her second Tony Award. She followed that with the live performance of the *Peter Pan* on television, winning an Emmy Award. From November 1959 through October 1961, she originated the role of Maria Von Trapp in *The Sound of Music,* capturing her third Tony Award.

Mary Martin was born in Weatherford, Texas, on December 1, 1913. Mary's father, Preston Martin, was a successful lawyer. Her mother, Juanita Presley, taught violin lessons. Mary, her sister Geraldine, and their friend Marion Swofford formed a trio that sang at the bandstand on the courthouse square on Saturday nights, dressed in bellhop costumes. It was the beginning of Mary Martin's quest to become a performer. When she was in high school, she began dating Benjamin Hagman, and they became sweethearts. When Mary left to finish school at Ward-Belmont in

Nashville, Tennessee, she soon was homesick for Weatherford, her family, and Benjamin. During a visit home, the couple persuaded their parents to allow them to get married on November 3, 1930. After ten months, she was pregnant and was forced to leave Ward-Belmont and return home to Weatherford, where her son Larry was born on September 21, 1931. At first happy to begin their new life together, it did not take long for Mary to become frustrated with her role as a wife. At seventeen, she was restless and bored and wanted more out of life. Her sister Geraldine convinced her to open a dance school. To learn more dance steps, Mary went to California to study dance at the Fanchon and Marco School of the Theatre. When she returned, the sisters opened a dance school in nearby Mineral Wells. Confiding in her father that she was miserable in her marriage, her father replied that she married too young. Shortly after, he began to prepare for divorce proceedings. In the meantime, Mary returned to California, leaving her young son in the care of her parents. Mary and Benjamin were divorced in 1936 when Larry was a five-year-old.

Young Larry lived with his maternal grandmother in Texas and California when his mother became a contract player for Paramount in 1938. In 1940, Mary Martin met and married Richard Halliday and, the following year, gave birth to a daughter, Heller. Larry was shipped off to the Black-Foxe Military Institute and later briefly attended Woodstock Country School, a boarding school in Vermont. When his mother resumed her Broadway career, Larry was once again living with his grandmother in California. A few years later, his grandmother died, and Larry joined his mother in New York briefly. In 1946, he rejoined his father in Weatherford, Texas, where he attended Weatherford High School, graduating in 1949. Although his father wanted him to follow in his footsteps and become a lawyer, Larry was more interested in theatre. He enrolled in Bard College, majoring in dance and drama, but dropped out after a year.

Larry's professional acting career began in 1950 with a role at the Woodstock Playhouse in Woodstock, New York. He also worked in Dallas at the Margo Jones Theatre as a production assistant and later appeared in *The Taming of the Shrew* in New York. In 1951, he joined the London production of *South Pacific*, starring his mother, and stayed in the show for nearly a year. In 1952, he received a draft notice and enlisted in the United States Air Force. Stationed in London, the majority of his military career was spent entertaining troops in the UK and at U.S. bases across Europe. After leaving the Air Force in 1956, he returned to New York and appeared in William Saroyan's off-Broadway play *Once Around the Block*. His Broadway debut occurred in the 1958 production of *Comes a Day,* followed by four other Broadway plays: *God and Kate Murphy*, *The Nervous Set*, *The Warm Peninsula*, and *The Beauty Part*. He also appeared in numerous live television productions, the first of which was in 1957, with Beverly Garland, in the crime drama *Decoy*. His film debut occurred in 1964 in *Ensign Pulver*, which featured Jack Nicholson, followed that same year with a featured role in *Fail Safe,* starring Henry Fonda. In 1965, he was cast as Major Tony Nelson, an astronaut who discovers a genie in a bottle in the sitcom *I Dream of Jeannie,* with Barbara Eden in the title role. This was the television series that established Hagman as a star and also brought him financial independence.

Shortly after our arrival at his Malibu Colony home, Hagman introduced us to his wife, Maj (a Swedish name pronounced 'My'), suggesting we change into swim trunks and go out to the beach.

The Pacific water was colder than I expected but refreshing after spending the afternoon in the announcer's booth at Dodger Stadium. As we strolled along the beach, virtually everyone we encountered spoke to Hagman. Each time, our congenial host introduced us to one of his neighbors. Some were names I immediately recognized. Each time he introduced us, the person we encountered immediately launched into a dialogue about what project they were working on, what script they had just read, or how they were having trouble structuring a deal. Nobody asked how the family was doing, what vacation plans they had, or anything of a personal nature. It was all strictly related to the business. As we were walking away from some writer who hadn't been able to get anyone interested in a script he had written, Hagman noticed that both Dierker and I had noticed an extremely attractive woman jogging on the beach, wearing a revealing bikini.

> "I want you to meet another neighbor, Dyan Cannon," Hagman said as he called out to Dyan. She asked what Larry had been up to as she approached us. "I've been at the Dodger game with these guys. This is Larry Dierker, a former pitcher with the Astros and now their color announcer. And this is Allen Morris. He is the television producer for the Astros."

> "Nice to meet you both. Who won the game?" Dyan inquired.

> "The Dodgers," Dierker replied, "But our boys put up a good fight."

> Then, Hagman turned to me and said, "You know Dyan as an actress, but she is also a producer. She is the only actress who has been nominated for Oscars for acting and producing. She is someone else who might have an interest in *Winter Ball*."

I remembered seeing her on the Oscar telecast in April when she was nominated for her performance in *Heaven Can Wait*. Now, we were standing together, nearly naked, on the beach in Malibu.

300

We stood on the beach with Dyan as I gave her my thirty-second elevator pitch for *Winter Ball*. She listened politely. As I spoke, I was marveling at how incredibly attractive she was. In my mind, I was trying to calculate her age. At that time, she was forty-two, but to me, she looked thirty-two.

"Have you read it?" Dyan directed her question to Hagman.

"Just their prospectus. I thought this could be a project Jerome could be interested in. It's a novel idea for a baseball picture. And there's a part for me in it," he said, smiling broadly.

"I'm going to Texas soon for a film with Willie Nelson *(Honeysuckle Rose)*," said Dyan. "And I just got a script for a film with Al Pacino *(Author, Author!)* that looks like fun. I don't know how well a baseball picture would do."

"It's not so much about baseball as it is about what a player goes through to become a successful ball player," Dierker interrupted.

I was struck, at the time, by how everyone we met was only talking about what projects they were or were not doing. I suppose that is true of every industry. For some reason, it struck me as particularly interesting that people in movies always talk about business. And why not? It was no different than what happened in my business. Every conversation I had with my contemporaries centered on what we were doing or were planning to do. I was beginning to realize that business is business, no matter what the field. Still, I was surprised they were not talking about other actors. Was I expecting gossip? Maybe. Actually, I had no idea what I expected, if anything. I was simply soaking up the atmosphere of being in Hollywood, talking Hollywood with Hollywood people.

As the sun was beginning to dip into the ocean, golden shimmers of light spread across the expanse of the Pacific. It was an incredible sight, and as we walked back toward Hagman's house, the flags that rimmed his deck were flapping in the breeze. I turned around to catch the sun just as it dipped below the distant horizon, and the sky was beginning to fade into a darker shade of blue. As we walked toward the house, Hagman explained to me how he had bought the property with the money he had made off of *I Dream of Jeannie.*

> "It's been a great investment. I rented the place to Julie Andrews and her husband, Blake Edwards, every summer for the past few years. They pay $15,000 for the summer, and I take my family to Sweden to visit my wife's family. We've only been back for a couple of weeks."

As we walked into the house, Gary announced that Maj said dinner would be ready in half an hour.

> "Just enough time for the spa," Larry Hagman said. He refreshed our drinks and led us to the spa.

He said it was designed by his wife and was supposed to massage different parts of the body for five minutes at a time. As we stepped in, I realized the bench where one sat was at different levels, with jets hitting different body parts. Where I sat was the highest level; Dierker sat to my left, slightly lower, although due to his being much taller than I, our heads were now at the same level. The water coming out of the jets was hot, quite a contrast to the cold ocean water. We had been in there for only about two minutes when another guest arrived. He greeted us and handed Larry Hagman a small box.

"Open it. I thought you might enjoy these," he said. Hagman opened the box, which was filled with mushrooms.

"These look wonderful," Hagman said, handing the box to Maj. "We can have these later," he said as Maj took the box into the kitchen, where she resumed preparations for dinner.

The new guest then stripped down and eased himself into the water next to me. "We haven't been introduced. I'm Joel Grey."

I had recognized him when he arrived. Hagman then introduced Dierker and explained that we were with the Astros and had been at the game together earlier in the day. He also explained that we were looking for a buyer for our film *Winter Ball.*

"So, what do you do?" Joel asked me.

"I'm a producer for the games. I arrange the crew that covers the game and travel with the team," I replied.

"And what do you do?" he asked Dierker.

"I'm the color announcer. I used to be a pitcher with the Astros," he replied.

"I think I've heard of you," said Joel to Dierker. "Weren't you right out of high school when you started playing pro-ball?"

"Yes. I was drafted when I was seventeen and pitched my first pro game on my eighteenth birthday," Dierker replied.

As we continued our time in the spa, I mentioned to Joel that I had done a research paper about his father, Mickey Katz, while in college.

"How did you know that name?" Joel asked, somewhat surprised.

"I was looking for an unusual subject for my thesis and settled on the Yiddish Theatre. When I started doing the research, I read an article about a clarinet and saxophone player working in Cleveland before the war. His name was Mickey Katz, and he eventually met Spike Jones, who invited him to Hollywood. Sometime after that, he recorded a comedy record based on 'Home on the Range.'"

"'Haim Afen Range.'" Joel said the Yiddish title.

"As I understand, before going to Hollywood, he started a band, *Mickey Katz and His Krazy Kittens,* touring with Betty Hutton in USO Shows across Europe during the war."

"He did. In fact, they gave him an officer's rank. That was as close as he got to military service. It was after the war that he first went to Hollywood. That was where he recorded 'Haim Afen Range.' It was a huge hit. Later, he produced a Yiddish stage revue called *Borscht Capades.* That was in 1948. I was in that show," Joel said, grinning. "It bombed!"

"I think I read that his band is in the Julie Andrews movie *Thoroughly Modern Millie,"* I said.

"That's true. They back Julie when she sings a Yiddish song at a Jewish wedding. I'm really surprised that you have heard of Mickey Katz."

"I'm surprised to be sitting in a hot tub with his son!"

As we sat there, Hagman told us it was time to rotate to the next position in the spa. As I moved to the next position, I slipped under the water while sipping my Scotch. I came up, now sipping the spa water from my glass.

"It looks like *Dallas* is a hit," Joel said to Hagman. "What do you think about it?"

"If it goes like it has, I think this series could get me well!" Hagman said, meaning that the success of the *Dallas* series could bring him enormous financial rewards. "We'll see how it does this next season. If it can stay on top in the ratings, I intend to cash-in!"

It would be at the end of the next season, March 21, 1980, when the famous "Who shot J.R.?" cliffhanger would captivate viewers worldwide. During the hiatus, when Hagman took off for his annual trip to Sweden with his family, he left *Dallas* director and executive producer Leonard Katzman with an ultimatum to raise his salary. It was a calculated gamble on Hagman's part. He was counting on continued publicity throughout the summer, fueled by speculation regarding his salary demands, to bolster his position with the CBS Network. It was CBS who would be paying for an increased salary. It was CBS who would reap the benefits if J.R. Ewing survived being shot and the show climbed even higher in the ratings. The only question that really mattered to CBS execs was, "Would the show survive without Hagman as J.R.?" The general consensus among CBS executives was that without J.R., *Dallas* would not likely survive another season. J.R. was *Dallas*. When the answer to "Who shot J.R." was provided to viewers on November 21, 1980, the show was seen by a worldwide audience of 350 million viewers. In the U.S., it received a 53.3 Nielsen rating and a 76% share with an audience estimated at 83 million people, more than the number of people who voted in the presidential election earlier in the month. The original *Dallas* series continued to climb in the ratings and would run for fourteen years, from 1978 until 1991.

When dinner was ready, Maj brought each of us a blue bathrobe. Climbing out of the spa, only Dierker and I were wearing swim trunks, to which Joel remarked, "You Texas boys are the modest type." As we changed into the bathrobes, Joel announced that he and his wife were meeting friends for dinner in Brentwood, where they were planning to buy a house. Since they were houseguests of the Hagman's, they planned to return later in the evening. In the meantime, the rest of us sat down at the dining table, looking like blue monks gathered for vespers and the evening meal.

I don't remember what Maj served us, but I remember switching from Scotch to some red California wine.

> "I have a friend who operates a vineyard in the valley," Hagman announced. "I think you will find this wine finishes well. Does anyone care to say grace?"

> When no one responded, I said, "Let us bow our heads. Father in heaven, we ask thy blessings on this meal and upon this gathering of friends and family. Forgive us our sins and grant us thy peace."

> Everyone then responded with "Amen."

Conversation during dinner centered on *Winter Ball*, with Dierker providing background on where the idea originated and his experiences playing *Winter Ball*. He related stories that had more to do with learning how to party than about learning how to be a better pitcher.

> "There was a lot of work done on perfecting pitches and working with a catcher about the role a pitcher plays in setting the pace of a game." Dierker explained, "that things might not come naturally but are really vital for becoming a successful pitcher in the majors,"

He said there was a great deal of drinking and smoking joints when the teams were not at practice or playing a game. One of his stories dealt with how the team managed to get out of the way of rebels who were in the process of attempting to overthrow the government of that particular country. It may have been Venezuela; I don't remember after all the intervening years that have passed. What I do recall is the team was in the midst of a game when the ballpark was suddenly filled with angry men carrying guns and shouting in Spanish. Dierker threw a full-count strike, ending the game. As the team made their way to the dugout, they were told to keep going and exited the stadium.

> "It was one of those things you don't want your mother reading about in the newspaper. You know how mothers worry!" Dierker said, laughing.

When our evening was over and it was time to leave, we got dressed and said our farewells. Gary was staying at his brother's house, and Dierker and I took the rental car and drove to his parent's house in Woodland Hills, where he had grown up. We slept that night in the bedroom he grew up in. It still had the look of a high schooler's room, complete with twin beds and pennants and posters hanging on the walls. In the morning, before we left for the airport and the flight back to Houston, we took a run, following the same route he ran when he was a high school athlete. We stopped every now and then, and he would relate a memory from his past of growing up in LA Suburbia.

I would not see Larry Hagman again until two years later, in 1982. By then, Hagman's gamble had paid off and he secured one of the most lucrative contracts in television history. Several scenes of the *Dallas* series were actually filmed at the Studios at Las Colinas and at locations in the Dallas area. Hagman took every opportunity to ingratiate himself into Dallas society. When shooting in Dallas, he attended many social functions. This particular evening was a fundraising dinner held on the largest soundstage at the Studios at Las Colinas, a movie-making complex that had been built to attract more movie business to the Dallas/Ft. Worth Metroplex. Hagman was the honorary chair for the event and was playing host to the metroplex movers and shakers who were paying a thousand dollars a plate for the dinner, which included a performance of a Broadway-bound production called *Movie Star.*

It was a musical revue conceived by Billy Barnes and costume designers Ray Aghayan and Bob Mackie. I was called in at the last minute to direct a four-camera shoot of the live production, which the play's producers intended to use to help attract investors. One of the leading actors in this production was Brad Maule, who was a fellow student when I was at Stephen F. Austin State University, and who would later play the role of Dr. Tony Jones on the daytime soap *General Hospital.*

A makeshift control room had been set up in a service corridor outside of the main studio where the dinner was taking place. I was standing by the camera monitors and recorders talking over headsets to the crew when I was suddenly tapped on the shoulder. I turned around and was greeted by Larry Hagman, who urged me come out and say hello to Maj. When I was called to direct, I didn't have time to go home and dress; therefore, I arrived wearing sneakers and wrinkled jogging sweats. I explained to Hagman that I was not properly dressed for going into the dining area, but he insisted, saying,

> "I am the Chairman of the dinner. I give you permission to come out and say hello to Maj, dressed as you are!"

We had a brief reunion at his table, where I am certain the dignitaries seated at Hagman's table were curious to know who the unkempt person was, speaking so familiarly with Larry and Maj. I stayed only a few moments and went to my position backstage to begin the show. The audience seemed to enjoy the performance, laughing at all the joke lines and applauding at great length after every musical number. *Movie Star* was an entertaining bit of fluff that paid homage to the glory days of Hollywood and the movie business. It was an appropriate selection considering the dinner was taking place on a real soundstage in a movie studio where part of America's number one television program was filmed. I am certain many in the audience came because of both the location and the opportunity of spending an evening with J.R. Ewing, the reprobate character Larry Hagman played so well. In the days following this evening, I edited the tape of the performance and sent it off to the producers. *Movie Star* would never make it to Broadway the following November as planned. *Winter Ball* also failed to find backing and went nowhere.

It would be three decades before I saw Larry Hagman again. In March 2012, he and Linda Gray, his co-star on *Dallas*, came to Tyler, Texas, to take part in "Black Tie and Diamonds, Dallas Style," at the Cowan Center on the campus of The University of Texas at Tyler. This fundraising event was designed to celebrate the individuals and organizations who had been instrumental in developing the Cowan Center as the premier entertainment venue of East Texas. The guest list was comprised of an exclusive group of

Tyler's leading socialites, who arrived and walked the red carpet, along with Larry Hagman and Linda Gray, as photographers flashed photos. It was just like a Hollywood premiere.

The reboot of the *Dallas* series was in production, and the stars were available (for a nominal fee) to make the ninety-minute limousine ride from Dallas to spend an evening with fans from Tyler. The planned evening included dinner on the stage at the Cowan Center. Susan Thomae-Morphew, the Executive Director the Cowan Center, called Jennifer Gaston, the editor at *Tyler Today Magazine,* inviting us to conduct an interview with Larry and Linda during the afternoon before the event. Jennifer and I arrived at the Cowan Center just as their limousine pulled up. As we settled at a table for the interview, while the staff was busily preparing for the evening event, Larry looked at me, saying,

> "I remember you! The last time I saw you was at a fundraiser at the Studios at Las Colinas," he flashed his mischievous smile and turned to Linda, and exaggerating the incident somewhat said, "He nearly drowned in the spa at my Malibu beach house." Turning back to me, he asked, "What have you been up to for the last thirty years?"

Thomae-Morphew had intended for us to spend about five minutes getting information for an article in the magazine. Instead, we spent nearly an hour, much of the time taken up with Hagman reminiscing about our past times together and explaining to Linda how we originally met and our subsequent meetings together. In between his explanations, I managed to ask enough relevant questions to write an article for the magazine. The whole time we were sitting there, Thomae-Morphew kept tapping her watch in an attempt to get us to wrap up. The more frustrated she became; the more Larry would launch into another subject. At one point he leaned over to me, whispering, "Is she always so nervous?"

Larry Hagman was an eighty-year-old liver transplant survivor when the *Dallas* reboot began production. He had endured several years of serious health issues, including surviving throat cancer in 2011. Despite not being as agile as he once was, he still had his quick mind and devilish sense of humor. He was looking forward to returning to the role of J.R. Ewing. However, not long after our final interview, in July 2012, he was diagnosed with myelodysplastic syndrome, a precursor to myeloid leukemia. Larry died the following November, two months after his 81st birthday.

Larry spent his life in the shadow of one of the theatre's most famous thespians, his mother Mary Martin. Through luck and hard work, he managed to become famous in his own right, probably becoming even more famous than his mother. He once told me,

> "Because of its world-wide syndication, *Jeannie* is bigger than *Dallas.* When I travel in Europe, more people recognize me as Major Nelson than they do as J.R. Ewing. Because I've had so much exposure on television, I became famous."

The level of his fame was once put into perspective by his mother. Larry tells about an evening during which he and his mother were together at a dinner,

> "An autograph seeker approached and asked her, 'How do you feel about your son being an icon?' to which she immediately replied, 'My son is a television star. I am an icon.' Her point was made even more clearly one evening when we both attended a performance by our mutual friend Joel Grey. At some point during the performance, Joel told the audience there were two celebrities in the audience he wanted to introduce. 'Ladies and gentlemen, you know him as J.R. Ewing, my friend Larry Hagman.' I stood up and

received a moment of polite applause and sat back down. 'With Larry is his mother, Mary Martin.' The entire room stood up and my mother was applauded for a show-stopping five minutes."

Perhaps the most important lesson I learned from Larry about fame, is how to handle it. One of the things he maintained throughout his life was a healthy respect for the legions of fans who frequently asked for his autograph. More than many celebrities in his position, he took the time to acknowledge his fans and spent time with them. In his 2001 memoir, *Hello Darlin' Tall (and Absolutely True) Tales About My Life*, Larry said that he would sign autographs for anybody who asked, but he made them tell him a poem, say a prayer, or sing a song in return.

"I thought that if I gave my signature away people didn't place any value on it. But if they had to work for it, and essentially pay for it, they got an experience they never would have gotten if I'd signed and we never interacted. Both of us walked away with something memorable."

He was grateful for the adulation of fans, even if he really never truly believed he deserved it. When I once asked him how he felt about his fame, he responded philosophically.

"I'm an actor. I can hardly compare myself to people whose lives are spent saving the lives of others, like a doctor; or those who help people in legal trouble, as my father did. There are so many who enter the acting profession and never make it big. I got lucky. For most of my career, I managed to keep working. And while I did a lot of projects strictly for the money, I am proud of several, ones that I believe, my contribution helped the picture. *Harry and Tonto* is one. Playing Art Carney's ne'er do well son was a terrific experience. It's a heart-warming story and Art deserved the Oscar he won for his performance. Working with Henry Fonda in *Fail Safe* was another experience that taught me a lot about the craft of acting. I managed to meet and work with some really talented and remarkable people because of this profession. I always learned from those experiences. Becoming someone who was recognized everywhere was gratifying, because it was a compliment and a sign that my work was appreciated. But it came to me because I was seen by so many people on television. Had I worked strictly in the theatre or films, I would never have achieved the level of fame that eventually came my way. Television did that."

I spent my life working in television without achieving the level of fame I sought. Was that because I was behind the camera instead of in front of it? Perhaps. Or, was it because of the types of projects I worked on? Maybe so. I managed to work on a handful of productions that had a national audience. Maybe, if there had been more of those, fame would have followed. Or, perhaps it was just not in the cards to attain the fame I wanted. Mother's words have always rung in my ears: "…there are more important things in life than being famous. You should aspire to be a good person."

Allen Morris

Chapter 29
Nancy Ames and Danny Ward:
The Forefront of the Event Industry

There was a time in the American theatre when the biggest attraction was always relegated as the last act on the bill. The reason was simple: no other act was likely to top it, and no other act wanted to follow it. I purposefully left this spot in my book for the final chapter because I wanted to end with recollections about two professional colleagues who became close friends. They are the proprietors of Ward & Ames Special Events, Inc., a special event management and production company that since 1982 has been responsible for producing large-scale events for nationwide corporate clients, major golf tournaments, charities and philanthropic organizations, including all of the Texas Medical Center institutions, to name just a few.

They have produced events for five Presidents of the United States, in and out of Washington D.C., as well as in Houston. Many of these events were connected to their dear friend, President George Herbert Walker Bush 41, and President George W. Bush 43. Several of these events also involved heads of state, innumerable foreign leaders, assorted dignitaries, governors and mayors as well as contracting iconic talents to perform at these events. Among the entertainers they engaged were Bob Hope, Andy Williams, Tony Bennett, Peggy Lee, Burt Bacharach, Gladys Knight, Bernadette Peters, Shirley MacLaine, Lionel Ritchie, John Mellencamp, The Beach Boys, Santana, Momix, Audra McDonald, Placido Domingo, Linda Ronstadt, Yo Yo Ma, Lady Gaga, Stevie Wonder, Imagine Dragons, and too many other performing artists to name.

I first met Danny Ward and Nancy Ames in the '70s when I was in Houston producing *#26 Morning Place* and *Paws for the Night* on KDOG-TV 26. At that time, Nancy had her own midday variety/talk show on KPRC-TV 2, the NBC affiliate. Danny, a native of Houston, was the musical director for Nancy's live performances, concert tours, and television shows. I first met them at an industry cocktail party, probably in 1977. Neither of them remembers meeting me, and why should they? I was a producer from a competing independent station, producing shows they had never heard of or seen. A year or so later, I met Nancy again when one of her friends, Warner Roberts, began a talk show on KDOG. Warner's show was produced by Terri Hartman, who was the daughter of Nancy's producer, Jonni Hartman. Not long after that, my boss, Al Footnick, started dating Terri. They eventually became Mr. and Mrs. Footnick. Al Footnick was a director whose early experience was at NASA, where he was responsible for what went on in the air during the Gemini program.

He directed many of the first national commercials that I worked on, including the Clio-winner I mentioned earlier in this book. I learned a great deal about directing by editing Al's commercials. His mentorship helped me progress in my career. It was Al Footnick who recommended that I be the producer for the Astros baseball team when Metromedia bought KDOG and renamed it KRIV. Al and Terri became close friends with Nancy and Danny. As I began writing this book, I began to think about James Burke's series *Connections* on PBS. In it, he delves into inventions that changed history and how progress over time was interconnected. It made me think about the connections among people, and specifically the people I have written about in this book, and their connections to one another. For instance, when I got to know Danny Ward, I discovered that he had gone to Waltrip High School. The connection there is my mother-in-law, Patsy Grubbs, who was the guidance counselor at Waltrip when Danny was a student there.

Danny was the second of four children, reared in a Catholic family that attended Saint Rose of Lima Catholic Church in the Garden Oaks neighborhood of Houston, which was located just north of what is now Loop 610 where it intersects with Ella Boulevard. A member of the Dominican Order of Saint Joseph, Sister Ann Agatha, taught Danny to play the piano.

> "When I was twelve or thirteen years old, I played the organ during masses," Danny remembers, "and that was my first endeavor at [musical] improvisation." By the time he was fourteen, he was playing two nights a week at Doyle's, an Italian restaurant, "…earning a whopping buck forty an hour. I was playing everything from jazz to popular songs and the standards."

His formal education was from the Houston Independent School District, at Waltrip High School, where he played for the theatre department, conducted the orchestra, played in the marching band, sang in the choir and spent time with his best friend Patrick Swayze, who was known as "Buddy" at that time. Buddy's mother Patsy was a teacher at Waltrip.

> "When I was a senior, I taught a sixth-period senior jazz band class. You could say that I was entrenched in music. Bert Roth was the band director at Waltrip, and he also directed the marching band at Rice University, where he brought me in as a high school student to play trombone and tuba. This was when Rice's "The Mob" band was running onto the field to get into position just in time to start playing 'Classical Gas,' and of course, in a Hot Dog formation.' It was a silly time for me, but I learned a lot."

Danny also played for Patsy Swayze's dance classes. Patsy was friends with Greg Harrison, who was the choreographer for the Gold Diggers on the Dean Martin Show. When the show came to Houston to audition potential new dancers for the show, Danny was asked to play for the auditions.

> "Francie Mendenhall got to be a Gold Digger, and Buddy became a big star in movies," Danny recalls.

After high school, Danny enrolled at the University of Houston,

> "But that only lasted two years. I was interested in figuring out how to make a living in music. I worked on how to accompany singers, and spent a lot of my time learning about composition, orchestration and other practical tools needed in music. I learned how to write for horns, vocals, and strings, which score worked best, and how recording sessions were done. The focus of the music department at U of H at the time was cranking out band directors for school districts and for developing musicians who wanted to make their careers playing in symphony orchestras. The school did not, at the time, have a curriculum that aligned with my professional music goals."

The early 70s in Houston offered local musicians with many opportunities for work. Because of his mastery of so many musical genres, Danny worked constantly. He played in a jazz trio, played with several different bands including rock bands and bands that specialized in the Big Band sound.

> "I had one of the first Arp 2600 synthesizers, a Minimoog, Hammond B-3, and other keyboards, which helped increase demand for my work as a musician."

It was a couple of years after that when he first met Nancy Ames, whose career had taken off after becoming the "That Was the Week That Was" girl on NBC in 1963.

Ames, nee Nancy Hamilton Alfaro, was born into Washington D.C. diplomatic society, the daughter of a prominent physician and the granddaughter of Ricardo Joaquin Alfaro, who served as the President of Panama from January 16, 1931, to June 5, 1932. Her grandfather was instrumental in drafting the Spanish language version of the United Nations Charter in 1945, co-authored its Bill of Rights, and was Chairman of the Legal Committee of the United Nations General Assembly that drew up the "Convention on Genocide" in 1949. In addition to multiple Ambassadorial posts, he served as Vice-President of the International Court of Justice in the Hague until his retirement in 1964.

Nancy graduated from the Holton-Arms School, and then attended Bennett College, studying architecture and design, and completed her formal education in Europe. Her career as a performing artist began with a role in Hal Prince's Broadway show *Tenderloin*. That led to singing in supper clubs, being discovered and managed by Harry Belafonte, and in 1963, Leland Hayward and Sir David Frost hired her for the signature singing role, TW3 Girl, in NBC's *That Was the Week That Was*. Based on Frost's original British version of the political satire with the same name, it ran first in the United States as a one-hour NBC special on November 10, 1963. Within two weeks of its airing, President John Kennedy was tragically struck down in Dallas.

Because a TW3 tribute show was the only outside program to air during NBC's 4-day coverage surrounding the President's funeral, it became a regular part of the NBC's mid-season schedule beginning on January 10, 1964.

> "I later learned that I was the only cast member to appear on every episode of *That Was the Week That Was* during its 2-year run," Nancy recalls, "It launched my career in television."

TW3 lampooned political figures and its satirical skits about the pressing issues of the day were ripped from the headlines. The opening of the show, sung with a comedic slant by Nancy, changed each week reflecting the top stories in the news with a comedic, and was often a scathing rebuke of the newsmakers themselves. It was a completely new approach to entertainment and was not immediately understood or accepted by audiences and critics.

The show slowly built a following; however, it was frequently pre-empted by political programming paid for by the Barry Goldwater campaign. In October of 1964, before that year's presidential elections, the show was bumped from its time slot three out of four times. It was pre-empted again on election day while all three networks covered Lyndon Johnson's landslide victory. The show eventually lost the ratings war to CBS's *Petticoat Junction* and ABC's *Peyton Place* and was canceled in 1965, allowing Nancy to accept more and more singing engagements and television appearances.

Despite its cancelation, the political satire format had been successfully established by TW3, paving the way for subsequent programs to include political satire as a regular feature within their formats. Chief among those immediate programs influenced by TW3 was the *Smothers Brothers Comedy Hour*. Having been a writer on TW3, Nancy ghost-wrote some pieces for it with Mason Williams and co-composed its iconic theme song. Throughout the sixties and mid-seventies, Nancy became a regular fixture on network television, performing on all the major variety shows of the era, including multiple appearances on *The Ed Sullivan Show, The Hollywood Palace, The Red Skelton Hour, The Andy Williams Show, The Dean Martin Show, The Tonight Show*; and on game shows like *Password*, and the daytime talk shows *Mike Douglas* and *Merv Griffin*. In 1968, she had a dramatic role on the NBC primetime drama *The Name of the Game*. Nancy did not limit her time to onscreen appearances; she also spent time in the recording studio, recording thirteen albums. In 1966, she broke the Billboard top 100 twice, first with "He Wore a Green Beret" (the answer to Staff Sgt. Barry Sadler's "Ballad of the Green Berets"); and again with "Cry Softly," later in the year. Fluent in Spanish, Nancy released an album called *Latin Pulse,* which consisted of ten songs, including several English language hits she translated into Spanish. Sony re-released *Latin Pulse* as a double CD with her *Spiced with Brazil* album on their Collectors' Choice label in 2005.

> "Not long after I moved to Houston, Jack Harris, the
> general manager at KPRC Channel 2, asked me to host a
> midday variety/talk show as its hostess, Joanne King
> Herring, was stepping down. *The Nancy Ames Show's*
> producer was Jonni Hartman, a pioneering dynamo in
> Houston television, and the mother of Terri Hartman
> Footnick and Lisa Hartman, who would later become
> famous in her own right as a singer and actress."

In 1974, Nancy was looking for a musical director for her concert engagements and show on Channel 2. That is when she first met Danny Ward.

> "Throughout my years in New York and Hollywood, I
> worked with some fantastic musicians and needed to find
> that kind of talent in Houston. Local band leaders I knew
> from my earlier performances in Houston gave me a list
> of pianists to interview. I met with some excellent pianists
> like Rob Landes, Bobby Holland, and a few others, but I
> didn't hear the breadth of musicianship I was looking for
> or sense that they were comfortable with my travel
> schedule. Then, I heard about a band that was playing in
> the Galleria-area, so I invited my friends Joan Schnitzer,
> Scotty Sanders, and a few others to go with me to hear

them," Nancy remembers. "As we listened to the band, I was beyond impressed with the music director/pianist. He was exceptional. I had rarely heard anybody play like that, and I had worked with some of the best in the business on variety shows and in recording studios. I told my friends, 'Oh my God, this guy is unbelievably talented!'" During the band's break, Nancy invited the pianist to join them at their table. "We introduced ourselves, and I asked him if he was interested in becoming my musical director. I explained what working on my tour would be like and what I needed as a performer. He thought about it for maybe two seconds and replied, 'Absolutely!' The rest is, as they say, history."

Nancy was finishing a tour with the Fairmont group of hotels before Danny joined as her Musical Director. Their first engagement together was for the opening of Disney World's Contemporary Resort Hotel in Orlando. He accompanied Nancy on her engagements for the duration of the variety era and when *The Nancy Ames Show* began on KPRC-TV. Danny accompanied musical guests and provided transition music going in and out of commercial breaks. On June 16, 1976, Nancy and Danny were married.

"A turning point in our early partnership came when Andy Williams appeared on my show to promote his upcoming concert with the Houston Symphony" Nancy recalls. "Naturally, Danny accompanied Andy on my show, and Andy was blown away. Then, he stole Danny from me," she says with mock anger.

Danny then spent eight years playing and conducting for Andy Williams for appearances world-wide. But when Andy was planning to open his Moon River Theatre in Branson, Missouri, and asked

Danny to join him there, he decided he'd had enough of traveling and returned to Houston and his family full time. During those on-the-road-years, Danny also played symphony and club dates with Bernadette Peters, Henry Mancini, Peggy Lee, Shirley MacLaine, Vic Damone, and Nancy.

> "When I began my career as a performer, I learned how turnkey production works in a professional environment, by just watching," Nancy said. "I realized that it is possible to parlay a career into a second career, using the assets gained from the first… to build the second! When I was touring, I was often booked for major events by wonderful production companies like Williams/Gerard and Caribiner. I saw how they managed the entire process and was fascinated by their attention to detail. There was nothing like those companies in Houston, so I thought Danny and I should build our own company to fill that void. In 1982, we started our company, Ward & Ames Special Events."

The division of responsibilities at Ward & Ames was established from the beginning. Nancy's role as Creative Director provides the visionary direction and thematic underscore for bringing their client's messaging to life. Utilizing her skills as a designer, she determines everything from color schemes to how sound and lighting can be used to the best advantage. She draws on her vast experience, learned from her first career as a performer, to create an event that enhances the audience experience, and ensures that it is entertaining as well as educational. Her prowess as an awarded cook enables her to design food and beverage menus while her background in interior design and architecture abets transforming a venue's look for myriad events.

Danny's role is that of Managing Director. Taking his background as a music director and conductor as the impetus, he coalesces the varied talents of staff and crew so they work together as one, an orchestra of technicians focused on a common goal: creating a perfect event.

Their company was initially thought of as an entertainment agency, but it rapidly evolved into a full-service production company, adding décor, lighting and sound design, video production and countless other aspects to their scope of services. Their first big event production was in the Astrodome for the City of Houston. "Cops Are Tops" was designed to celebrate the contributions of the Houston Police Department, so Nancy contacted and secured the entire cast of the hit television police series at the time, *Hill Street Blues,* to salute the HPD. It was a huge success, filling the Astrodome and giving Houston a glimpse into the level of expertise that would soon become the hallmark of Ward & Ames.

Their second large event was for the 100th anniversary of the Amoco Company, which had been founded by Standard Oil in 1889 as a subsidiary of **American Oil Company**. Nancy's theming and architectural chops designed and brought to life "The World of Amoco, A Centennial Celebration" highlighting its global footprint. It was installed at the Astro Arena Complex, encompassing both the expansive right wing of the structure and the central Arena. The immersive event took visitors across the world with interactive displays of the various aspects of the company's forays in chemical and oil research and development. Again, Ward & Ames set a new standard of excellence for incorporating messaging into an environmental design, utilizing décor, lighting, sound, and visuals to create a uniquely experiential event.

During the past forty-two years, Ward & Ames developed long-term relationships with clients such as Kohler, Liberty Mutual

Insurance, Chevron-Texaco, BHP, Hess Energy, The Greater Houston Partnership, Mahindra, Emirates Airlines, Comcast, Texas Children's Hospital, Houston Methodist Hospital, MD Anderson Cancer Center, Memorial Hermann Healthcare, UT Health, Baker Botts LLP, United Way, The University Of St. Thomas, The Texas State Society of Washington, D.C., Major League Baseball, The Office of George H. W. Bush, Barbara Bush Foundation for Family Literacy and her eponymous Houston Literacy Foundation, among countless others. Ward & Ames' intuitive creativity and innate marketing and messaging skills have helped raise several hundreds of millions of dollars for worthwhile philanthropic organizations. Giving back to the community is an entrenched part of the Ward & Ames culture, shared by its employees.

My first working experience with Ward & Ames came about after Tropical Storm Allison stalled over the Gulf Coast in 2001, wreaking havoc on the greater Houston area. Three companies were asked to work together with the United Way of the Texas Gulf Coast to put together a fundraising campaign to help those families who had been devasted by the storm. Belay Media, Texas Video and Post, and Ward & Ames answered that call, with Danny Ward taking the lead role in coordinating the efforts to produce a star-studded televised concert that was held on the playing field of Minute Maid Park. Using their connections in the entertainment field, Nancy and Danny convinced Houston natives Clint Black and his wife, Lisa Hartman Black, to co-host the event. He then assembled an all-Texas cast of performers that included Lyle Lovett, Pat Greene, Kevin Black (Clint's brother), La Mafia, Yolanda Adams, a gospel choir, and a host of other performers. I wrote a short feature that was used to help raise funds from Houston-based corporations to underwrite 100% of the expenses incurred to produce the telethon. I also directed on-location interviews, sharing how the tragic storm made an impact on families throughout the region.

The feature was entitled "One Houston United: The Night the Rains Came." It was the opening segment of the program, which, in an unprecedented turn of events, was aired simultaneously on five Houston television stations: all three network affiliates and two independent stations. A year after airing, that feature received a national Emmy Award from the National Academy of Television Arts and Sciences. During the night of the performance, volunteers from each of the participating television stations manned phone banks installed at the ballpark, alongside national and regional luminaries, taking in pledges of more than $3.5 million. Every dollar raised went directly to families affected by the storm. Months later, additional funds were underwritten by one of the original sponsors.

Not long after we had collaborated in producing the "One Houston United" event, I received a call from Danny asking if I would be interested in writing a video script for an upcoming production his company was undertaking. This assignment was to write profiles of Nobel Prize Winners from Houston. It was an intriguing project that allowed me to meet with several of the local Nobel Laureates and the beginning of a relationship with Ward & Ames that has continued for twenty-five years. During this alliance, I have been tasked with writing profiles for video tributes of CEOs, civic leaders, and politicians. In addition, I have occasionally written short speeches for some of their clients, including a couple of remarks presented by former President George H.W. Bush and his wife Barbara.

In 2018, as a member of the Executive Committee of the Lone Star Chapter of the National Academy of Television Arts and Sciences, and as a National Trustee for NATAS, I had the honor of nominating Nancy Ames for induction into the Gold Circle of the Academy, in recognition of her more than fifty years working in the television industry. I produced a short profile about Nancy's career that was shown before she was introduced to accept the honor. It was a memorable evening, and I was honored to sit next to Nancy during the dinner with the Ward & Ames staff who were also in attendance. Not surprisingly, Nancy received a standing ovation when she was introduced by the Chapter President Martha Kattan and Award's Committee Chair Evelyn Escamilla. When the applause finally died down, Nancy graciously thanked the Academy for the unexpected honor and remarked, in her usual self-deprecating style,

> "I am also very humbled and grateful for the fact that
> there are more than three or four people in the audience
> who know who I am."

She expressed her good luck at having the opportunity to have begun her career first on Broadway, and then her big break on NBC's *That Was the Week That Was.* She expressed her gratitude at having been at the right place and time during the era of variety shows on television, and listed a few of the people with whom she worked at the beginning of her career, including Henry Fonda, Mel Brooks, and Alan Alda, whose first national television appearance was also on *That Was the Week That Was.* After expressing her gratitude for appearances on *The Ed Sullivan Show, Andy Williams,* and *Dean Martin Shows,* and the gamut of variety shows during that era, she then spoke of the second iteration of her career, which was hosting the midday talk show on KPRC Channel 2 in Houston. She lovingly called out her husband Danny, and thanked him for working with her in the performing years of her career, and for the blessings of sharing their time together in marriage and business. Finally, Nancy graciously recognized the members of the Ward & Ames team in the audience and complimented them on the work they do to help make Ward & Ames successful. She ended her acceptance, saying,

"Thank you all so much for being here this evening." She then spoke sincerely to the members present, "I wish you all the same joy and luck that I've had in my career, and be grateful to God for everything that we have. Thank you again, and goodnight."

Five years after that wonderful evening, I asked Nancy if she had sought fame at the beginning of her career. It was not a question she had given much thought to since the early days of her career. When she answered, she was pragmatic.

> "Not chasing fame is probably one of the reasons I didn't try to prolong my performing career," Nancy said without revealing whether she wanted fame. "After living that lifestyle on both coasts for the better part of twenty years, I was tired of traveling," she said, reflecting on her move to Houston in the early 70s, adding, "I had a daughter I wanted to enjoy raising in my newly adopted hometown."

Danny had a different answer.

> "When I was young, all I wanted was to make my career in music. Sure, I wanted my talent recognized because that meant getting more bookings. But no, I was not concerned with becoming famous. As far as I am concerned, we have one famous person in the family, and that is Nancy."

I disagree with Danny on that point. I think he has achieved a modicum of fame, whether he wanted to or not. He is well-known for his ability to manage the projects the Ward & Ames company produces for their clients. And the performers he hires know that he is an accomplished musician in his own right; therefore, they listen when he speaks. In the events production field, Danny has a level of fame that eclipses his competitors. Still, he doesn't stand in the limelight. Instead, Danny always stands in the background, letting Nancy take the bows. And he never misses an opportunity to sing her praises. At the end of an event, when the client approaches him and compliments him on the event's success, Danny will immediately reply, "Well, we have Nancy to thank for that."

Part of the reticence Nancy displays when talking about her fame is grounded in her upbringing, where she was taught to think of others first and not to be self-centered. She came from a family whose careers were centered on serving others. In a way, she considered her career as a performer to be serving others by entertaining them.

> "The first time I realized I was gaining a little fame was when I heard my songs on the radio. After I started performing on television, people began to recognize me on the street and call me by name," she admits modestly. "I tried to handle the little fame I enjoyed with humility and grace. I was aware of my obligation to respect my fan base; I didn't ignore autograph seekers, and I hope I always treated them with dignity and gratitude."

While fame was helpful in her career, Nancy was affected by its negative side. Getting stalked by some fans produced a paralyzing fear.

> "That convinced me I would not miss being famous," she says. "In small doses, I believe fame can benefit the person being admired, as long as it is contained. Overdoses of fame can turn a normally kind person into an arrogant fool or obnoxious narcissist. I was conscious of that fact and worked hard to avoid falling into that trap."

Today, Nancy does not consider herself to be famous, except for those few who can remember her from her performing career. She says she is always amazed when someone tells her they had seen her recently on a rerun of *The Ed Sullivan Show,*

> "That's enough to boost my self-esteem. What I enjoy now more than fame is the sense of respect I get from clients, colleagues, and friends who value my opinion, creativity, and wisdom gained from my experience. When I pontificate or become dogmatic, I go through a normal amount of self-loathing for those overbearing moments!"

Chapter 30
Epilogue

One of my favorite lines from a play is in *The Sound of Music*, Act I, Scene 6, in which the character Max Detweiler states, "I like rich people. I like the way they live. I like the way I live when I'm with them." I feel that way about famous people. I like the way they live, and I like the way I live when I'm with them. Admittedly, my lifelong ambition to be famous was a shallow goal. Throughout my quest, I never denied that fact. Despite the admonition of my mother when I was a five-year-old and despite my efforts to adopt aspirations toward becoming a better person, my desire for fame never diminished. What baffles me is that the goal was always just beyond my grasp. I was cast in leading roles when I was young and still a child. I loved performing in front of an audience or the camera. There was such an exhilaration when I heard applause. It was intoxicating, and I enjoyed those moments. But eventually, the parts I auditioned for stopped coming. That is when I consciously started developing my talents behind the camera. For me, directing became an acceptable alternative to performing. As a young adult, unable to resist the lure of the stage, I was able to get good parts in dinner theatre productions. But the money was not as good, and the opportunities for performing were inconsistent. I had become accustomed to getting a regular paycheck by working on television.

From the beginning of my career, it seems I was always the youngest person on the set. Suddenly, without warning, I became the oldest. Where did time go, and why was I unaware of its passing? In the early days of my career, nearly every project I worked on received accolades from my peers and won awards. I never understood why that recognition didn't produce the results I thought it would. There was a time when I thought perhaps it was my ambition. I thought maybe my self-confidence was mistaken for arrogance. I worked hard to learn my craft and became good at it. More importantly, I treated the crews with whom I worked with respect. I always made a point to thank everyone on the crew when we completed a production, whether it was a television commercial or a live event; the success was always a team effort. I made certain that when a project was up for an award, everyone who contributed their talents was listed in the credits. When the awards came, why were they not accompanied by fame?

My close friend Al Raya is an actor. When I was discussing the nature of fame with Al, he made a good point with a rhetorical question: "Is there a door we must go through to access a formula for success and fame in this subjective business—an unknown formula that we stumble upon? Does this formula consist of ingredients only known to destiny?"

Like me, Al had a desire to be famous since his early childhood. In his early adulthood, he went to New York to make his way in the theatre. He got a few parts off-off-Broadway and a bit part in the soap opera *Love of Life*

> "I came close to stepping through the door that would give me access to the kind of fame and success I so deeply wanted," he says wistfully. "No matter how hard I pushed myself toward that goal, and no matter how much I desired it, time got it my way."

In Al's case, he had a wife and child to provide for, and he had to divert the time needed to seek fame into taking care of his family. "I'll get back to it later," he thought. But later never comes.

> Al believes that the essence of mystery is time. No one of us can affect time—we can't alter it or influence it; we can't adjust time in any way. We must adapt ourselves to time as it governs our lives.

"Maybe we find fame where we live," Al pondered."I think about the number of times I came close. No matter how hard I pushed myself toward that goal and no matter how much I desired it, time got it my way," Al explains.

The mystery of time is a force that moves each of us based on our actions, thoughts, and beliefs. It is our persona, and no matter how committed we are to becoming successful or famous in any endeavor, if our ingredients don't line up or match up with that unknown formula, that particular vision of fame that we have created for ourselves will be lost in time. That is the conclusion that came to Al. He now reflects on the number of times he has performed for small groups, such as performing sleight-of-hand magic at the Dallas Anatole.

"I realized that for a brief hour and a half, I was famous in the eyes of that audience. It was not the fame I wanted, but it was a kind of fame. Perhaps that is the fame I must content myself with, being a star in my backyard, so to speak."

As we discussed the nature of fame, Al asked me questions: "Do you think people who have both success and fame are happy? Can you be happy without fame? Are we supposed to make a choice between fame and success and happiness? Or are we supposed to be content with what we have? Can we find fame in small moments? What about choosing between happiness and success and fame?"

Those questions are difficult for me to answer. The difficulty comes from separating myself in reality from that young kid who decided he wanted fame like Mickey Mantle had. I have enjoyed a most unusual career, one in which I have spent fifty-plus years in the company of famous people. Did I achieve success? I made a good living. Did I achieve happiness? Yes, I think I have been a happy person all of my life. I am one of those fortunate people who has worked in a field that I love, doing something I enjoyed, and for the most part, was in charge of my schedule and was able to pick and choose the projects on which I wanted to work. What more could I ask for? Fame!

If I think about it and apply the logic Al Raya did, then perhaps I did achieve a modicum of fame. I suppose I achieved some level of fame among the people who have been my clients. I know I have a reputation among my clients as being at the top of my game; otherwise, why would they continue to seek me out when they need someone who can do what I do? I think about the number of times I have shown up to work with a new crew, and they tell me they have heard of me and are looking forward to working with me. That must be evidence of some level of fame. Then, too, there are the awards that line the bookcases in my office. Are they not also evidence that I have achieved some level of fame?

So, what if I don't have the level of fame that Martin Scorsese has? Can he do what I do? Of course, he can. But would he want to? He has bigger fish to fry. I get the jobs no one would dare to approach Scorsese with. I work in a part of the business to use a baseball analogy that is relegated to the second-string players. What is wrong with being the best player on the second string? Nothing. Eddie Mathews hit 46 home runs in 1959, the most hit that year. Jim Lemon hit 33 home runs in 1959, ranked 8th compared to 9th-placed Mickey Mantle, who only hit 31. Rocky Colavito was #3 in 1959 with 42 home runs. Does anyone, other than die-hard Cleveland Indians fans, remember Rocky Colavito?

"There are more important things in life than being famous. You should aspire to be a good person. Fame is fleeting. Character lasts." Those words are always ringing in my ears. I should be grateful for what I did achieve. And I am. I have a wonderful wife, six children, and nine grandchildren, all of whom fill me with great pride. That's what matters in life.

As I write this on July 9, 2024, I am reminded that this coming August 29th would have been my father's 104th birthday. My father invented a camera that eliminated the need for a dark room in offset printing. He did not become famous for it. And within just a few years after he patented it, Xerox came up with an invention that made his invention obsolete. Still, I take great pride in the fact that my father invented a camera that eliminated the need for a dark room in offset printing. More than that, I am proud of my father's accomplishments as a man of honor. He slogged his way from North Africa to the invasion at Anzio and took photographs to document the liberation of the concentration camp at Buchenwald. He was proud to have served his country, but it was not something he spoke about very much. It was a duty he was required to perform, and he did it. Enough said.

After the war, he met my mother. They were married and together reared four children. He always treated my mother with great respect and instilled in both of his sons the necessity of always taking care of our mother and our sisters. He did his best to teach us how to be gentlemen, to never back down from a fight when one was inevitable, and to treat everyone with dignity and respect. He had flaws, like we all do, but none that mattered in the final analysis. He had character and honor. He once told me that honor was the one thing a man can never regain once it is lost. He said, "Your honor must be protected, always."

Achieving honor is worthwhile. Achieving fame does not compare to that. Becoming famous is a by-product of how one lives one's life. Living with honor *is* life. It's okay to be famous as long as one lives an honorable life. One can live without fame but not without honor. I am somewhat ashamed that I lived so much of my life seeking to achieve fame. There were so many more worthy goals to aspire toward. Perhaps it is a good thing that achieving fame eluded me. Still…

About the Author

Allen Robert Morris turned 70 in 2024. He spent his career perfecting his ability to direct. Beginning with live television, he ventured into creating live events, ranging from corporate theatre to concerts to working with live actors. He mastered the art of documentary filmmaking by traveling across the globe, from capturing stories about war in the Middle East and interviewing world leaders, to documenting efforts to preserve the South American Rain Forest. Two of his most-honored films are *One Man, Four Lives,* about Holocaust survivor William J. Morgan who assumed four different identities to escape the Nazis in World War II, and *An American Rhapsody*, which is the history of the United States, from its founding to the election of Barack Obama as president, set to the music of George Gershwin's "Rhapsody in Blue," performed by Leonard Bernstein. His work has been honored with every major award from the advertising industry and both regional and national Emmy Awards.

He has published four books, under the pseudonym Robert Marlin, and contributed multiple articles in every issue of *Tyler Today Magazine* for the past twelve years. His extensive experience working with the famous and near-famous for more than fifty-years qualifies him as an expert in the field of celebrity. He has worked directly with several hundred and has met hundreds more. "Working closely together over an extended period of time, creates an intimate relationship; sharing private thoughts and developing confidences that remain long after the project has been completed," Morris says. "Keeping those confidences is how long-term friendships develop. If I've learned anything from the celebrities I've worked with closely, it is that they are almost always looking for someone in whom they can develop trust. They seem to cherish our friendships because it is so rare in their lives."

INDEX